JUST AROUND MIDNIGHT

Just around Midnight

Rock and Roll and the Racial Imagination

JACK HAMILTON

HARVARD UNIVERSITY PRESS

Cambridge, Massachusetts // London, England // 2016

Second printing

Library of Congress Cataloging-in-Publication Data

Names: Hamilton, Jack, 1979– author.
Title: Just around midnight : rock and roll and the racial imagination
    / Jack Hamilton.
Description: Cambridge, Massachusetts : Harvard University Press,
    [2016] | Includes bibliographical references and index.
Identifiers: LCCN 2016013926 | ISBN 9780674416598 (hard cover : alk.
    paper)
Subjects: LCSH: Rock music—Social aspects. | Rock music—1961–1970—
    History and criticism. | Music and race—United States—History—
    20th century. | Music and race—Great Britain—History—
    20th century. | African American rock musicians.
Classification: LCC ML3534 .H336 2016 | DDC 781.6609/046—dc23
    LC record available at https://lccn.loc.gov/2016013926

For Neil Chamberlain (1981–2010),
and my parents

Contents

JUST AROUND MIDNIGHT

Dreams and Nightmares

IN JANUARY OF 1973—the same month that the Rolling Stones were banned from touring Japan due to prior drug convictions, the same month that a band called Kiss (or KISS) played its first gig in Queens, and the same month that a young New Jerseyan named Bruce Springsteen released his debut album on Columbia Records—*Harper's* magazine published an essay by future Pulitzer Prize–winner Margo Jefferson entitled "Ripping Off Black Music." The piece was partly a broad historical overview of white appropriations of black musical forms, from blackface minstrel pioneer T. D. Rice through the current day, and partly a more personal lament over what Jefferson, an African American critic, had come to see as an incorrigible and endless cycle of cultural plunder. The article's most striking moment arrived in its penultimate paragraph:

The night Jimi died I dreamed this was the latest step in a plot being designed to eliminate blacks from rock music so that it may be recorded in history as a creation of whites. Future generations, my dream ran, will be taught that while rock may have had its beginnings among blacks, it had its true flowering among whites. The best black artists will thus be studied as remarkable primitives who unconsciously foreshadowed future developments.[1]

That Jefferson's "dream" came true is so obvious it seems self-evident. According to anthropologist Maureen Mahon, by the mid-1970s young black musicians who wanted to play songs by Led Zeppelin and Grand Funk Railroad recalled being ridiculed by white and black peers.[2] In July of 1979 thousands of white rock fans rioted at Chicago's Comiskey Park at the now mythic "Disco Demolition Night," burning disco records in what many since have described as an antiblack, antigay, antiwoman, reactionary uprising.[3] In 1985, the Hollywood blockbuster *Back to the Future* featured a climactic sequence in which history is altered so that Chuck Berry's "sound" is retroactively invented by a Van Halen–obsessed white teenager.[4] By 2011, when a popular New York "Classic Rock" radio station held a listener poll to determine the "Top 1,043" songs of all time, only twenty-two—roughly 2 percent—were recordings by African American artists, and sixteen of those twenty-two were by the late Jimi Hendrix (the "Jimi" of Jefferson's dream), the lone black performer whose place in rock music hagiography is entirely secure.[5]

Jefferson's words above were accurate, and it's tempting to call them prophetic, but they weren't: Jefferson's nightmare had in fact come true before she wrote her article, even before "the night Jimi died." When Hendrix passed away in 1970, one prominent obituary pointedly described him as "a black man in the alien world of rock," and throughout Hendrix's tragically brief stardom the guitarist's race had been an incessant topic of fascination among fans of the music that had once been known as "rock and roll."[6] Even in the late 1960s, the hypervisibility of Hendrix's race confirmed a racial imagination of rock music that was quickly rendering blackness invisible, so much so that at the time of his death the idea of a black man playing electric lead guitar was literally remarkable—"alien"—in a way that would have been inconceivable for Chuck Berry only a short while earlier.

This is a book about how this happened, how rock and roll music—a genre rooted in African American traditions, and many of whose earliest stars were black—came to be understood as the natural province of whites. Moreover, this is a book about how and why this happened during a decade generally understood to be marked by unprecedented levels of interracial aesthetic exchange, musical collaboration, and commercial crossover more broadly. Many of the most famous moments of 1960s music are marked by interracial fluidity: a young Bob Dylan's transformation of a nineteenth-century antislavery anthem, "No More Auction Block for Me," into the basis for a song that would become one of the most indelible musical works of the American civil rights era; or the revolution of Motown Records, in which a black American entrepreneur actually bet *against* the racism of white America and won, and in doing so created the most successful African American-owned business in the country. Or the previously unimaginable inundation of groups from England, most notably a quartet from Liverpool called the Beatles and a quintet from London called the Rolling Stones, both of whom were tireless evangelists for black American music and would soon hear their own songs performed, frequently, by the very musicians they once idolized. And of course there was Aretha

Franklin, the Memphis-born and Detroit-raised daughter of one of America's most famous black preachers, who linked up with a band of white southerners and transformed R&B music; and Jimi Hendrix himself, a black man from Seattle who'd joined up with a couple of white Englishmen in London, and transformed the possibilities of the electric guitar.

If, then, by the time of Hendrix's death, rock and roll music had in fact "become white," how did this happen, and why? And perhaps most importantly, if rock and roll music did "become white," what does it even mean to say such a thing? What ideological forces and cultural logics conspire to elide the audible imaginary of music with the visual imaginary of race? These are questions that we often assume we know the answers to—after all, to describe a singer as "sounding black" or "sounding white" is to gesture toward entire universes of ill-defined but widely understood aesthetic criteria—and yet we rarely take the time to really ask them, to peel back everything that makes such descriptions both nonsensical and strangely commonsense. If we fix our eyes and ears and step back far enough, the repeated disruptions and reconstitutions of this elision of race and sound begin to resemble something like the history of American music itself.

This book sets out to tell two different yet interconnected stories simultaneously. The first story is of audience and discourse, the processes through which a musical culture rooted in interracialism came to imagine whiteness as its most basic stakes of authenticity. A fundamental panic that engulfed rock and roll's emergence was that the music's overtones of racial intermixture would threaten the social order: the infamous "Help Save the Youth of America: Don't Buy Negro Records" flyers circulated by White Citizens' Councils in the American South during the 1950s were not so much about stopping the circulation of black music in general, but rather about stopping the circulation of black music to young whites.[7] And yet by the end of the 1960s the music had lost this character of racial disruption, to the point that black involvement was seen as flatly incongruous.

This is a story of the forced marriage of musical and racial ideology, how ideas that people had long held about the innate qualities of "black music" and "white music" were fractured and then remade in newly powerful ways. This story takes place in many locations and through many conduits, and it follows the rise of a young generation of listeners eager to comment upon the sounds they were hearing, which culminated in the rise of a new literary figure: the rock critic. "Written criticism, as much as musical criteria," Guthrie Ramsey reminds us, "clearly determines the pedigree of a genre."[8] In America the "institution" of rock criticism would come to be largely synonymous with *Rolling Stone* magazine, started in San Francisco in 1967, and the magazine's enormous success was a pivotal happening in the history of popular-music media. But people had been writing about the new music coming from Detroit, London, Liverpool, Greenwich Village, and elsewhere for nearly as long as they'd been hearing it, in local and national newspapers, in alternative weeklies and august prestige publications, in pioneering books and tiny, passionate fan magazines. In all of these venues, discussions and debates were held over what this music should, and shouldn't, sound like, be like, *look* like, and it is in these conversations, in their gathering ideologies and creeping omissions, that we can see the color of rock and roll begin to change.

The second story is of music itself, the ways that artists and performers during this period negotiated and traversed racial divides to degrees unprecedented in the history of popular music. In some sense this is a counterhistory to the one above, an attempt to recover the resonances and possibilities in musical compositions, performances, and recordings, piecing together previously missed connections to reveal what Josh Kun calls "audiotopia": "an enacted, lived utopia that struggles against the constraints of racialization and nation-building."[9] This story sets out to "hear together" musicians who have long been thought of as disparate but who weren't necessarily thought to be so at the time, least of all in their own minds. For instance, one would never hear the Supremes on a "rock" radio station in the twenty-first century, yet in May 1965, when *Time* magazine ran a story entitled "Rock 'n' Roll, Everybody's Turned On," the Supremes were on its cover. Similarly, Bob Dylan's credibility as a rock icon is unimpeachable, but in 1964—the year Sam Cooke released "A Change Is Gonna Come," his landmark civil rights anthem inspired by Dylan's "Blowin' in the Wind"—no one would have thought to describe Dylan as a "rock and roll singing star," as the *Chicago Defender* described Cooke while reporting on the singer's death that same year.[10]

Criticism, historiography, and popular discourse generally have accepted a view of popular music in the 1960s as split according to genre and, more tacitly, race: on one hand is rock music, which is white; on the other, soul music, which is black. We hear Creedence Clearwater Revival's 1970 version of "I Heard It through the Grapevine" as classic rock—the 662nd greatest classic rock song of all time, according to the aforementioned radio-station poll—and we hear Marvin Gaye's slightly earlier version as something else, even though Gaye's version spent seven weeks atop the charts in 1968 and 1969 and was clearly far more popular in its day among white *and* black listeners. As the above paragraph suggests, these divisions didn't happen as naturally as we're often inclined to think: they took work. As Franco Fabbri and Simon Frith have both argued, popular-music genres are a collapsing of sociological and ideological arguments, indicating the social positions of performers and audiences while also describing the ways these communities position themselves within, and project themselves to, the larger world.[11] Rock and roll became white in large part because of stories people told themselves about it, stories that have come to structure the way we listen to an entire era of sound.

In telling the story of those stories, I want to suggest ways to hear this music differently, more complexly, and more clearly: in other words, to hear it *better*. As Ingrid Monson has written, "Music is full of ideas that are evaluated by audiences and musicians, that acquire authority and prestige within particular aesthetic landscapes, and that are perceived to 'say something' substantive about human experience and feeling."[12] This statement seems particularly true of popular music, where processes of production, circulation, and reception are wide-ranging and fluid, and where the acquisition of authority and perception of what music "says" are often determined by ideological forces that far exceed the practice of musicians themselves.

In American music the construction of race has long been among the most powerful of these forces, and to best explore this relationship I have embraced the term "racial imagination" as set forth by Ronald Radano and Philip Bohlman, a concept that accepts a notion of race as profoundly extra-visual, but avoids ideas of fixed racial essence and suggestions of race as a purely psychological construction. If race is a category that is constantly being produced and reproduced by social forces—as "racial formation" theory has long held—then race must be considered alongside forms of cultural production, particularly during a period in which popular music's real and imagined relation to social forces took on unprecedented intensity.[13] "Racial imagination," Radano and Bohlman tell us, "is forever on the loose, subject to reformation within the memories and

imaginations of the social as it blurs into other categories consti-
tuting difference," thus becoming "a signification saturated
with profound cultural meaning and whose discursive instability heightens its affective power."[14] Josh Kun puts this in
the terms of popular music specifically, noting that "race and
popular music have always been experienced not alongside each
other, not as complements, supplements, or corollaries of each
other, but through each other."[15]

As the subtitle of this book suggests, the term that I choose
to use to describe almost all of the music in these pages is "rock
and roll." There has often been a presumed generic gap between
"rock and roll" and "rock," the former indicating the teen-driven
dance music of the 1950s and early 1960s, the latter something
distinctly more high-minded. As one critic has it, "rather than
rock being just another mainstream music, it emerged in the
mid-1960s as a way of *stratifying* mainstream musical consumption, as a means of creating higher and lower levels of popular
music."[16] By the end of the 1960s this distinction was already
being naturalized, either implicitly or explicitly, in some of the
earliest and most foundational histories of the music.[17] I am not
so much out to deny that this shift happened—all music changes,
after all—but rather to push at received tales of when it happened, and how.

I am skeptical of these tales, and this book reflects this skep-
ticism, in its content and its structure. For instance, as Chapter 2
shows, the most well-worn pairing *qua* dichotomy in rock history, that of the Beatles and Rolling Stones, emerged in this period, but this was largely a creation of media.[18] Particularly in the
early years of their stardom, the contemporary music that the
Beatles spoke of most enthusiastically was Motown: when
Melody Maker asked John Lennon in 1964 to name a current hit

he wished he'd written, he responded with Marvin Gaye's "Can I Get a Witness."[19]

Thrice-Told Stories

The "whitening" of rock and roll music is a subject that has generally been approached in one of three ways. The first is by casting the music's re-racialization as just one more iteration of a broadly transhistorical phenomenon of white-on-black cultural theft. In this telling, the appropriation of black musical styles by performers ranging from Elvis Presley to John Lennon to Janis Joplin is held as conceptually and ethically contiguous with a singular tradition of plunder most fundamentally exemplified in the practice of blackface minstrelsy. In its most reductive instances, this formulation rests on ideas of cultural ownership, essentialist originalism, and racial hermeticism: a belief that there is a clear and definable boundary between "black music" and "white music" in America that resists porosity.[20] This belief does not hold up under basic scrutiny, and by abstracting black and white sound to monoliths it obscures the fact that, as Karl Hagstrom Miller has written in his study of race and the early folk and pop-music industries, "the differences *within* African American or white music cultures were more extreme than the differences *between* black and white music cultures."[21] This statement is just as applicable—if not likely more applicable—to the United States and United Kingdom of the 1960s as it is to the American South of the early twentieth century.

Less strident iterations of the "theft" narrative tend to employ minstrelsy as more of an explanatory metaphor. The publication of Eric Lott's *Love and Theft* (1993) occasioned an ongoing explosion in critical and historical interest in minstrelsy, and the notions of counterfeit and thievery so explicitly on display in minstrelsy have obvious rhetorical utility when surveying the history of a popular-music industry that's tended to grossly overcompensate white appropriators over black originators, from Paul Whiteman to Pat Boone to Iggy Azalea.[22] But the minstrelsy metaphor is still flawed on several fronts. First, its transhistoricism leaves little room for *differences* between appropriations and exclusions, and it fails to reckon with the ever-changing character of both racial thought and expressive culture itself. As Lott and Alexander Saxton before him demonstrated, Northern antebellum blackface minstrelsy enacted and articulated a variety of specific cultural and political concerns that were surely different from those enacted by Elvis Presley, to say nothing of Mick Jagger.[23] Abstracting minstrelsy into a soft, ahistorical formation that takes place primarily at the level of the imagination risks underplaying the real violence and inequities enacted by the history of actual blackface minstrelsy, as well as misunderstanding the diverse array of contexts and intentions that have informed white flirtations with nonwhite culture throughout American history.

Moreover, while other African American popular musical forms like jazz, blues, and most recently hip-hop have long histories of white appropriation, the "canons" of these musics remain overwhelmingly black, whereas rock music has all but purged its hagiography of black musicians. As Elijah Wald writes, "It is a profound irony that the attempts to make highbrow art out of jazz in the 1920s . . . is generally recalled by historians as an embarrassing wrong turn, whereas the attempt to make highbrow art out of rock 'n' roll in the 1960s . . . is generally viewed as a step forward for the genre, which has been led by white artists ever since."[24] This seems a crucial difference: no black-derived musical form in American history has more assiduously moved to erase and blockade black participation than rock music. When rock ideology purged itself of (visible) blackness it was foreclosing not simply African American performers but an entire young tradition of interracial fluidity.

The second way that the "whitening" of rock and roll music has been addressed has been to place the onus of separation on black performers by arguing that, as the 1960s progressed, black music effectively self-segregated. In this narrative, the broad trajectory of black popular music is often directly linked to—if not conflated with—the broad trajectory of the civil rights movement, in which discourses of self-determination and, in more extreme cases, outright separatism became more pronounced in the later part of the decade. This is an intriguing argument with no small amount of truth, and of course there have been a number of excellent and important histories of 1960s rhythm and blues music's relationship to the civil rights movement.[25] As Chapter 4 here discusses, in the late 1960s the near-simultaneous ascendances of Aretha Franklin and Janis Joplin to superstardom helped produce a flurry of debates over "soul," which were often themselves musical proxies for broader cultural and political discourses.

That said, there are multiple flaws to the self-segregation narrative, starting with the fact that it tends to conflate music and activism when the specifics of musicians' political commitments were often hazier. James Brown's 1968 hit "Say It Loud—I'm Black and I'm Proud" spent six weeks atop the R&B charts and was a groundbreaking musical anthem of black power; less than six months after its release, Brown performed at Richard Nixon's inauguration. Conversely, a performer like Nina Simone, who was outspoken in her political commitments and whose fierce dedication to the civil rights movement explicitly informed her music, operated mostly outside both the black and white commercial mainstreams. Suggesting that R&B music self-segregated implies that "R&B music" is a singular, unvarying monolith, a reduction that partakes in what Emily Lordi identifies as a tendency to "treat entire genres of music ... as metaphors for culturally specific values like community."[26] Even more importantly, the self-segregation narrative excuses the majority (white) side from any responsibility for the disappearance of black artists from rock music: for all of the late 1960s celebrations of "soul" on the part of African American writers, the belief that black music should be kept separate from white was also proselytized by white writers, and white critics were often just as vocal in policing boundaries of black musical authenticity.

Which brings us to the third, and by far most common, way that the "whitening" of rock and roll music has been discussed: simply not at all. The history of rock discourse is marked by a profound aversion toward discussions of race, and attempts to reckon the music's racial exclusivity have often been met with hostility, particularly at the level of fandom. When Lester Bangs wrote an infamous cover story entitled "The White Noise Supremacists" for the *Village Voice* in 1979 about the racism of New York's punk and new wave scenes, he was met with outrage and accusations of betrayal; when Sasha Frere-Jones wrote a similarly controversial piece for the *New Yorker* on the whiteness of "indie rock" in 2007, he was widely pilloried in the rock blogosphere.[27] Neither of these essays are perfect works (particularly the Bangs), but the dismissiveness and sometimes outright vitriol with which they were met speak to the extent of rock's peculiar racial denialism.

In historiography this denialism conceals itself more subtly. The most common way is a tendency toward stories of individual rock "genius" that foreclose discussions of race by celebrating individual artistry and intellect. While many black performers of the 1960s have often been relegated to booklength histories of black music generally, white artists like Bob Dylan or the Beatles receive their own increasingly lavish biographies and hermetic critical treatments of musical output.[28] In this disparity we see a sort of critical corollary to what Fred Moten describes as "white avant-gardism whose seriousness requires either an active forgetting of black performances or a relegation of them to mere source material."[29] From an even broader standpoint, the recognition of white people as individuals while recognizing nonwhite people only in relation to collectives is a hallmark of racism across all areas of culture: one might argue that the entire history of white supremacy rests upon it.

An alternative to this "Great Man" tendency is a sort of nostalgic populism that glorifies rock and roll music for its democratizing "folk" elements. In these formulations rock music is often folded into a quasi-mythic lineage of American proletarian expression, with class trumping race in narratives that claim rock and roll music as an inherently and nobly working-class form. Leaving aside that even a quick glimpse at history makes this difficult to corroborate—for each Elvis Presley, son of a Mississippi truck driver, there is a Buddy Holly, scion of relative affluence in Texas—the working-classing of rock and roll tellingly manifests some of the same anxieties that haunted the New Left of the 1960s, a movement in which radical political ideology often rested uneasily against the middle-class background of its leaders.[30] In the years since, the fantasy of rock music as a fundamentally proletarian (and hence subtly raceless) form has sometimes haunted left intellectuals' writing on the music, within and outside the academy. An object lesson in this is the case of Bruce Springsteen, a figure whose salt-of-the-earth persona has helped him carve out a niche as rock's "everyman" for a rabid fanbase that sprawls to include, at the time of this writing, even the conservative governor of New Jersey, Chris Christie. Springsteen's populist heroism is cited in terms of everything from his progressive politics to his geographical origins to his class background to his grueling performance style, all while his whiteness remains generally undiscussed.[31]

And yet racial imagination did reveal itself in Springsteen fandom, obliquely yet powerfully, after the 2011 passing of his longtime saxophone player, Clarence Clemons, the lone black member of the E-Street Band. Eulogizing Clemons for the *New Yorker*, editor and Springsteen fan David Remnick described him as "a vessel of many great soul, gospel, and R&B players who came before him" and "an absolutely essential, and soulful, ingredient in both the sound of Springsteen and the spirit of the group."[32] In this passage, language like "soulful ingredient" ascribes a sort of black musical magic to the figure of Clemons, a magic in turn transferred to Springsteen by association, through some mystical "spirit of the group." It's a move that subtly strips Clemons of agency ("a vessel") in order to enfold him into a fantastical rhetorical lineage—there is no real gospel saxophone "tradition" to speak of—that in turn confirms Springsteen's white heroism. Clemons's presence (or, now, his absence) affirms the centrality of Springsteen's whiteness while foreclosing discussion of racial inequality, rock's equivalent of the "but some of my best friends . . ." argument.

The enormously powerful and enormously vague conceptual engine that powers all of the various omissions, fallacies, and obfuscations described above is "authenticity." Rock ideology, the foundations and emergence of which are in large part the subject of this book, is first and foremost an ideology of authenticity. By this I do not just mean an understanding between performer and audience that what is being performed and expressed is "real," although I do partly mean that.[33] I also mean that rock's ideology of authenticity functions as a way of delineating what constitutes "real" rock music, including who is authorized to play that music and who is authorized to talk about and listen to it. Keir Keightley argues that rock's obsession with authenticity is a symptom of its vexed relation to commerce, what Keightley calls "rock's constitutive paradox—that it is a massively popular anti-mass music."[34] By emphasizing "realness," the music was (and is) able to convince itself that its commercial success was the reward of heroic expression rather than business calculation, a fervid and complicated belief that this book explores in some detail. I also follow Philip Auslander in treating rock authenticity as both "an ideological concept and as a discursive effect," one that is "essentialist, in the sense that rock fans treat authenticity as an essence that is either present or absent in the music itself."[35] In other words, rock music takes the reality of its own "realness" for granted, and by the end of the 1960s "real" rock music had been colored white. Playing and consuming rock music offered new ways into being a "real" white person— most often a white man—and in many quarters being a white man had become a precondition for making "real" rock music.

Along with these new (yet old) ideologies of white musical authenticity came new (yet old) ideologies of black musical authenticity. Whereas artists like Bob Dylan, the Rolling Stones, and Janis Joplin were lauded for casting off the shackles of racial conformity, artists like those at Detroit's Motown Records, whose R&B-to-pop "crossover" formula was the most significant American musical achievement of the decade, were derided for being insufficiently black. In these formulations, cosmopolitan versatility among African American artists was not heard as identity transcendence but rather as racial betrayal, in accusations that were frequently lobbed by white critics. Again, perhaps the most tortuous example of this was Jimi Hendrix, who during his career was judged by many as a fraud or sellout, his blackness rendering his music as inauthentically "rock" at the same time that his music rendered his person as inauthentically black.

What these ideologies reconstructed in tandem was a sonic worldview in which black musical authenticity was defined in relation to a set of imagined aesthetic strictures imposed onto a group, while white musical authenticity was seen in terms of individuality. In rock music the very act of imaginatively engaging with and "putting on" black musical authenticity while keeping black bodies at arm's length became, simply, a new way of being white. The laughed-off response to why we don't speak of "white musical authenticity" is that such a thing is jokily stereotyped as undesirable, but the real reason is that rock ideology rendered it so fluid that it escapes all definition and confinement—in the twenty-first century it's difficult to imagine anyone listening to a white rock band and fretting that they weren't white enough, as certain people did over the Rolling Stones in the mid-1960s. All of this is a rather perfect reflection of one of the central features of American racial thought, the belief that, in Patricia J. Williams's formulation, race is something that everyone "has" except white people.[36]

Hearing and History

Like all writers, I bring my own background to bear on this material. I began playing music at age six and have spent much of my adult life as a working musician: as such, my first inclination has always been to approach music as lived practice, to figure out how it works and why it works. Accordingly, I try to never lose sight of the fact that almost all music originates with people in a room together, at a specific time and in a specific place, and that music is an activity and an action before it is anything else.

I have also worked extensively as a music critic, which has made me keenly aware both of the potentials and pitfalls of writing about music and of the way that both writing and reading about sound can structure and inform our experiences of it. One aim of this book is to listen to music against and alongside the stories we've told ourselves about it, to respect it as performance and art and a mediated moment in audible time. I have thus drawn inspiration from Alexandra Vazquez's model of "listening in detail," which Vazquez describes as "to listen closely to and assemble that inherited lived matter that is both foreign and somehow familiar into something new" and, in so doing, "making criticism a creative activity."[37]

I frequently employ my own music-critical tools here: if there are passages of this book that read like music criticism, this is by design, and I've tried to keep musical analyses legible and lively for nonspecialists while respecting musical recordings as audible texts and foregrounding their autonomy from what people may—or may not—have said about them. As Theodore Gracyk argues, rock culture is most fundamentally concerned with records themselves, while Auslander suggests that, despite our imaginings of rock stardom as a performed effect, rock authenticity is in fact located *between* recordings and performance in a strangely self-validating cycle. While recordings, and albums in particular, are fetishized by rock fans, the ability to "play live" is also seen as paramount, in order to prove one is not simply a market creation. And yet live performances by bands are frequently evaluated *in comparison* to the album: if a band or artist is seen as unable to replicate the sounds heard on its album, authenticity is rendered suspect.[38] Given the centrality of recordings to

rock ideology, this study takes sound recordings and the discourses around them as its primary objects of analysis. For the
most part I am more interested in specific works from the artistic lives of performers during this period, rather than personal biographies or holistic evaluations of their careers.

What Was Rockism?

In the twenty-first century, music-critic circles—circles in
which, as noted above, I frequently travel—have been marked by
ongoing debates over what is pejoratively known as "rockism."
Rockism is an ideology that holds the rock "canon" as the epitome
of popular-music-as-art and that, as Eric Weisbard has nicely
glossed it, connotes "a fixed language of guitars, bass, and drums,
nostalgia for the peak years of Dylan and the Stones, and ideals
of sweaty authenticity."[39] The line between "rockism" and
"racism" is rarely a bright one: as Kelefa Sanneh asked in a widely
discussed 2004 *New York Times* article on the subject, "could it
really be a coincidence that rockist complaints often pit straight
white men against the rest of the world?"[40] Rockism is often juxtaposed against the cheekily named "poptimism," a critical disposition that rejects rockism's presumption of rock's inherent
supremacy and that champions other popular forms that
rockism tends to deride: disco, hip-hop, electronic dance music,
or Nashville country, to name just a few.

As is the case in most such debates, both sides have often car-
icatured the other, and I'm not sure there's a twenty-first-
century music critic of any real influence who conforms to the
stereotype of "rockism" as laid out in antirockist screeds, nor is
there anyone I know of who squarely conforms to the "popti-
mist" stereotypes laid out in antipoptimist screeds. In my own
writing I've generally avoided these debates for a number of rea-

sons, one of which is that I don't actually think hardcore rockism exists anymore as a viable critical disposition: the force with which the term now lands as an epithet suggests the poptimists have more or less won. It's almost impossible to imagine a contemporary critic of any clout publicly suggesting that, say, Coldplay's music is more worthwhile than Kanye West's solely because the former play guitars, or some equally silly canard.

But I certainly believe rockism *did* exist, and still exists among certain fan communities and audiences (and certain museums in Cleveland), and the fact that it no longer has a serious voice among twenty-first-century music critics—an awfully small percentage of the music-listening public—does not mean that it is no longer germane to musical understanding and to musical history. In many ways this book is the story of rockism's emergence, and its indebtedness to ways of thinking and listening and writing that well predate rock music itself. As such, some will look at some of the artists considered in these pages—Bob Dylan, the Beatles, the Rolling Stones, and Janis Joplin—and argue that this book is reinscribing the rockist canon, which to a certain degree it is. But rockism isn't much else *but* a canon, and it's crucial that the foundations of this canon are some of the most famous musicians in history. Keightley notes that rock is different from many other forms of popular music in that it can't be understood in terms of a crossover: rock did not *enter* the mainstream from elsewhere, but rather it was born there.[41] To write an "alternative" canon of rock music in this period would ultimately be to write about something different than rock music itself. Rather, this book seeks to expand this canon to a degree that challenges and defamiliarizes the ways we have come to think about music in general during this period.

In each of my chapters I strive to respect both music and race as lived realities that are also constructed by powerful imaginative work. If, as Radano suggests, we should pay attention to the "comprehension of black music as a form constituted within and against racial discourses," the same approach must be said of what we've come to receive as "white music" as well.[42] Chapter 1 focuses on connections between Sam Cooke and Bob Dylan in the early 1960s, most centrally evidenced by Cooke's landmark composition "A Change Is Gonna Come," partly inspired by a twenty-one-year-old Dylan's "Blowin' in the Wind." Cooke and Dylan have since been positioned as foundational figures in soul and rock music, respectively. By analyzing moments of overlap between these artists as well as the ways they were discussed at the time and in years since, I expose the ideological agendas underlying these genre formations while highlighting the interracial aesthetics of two of the decade's most influential musicians, one of whom met his premature demise in late 1964, the other of whom is now regarded as one of the most significant musicians of the twentieth century.

Chapter 2 travels across the Atlantic to explore the intermingling of musical and racial imagination in England during the long moment before the Beatles touched down at a newly renamed John F. Kennedy Memorial Airport in 1964. By looking at four British youth cultures that sometimes shared little else than an obsession with African American music—the teddy boys, "trad" jazz, skiffle, and British blues—this chapter reveals the degree to which young Britons' relationship to popular music was filtered through racial fantasies that were distinctly homegrown. While much of this chapter deals with music and musicians who remain relatively unknown in the United States, such as Ken Colyer, Lonnie Donegan, and Alexis Korner, I also explore the impact of their legacies on the Beatles and the Rolling Stones, whose stateside arrivals brought American audiences new ways of thinking about music, masculinity, and race.

The Beatles' emergence transformed 1960s popular music on nearly every conceivable level. Chapter 3 focuses on them and explores their creative interactions with Detroit's Motown Records. While this influence is most famously heard in the "covers" of Motown songs that appear on the Beatles' early American and British LPs, this chapter shows that the relationship between the Beatles and Motown was multilayered in its reciprocity and stretched throughout the 1960s, spreading to include the influence of Motown bassist James Jamerson on *Rubber Soul* and *Revolver* and finally Stevie Wonder and Marvin Gaye's drastic reimaginings of Beatles compositions at the dawn of the 1970s. In doing so I also aim to redress long-standing misapprehensions of Motown itself, as the label's crossover aspirations caused many commentators to label it inauthentically or insufficiently "black" in comparisons to other R&B music of the period. The interplay between Motown and the Beatles shows the way interracial crossovers heard as cosmopolitanism for white artists have frequently been heard as diluted accommodationism for black artists.

The policing of racial authenticity in music gained new energy in the late 1960s. During this period the concept of "soul" became a fixation of popular discourse, and Chapter 4 examines this phenomenon in relation to the singers Aretha Franklin, Janis Joplin, and Dusty Springfield. Franklin and Joplin were often made to stand as polar extremes in these debates, with Franklin held as the embodiment of soulful authenticity and Joplin made into a flashpoint for arguments over whether "soul" was a racially exclusive proposition. British pop star Springfield never became a household name stateside but enjoyed a surprise hit in 1968 with "Son of a Preacher Man," a song originally written for Aretha Franklin and recorded by Springfield with members of Franklin's band. Through these musical and discursive convergences, I show that the discourse of soul was a way to use music to talk about race and vice versa, and that its authenticity fantasies sometimes drowned out the music it purported to celebrate.

Chapters 5 and 6 look at Jimi Hendrix and the Rolling Stones, respectively, two artists whose relationships to race and rock and roll were arguably the most complex of any during this period. Hendrix was an African American lead guitar virtuoso in an increasingly white rock landscape in which white critics and commentators were often explicitly pushing black musicians to the margins. Chapter 5 explores his emergence and too-brief stardom against the continuing rise of rock writing as a form, as well as the various crises that Hendrix's blackness provoked for rock ideology's emergent self-understanding. I also discuss Hendrix's pioneering efforts to both critique and represent violence through music, a creative fixation that, I will argue, grew out of his artistic urges to forge musical utopias out of lived dystopias. The end of this chapter considers the emergence of one of rock's most significant post-Hendrix guitar heroes, the Mexican-born Carlos Santana, whose Latino identity and cosmopolitan musical style offered one of the first great challenges to rock's hardening racial imagination.

Chapter 6 explores the Rolling Stones, arguably the most racially controversial rock band in history (a lyric from their spectacularly troublesome 1971 hit "Brown Sugar" provides the title for this book). The Rolling Stones were a white British band obsessed with African American music who continued to perform alongside black musicians to increasingly unusual degrees as the 1960s came to a close, and the group insisted on black music's continuing relevance to rock and roll. Like Hendrix, the Stones' creative output in this period was marked by a fixation with violence that dovetailed with ideas about the band as "threat" that had circulated since their emergence into stardom earlier in the 1960s. Late 1960s classics such as "Jumpin' Jack Flash," "Street Fighting Man," and "Gimme Shelter" voraciously pursued the intersection of rock and roll music and violence, often through explicit engagements with black musicians and black musical forms. While creatively invigorating, these flirtations with violence exceeded the boundaries of musical practice with the murder of Meredith Hunter at Altamont in December 1969, an event for which the Stones were widely vilified and which quickly came to be imagined as a symbolic death rattle for the 1960s. Both the Stones' and Hendrix's pioneering experimentations with musical violence—experimentations that can also be heard as critiques of encroaching white hegemony, and demonstrations that rock music in this period was, in the words of Michael Kramer, "utopian and sinister in equal parts"—were ultimately appropriated and absorbed by rock ideology in order to confirm its own white masculinist exclusivity.[43]

I would now like to acknowledge some of the many things that this book does not do. For starters, I am acutely aware of the fact that this book reproduces a dyadic and by now thoroughly antiquated notion of race. As Josh Kun writes, "Rock discourse has traditionally been deployed within the outmoded racial binary of black and white, with the vast majority of discussions of rock's relationship to race never going far beyond the more familiar and ready-made vocabulary of U.S. blackness and whiteness," and from a somatic standpoint the story I tell here is overwhelmingly black-and-white.[44] But the fact is that racial-cum-musical discourse in this period was almost entirely conducted on these grounds, at least within the critical and commercial mainstream. The first resounding challenge to this binary, Carlos Santana, ascended to stardom at the tail end of the period covered here, and his emergence is considered in Chapter 5.

Furthermore, by focusing on recordings and print media, I do not write very much about radio, television, or film, all of which were surely hugely important media for the dissemination of popular music, and ideas about popular music, during the period I'm writing about. Fortunately, there is a growing field of scholarship on these areas, starting with Eric Weisbard's *Top 40 Democracy,* a fantastic history of how radio formats have shaped our ideas about musical genres and the identities those genres seek to reflect and produce. In terms of television, Gayle Wald's book on Ellis Haizlip's pioneering public television show *Soul!* and Matthew Delmont's book on *American Bandstand* and Philadelphia are just two recent examples of important work on music and television during this period.[45]

In selecting my subjects there are also invariably artists I've had to leave out, and bodies of work that are not addressed thoroughly in these pages could make for an enormous and impeccable record collection. Sly and the Family Stone, Curtis Mayfield, and the Band are just three artists from this period whom I would happily write a second (and third and fourth) book about, but they don't substantially make it into this one. Stax Records is only sporadically considered here, partly because the label has already received a masterful history at the hands of Rob Bowman and partly because Stax has too often functioned as the be-all, end-all of utopian musical integrationism, a shorthand that Charles Hughes's recent work on Southern soul has productively challenged.[46] James Brown is another omission, but Brown too has been written about extensively elsewhere, and he never really inhabited the "crossover" ethos that this book probes, in all its various meanings (Brown, for all his successes, never had a number 1 pop single).[47] Similarly, the Doors, the Grateful Dead, the Who, and Cream are all artists more than worthy of someone else's story, but at present they can't be mine.

Finally, I want to emphasize that this book does not set out to redefine or re-delimit either white musical authenticity or black musical authenticity: I am deeply skeptical of any concrete ontology or explanatory usefulness of one or the other. A central motive of this book is to disrupt the stories that we have told ourselves about what we've partitioned as "black music" and "white music" and to identify what we are actually talking about when we say these things, particularly with regards to this period, one of the most significant in the history of popular music. Among the figures discussed in this book, Aretha Franklin sang "My Country 'Tis of Thee" at the first inauguration of the first African American president of the United States, Bob Dylan has won so many honors that new ones are being invented on his behalf, and John Lennon has been dead for more than thirty-five years yet might still be more famous than both of them.[48]

A shared trait of nearly every artist considered in these pages, white or black, male or female, American or British, is that he or she provoked a crisis in ideas about musical and racial authenticity, crises to which the racial imagination of 1960s musical discourse was forced to respond. Another shared trait is that none of them, regardless of skin color, ever set out to make music that was "white," and all saw themselves as deeply and fundamentally indebted to black American musical traditions. Like much of white supremacy itself, rock music's musical-racial ideology of white authenticity has long taken its power precisely from the fact that it conceals and outwardly denies its own existence. This began in a period when age-old stories that people had told themselves about race and its relation to sound, performance, and the businesses of sound and performance were pushed to a point of rupture. Faced with this rupture, the old stories were retailored to fit the extraordinary times that had brought them to crisis.

CHAPTER 1

Darkness at the Break of Noon

Sam Cooke, Bob Dylan, and
the Birth of Sixties Music

> *I was born by the river*
> *In a little tent*
> *And just like that river I've been running ever since.*
>
> —Sam Cooke, 1964

> *He not busy being born*
> *Is busy dying.*
>
> —Bob Dylan, 1965

IN LATE 1963, Sam Cooke found himself at another crossroads in a lifetime full of them. In 1950, a nineteen-year-old Cooke (then Cook) had become the lead singer of the Soul Stirrers, perhaps the most famous gospel group in the country. Seven years later he added an "e" to the end of his name and wrote and released a secular single called "You Send Me"; stunningly, the record soared to the top of the *Billboard* Pop singles chart, making Sam Cooke the most successful gospel-to-pop crossover artist in American history while expediting his departure from the Soul Stirrers and scandalizing his religious fanbase. Shortly thereafter, he signed with RCA Records, the same label that recorded Elvis Presley, Lena Horne, and Perry Como, and enjoyed a consistent string of hits well into the early 1960s.

By 1963 Cooke's attention was increasingly drawn to politics and to the growing network of protests and struggles rooted in the American South. Cooke had long been attuned to issues of civil rights, but as the year wore on and Martin Luther King delivered his famous "I Have a Dream" speech in Washington, D.C., that August, Cooke sensed that the stakes were rising. Fueling his urgency was his growing obsession with a song called "Blowin' in the Wind," written by then-twenty-year-old singer and songwriter named Bob Dylan and released in May 1963 on his second studio album for Columbia Records, *The Freewheelin' Bob Dylan*. Peter, Paul and Mary's version of the song, released for Warner Brothers on June 18, 1963, reached number two on the Pop charts and sold 320,000 copies in its first eight days, making it the label's fastest-selling single in history.[1]

Cooke's longtime friend and collaborator J. W. Alexander later recalled Cooke expressing wonder at "a white boy writing a song like that"; shortly thereafter, Cooke invited Alexander to his house and played him a sketched-out version of a song he'd been working on.[2] A curious mixture of gospel imagery and secular fury—this early draft referred to a white segregationist as a "motherfucker"—it was unlike anything the singer had yet written, closer to the "protest" or "topical" music of Dylan than the mass-marketed pop that had garnered Cooke his lasting success.[3]

Cooke finally recorded a completed version of the song, now titled "A Change Is Gonna Come," in late January of 1964, by which time it had morphed into a stunning mix of influences. Its church-infused vocal text was set to sophisticated pop chord changes, all nestled against a ravishing backdrop of strings, brass, and tympani. In early February Cooke performed the song on Johnny Carson's *Tonight Show*, although as his biographer, Peter Guralnick, notes, the singer had at first strenuously objected to the suggestion and had to be persuaded to do so by his manager, Allen Klein.[4] The studio version of "A Change Is Gonna Come" was first released without much fanfare in March of 1964, appearing as the first track on the second side of Cooke's latest RCA album, *Ain't That Good News*.

Cooke would not live to hear "A Change Is Gonna Come" become arguably the most enduring song of his career and a seminal musical moment of the intensifying civil rights movement. In December of 1964 the singer was murdered in Los Angeles; just days after, "A Change Is Gonna Come" was released in single form, initially as the B-side to "Shake," although the song soon began climbing the R&B and Pop charts on its own. Less than four months later, Bob Dylan issued his own symbolic resignation letter from the folk community with the release of the half-electrified album *Bringing It All Back Home*. This was followed in the summer of 1965 by *Highway 61 Revisited* and its groundbreaking lead single, "Like a Rolling Stone," a six-and-a-half-minute opus that reached number two on the *Billboard* charts and finalized Dylan's shift from folk wunderkind to full-blown pop icon, a transformation that would have massive ramifications for popular music.

This chapter draws connections between Sam Cooke and Bob Dylan, two musical legends of the 1960s, and endeavors to hear them together, in a sense. On the surface the two would seem to have little in common, and aside from the remarkable but not entirely unexpected influence of "Blowin' in the Wind" on Cooke—it was, after all, a hugely influential song—there's been scant discussion of any similarities or affinities shared by the two men in this period. Dylan was a lapsing folkie from Minnesota by way of Greenwich Village; Cooke, a lapsed gospel superstar who'd become one of the most powerful figures in black popular music when Bob Dylan was still a high schooler named Robert Zimmerman, playing Little Richard–inspired piano in garage bands. At one point in his 2004 memoir, *Chronicles, Volume One,* Dylan mentions Cooke and specifically "A Change Is Gonna Come" but only in passing, a casual allusion that might be a sly return-of-favor but that disappears as quickly as it arrives.[5]

And yet I want to suggest that these two figures have functioned in similar imaginative ways for audiences and writers, both in the period outlined here and in the years since. The discussions that have surrounded Bob Dylan and Sam Cooke—and, just as significantly, the silences that have surrounded them as well—speak to broader ideologies that have partitioned 1960s music by disguising racial difference in the language of musical difference. These two artists share far more than has been acknowledged: from their ceaseless assaults on expectations of form and genre, to their controversial defections from the traditionalist musical communities from which they sprang, to their fiercely individualist pursuits of artistic autonomy.

Dylan and Cooke loom as totemic figures in the two most important genre stories of 1960s music, that of "rock" music and that of "soul" music, respectively. A 1968 posthumous compilation of Cooke's RCA material was titled *The Man Who Invented Soul*; thirty-two years later, the same appellation appeared on the first-ever deluxe box set of the singer's material.[6] While this

claim is clearly burdened with hyperbole, Cooke's unprecedented and massively successful 1958 crossover from gospel
stardom to mainstream American pop stardom indeed created
new possibilities for African American performers in American
popular music and led to an explosion of gospel-trained singers
storming the Pop charts through the 1960s, including such
names as Marvin Gaye, Wilson Pickett, and Aretha Franklin, to
whose family's home Cooke was a frequent visitor.

Similar to Cooke's gospel-to-pop crossover, Dylan's decision
to turn his back on the folk revival and pick up an electric guitar
and rhythm section in 1965 has been cast by many as a seminal
moment in the birth of serious rock music. In broad terms it happened in three moments: first in the studio on *Bringing It All
Back Home*; then live at the Newport Folk Festival in June of
1965, a legendary performance that the historian Elijah Wald
has dubbed "the night that split the Sixties"; then, finally, in the
startling and decisive commercial and cultural breakthrough of
"Like a Rolling Stone" later that summer.[7] "Like a Rolling Stone"
has often been heralded as marking a new era of rock-and-roll
musical history, an idea that began to take root almost immediately after the song's release. In the words of one writer, "Like a
Rolling Stone" is widely heard as "the moment when pop (ephemeral, trivial) mutated into rock (enduring, significant)."[8]

Bob Dylan is the most written-about and critically assessed
artist of the rock and roll era. As the opening sentence to the
introductory essay in the *Cambridge Companion to Bob Dylan*
confidently states: "No other figure from the world of American
popular music, of this or any other era, has attracted the volume
of critical attention, much of it quite original and perceptive, that
Bob Dylan has."[9] Dylan's lyrics have been parsed by critics and
scholars and anthologized in collections of American poetry
since the mid-1960s, his position in American life figured and re-

figured by critics and historians, within the academy and without.[10] Dylan's aforementioned 2004 memoir was named one of the best books of the year by the *New York Times,* the *Washington Post,* and the *Economist,* among other publications, and was a finalist for the National Book Critics Circle Award. In 2008 the Pulitzer Prize committee awarded Dylan a special citation for "his profound impact on popular music and American culture, marked by lyrical compositions of extraordinary poetic power."[11]

Conversely, for all of Sam Cooke's generally agreed-upon significance—the first sentence of the *All Music Guide*'s entry for Cooke declares him both "the most important soul singer in history" and "the inventor of soul music"—he is a surprisingly underdiscussed figure.[12] Before Peter Guralnick's magisterial 2007 biography, *Dream Boogie: The Triumph of Sam Cooke,* there was only one full-length biography of the singer in existence, Daniel Wolff's *You Send Me: The Life and Times of Sam Cooke* (1995), cowritten with Cooke's former associates S. R. Crain, Clifton White, and G. David Tenenbaum. At the time of this writing there are no academic monographs devoted to Cooke, and only a few scholarly articles have addressed the singer.[13] Cooke is an artist whose brilliance is readily conceded but whose music itself—much of it, at least—has tended to provoke reactions ranging from disdain to pointed silence. This chapter addresses the relative paucity of attention paid to the singer, and argues that this void betrays a deep and long-standing ambivalence toward Cooke's work and career.

I will show that in many senses the stories that we have told ourselves about Bob Dylan and Sam Cooke mirror the stories that we have told ourselves about the respective genres that they have come to embody, and that the ideological underpinnings of these genres have been passed down into discussions of these artists. In the years since the careers of Dylan and Cooke briefly but significantly converged around "Blowin' in the Wind" and "A Change Is Gonna Come," the separation of these two artists' legacies—and, to a large extent, the separation of the genres they stand in for—has been enacted around a powerful and perilously vague concept: authenticity. On one hand, Cooke's relative marginalization in criticism and historiography is largely the result of his instability within discourses of black musical authenticity, where his crossover triumphs are often heard as "selling out"; on the other hand, Dylan's centrality to rock ideology is the result of an authenticity construct that has long claimed the singer-songwriter himself as its benchmark, to a wide array of uses and ends.

I want to argue that these ideologies not only are faulty and disingenuous, but also bear such a strong familial relation to each other that they are essentially mirror images that sustain and reinforce each other, linked by a history that stretches back much farther than the music that they purport to describe. By considering Dylan and Cooke together, I want to disrupt a troubling and ongoing tendency to listen to and analyze these artists in racially reductive and overdetermined ways, and in doing so offer an alternate path into understanding their music that rescues a moment when "change" was in the air, the ears, and the songs themselves.

The Making of Sam Cooke: Commerce, Religion, and Black Musical Authenticity

In the early morning hours of December 11, 1964, Sam Cooke was shot to death at a $3-a-night motel in a dilapidated neighborhood of Los Angeles. It was the most momentous rock-and-roll death since Buddy Holly's, but because of the timing and circumstances of the shooting, news of Cooke's death was slow to spread, and details sketchy as they emerged. Hotel employee Bertha Franklin confessed to pulling the trigger but claimed self-defense, alleging that a drunken and enraged Cooke had broken down the door to her office and physically accosted her, and on December 15 a coroner's jury ruled the singer's death a "justifiable homicide."[14]

Reaction to Cooke's death, particularly in the African American community, was fraught and skeptical, with rumors of a "frame-up" circulating so persistently that Los Angeles police were forced to issue a formal denial.[15] A letter to the editor of the *Chicago Defender* written by a high school student who identified herself as "Frances L." declared of the verdict: "There have been so many things overlooked. Why? I know the answer, and so does everyone else. If it had been the Beatles or Ricky Nelson, the investigation wouldn't stop until the truth was known. Will the Negro ever get a equal chance—even in death?"[16] Others accepted Franklin's story and even seemed to blame Cooke for his own demise: "If he hadn't have left God, left the church, it never would have happened," Reverend Clay Evans of the Fellowship Missionary Baptist Church in Cooke's hometown of Chicago later declared.[17]

In death as in life, Sam Cooke was many things to many people. To some he was a handsome and clean-cut pop idol; to others, a fallen star who had left gospel music for the material rewards of rock and roll; to still more, a shining example of African American pride and independence, a self-made entertainer and businessman whose groundbreaking successes helped alter the racial dynamics of the entertainment industry. In the years since his passing, Cooke's stature as both a major American vocalist and a transformative influence on the history of popular music has only grown. As Craig Werner eloquently puts it, his was "a voice that possessed a unique ability to call forth strong responses from the black folk attending the gospel show that night in California and from the teens, black and white, who heard it on their transistor radios."[18]

For all of this influence, however, Cooke's position in musical historiography is an uneasy one. As was the case during Cooke's life, evaluations of the singer's posthumous legacy are plagued with anxieties over this very crossover. In his widely read, polemical history of midcentury African American popular music, Nelson George complained of "the obnoxious studio input of white producers" on Cooke's music, even though it is well documented that Cooke was largely in charge of his own studio production.[19] The historian Brian Ward has assailed George's accusations of interracial interference but still laments the "glutinous strings and perfunctory female choruses" of Cooke's "pop" material, while the critic Dave Marsh writes that in Cooke's transition from gospel to pop, "the aesthetic purity of [his] music had been sullied."[20]

Such statements evince critical discomfort toward certain musical choices that Cooke made: they hear the singer's embrace of a more "pop" aesthetic as dilutive and inauthentic. This dilution/purity dialectic has a long history in discussions of black music but was perhaps most prominently articulated in Amiri Baraka's (then LeRoi Jones's) landmark study *Blues People: Negro Music in White America*, first published in 1963, the year Sam Cooke heard "Blowin' in the Wind."[21] In Jones's telling, black music's proximity to what the writer held as white influence— aesthetic or commercial—was seen as a compromising if not entirely destructive force. "The most expressive Negro music of any given period will be an exact reflection of what the Negro himself is," Jones declared, a provocative if tautological statement dependent upon the author's own specific criteria of racial authenticity.[22]

In such purity-versus-dilution appraisals, Cooke's recording career is roughly viewed as having three stages: a gospel stage, in which the young Cooke sang lead for the Soul Stirrers, one of the most successful gospel quintets in the country, from 1950 to 1957; a move to pop that found Cooke forsaking his gospel roots in search of mainstream success with songs such as "You Send Me," "Wonderful World," and "Cupid"; and a final return to a gospel aesthetic, in which Cooke reembraced his past and reached his apotheosis, musically evidenced by his civil rights masterpiece, "A Change Is Gonna Come." As the musicologist Mark Burford sums it up, "Music critics, biographers, and cultural commentators alike have demonstrated a remarkably consistent fealty to a narrative of gospel triumphalism that basks in Cooke's legacy of laying the foundation for 1960s soul music in spite of the insidious lure of fifties pop schmaltz."[23]

Instead of allowing the story of Cooke's life and work to be fragmented by anxieties over autonomy and authenticity, we would do better to examine Cooke's career as a holistic endeavor united by an ongoing aesthetic experimentalism. To characterize Cooke's crossover in terms of compromise and dilution forecloses the very artistic autonomy whose supposed loss is lamented by certain of Cooke's critics; what's more, it perpetuates notions of "authentic" black musicality that are rooted in imaginings of black music as primordial and premodern, definitively divorced from the market and ambitions of mobility. As Ronald Radano has argued, these authenticity fantasies presuppose the existence of an ideal purity that exists outside of history, and draw from a legacy of racial thought rooted in ideas of cross-cultural impossibility and unequal difference.[24]

I want to argue that the "problem" of Sam Cooke, the problem that accounts for the striking critical ambivalence—or, most often, silence—that surrounds him is one of race, the unwieldy collision of musical and racial imagination. Cooke is made to stand in for a host of anxieties about a black singer's obligation to his race, not in the political sense of a broader African American community—Cooke both felt this obligation and strove to fulfill it—but in the vague and mystical notion that there is and ought to be an immutable connection between skin color and artistic capacity. In an essay published only a few months prior to Cooke's recording "A Change Is Gonna Come," Ralph Ellison wrote that "no matter how strictly Negroes are segregated socially and politically, on the level of the imagination their ability to achieve freedom is limited only by their individual aspiration, insight, energy and will."[25] Cooke's career is a study in individual imagination, one misunderstood by far-reaching systems of thought that would quietly seek to limit its possibilities.

Sam Cook arrived into the world on January 22, 1931, in Clarksdale, Mississippi, the fifth child born to Reverend Charles Cook and his wife, Annie Mae.[26] Shortly before Sam's second birthday Charles announced intentions to move the family to Chicago, where he founded a congregation at the Christ Temple Church in Chicago Heights, an ethnically diverse suburb thirty miles outside of the city. Charles also took employment at the Reynolds Metals plant, where he would work long enough to reach the position of shop steward, and where his income eventually allowed him to move his family to a comfortable apartment in the four-story Lenox building at 3527 Cottage Grove Avenue in Chicago. By the age of six, Sam was singing tenor among four of his siblings in a five-member gospel group called the Singing Children: at the height of their popularity, the group had a manager, a booking fee, and a chauffeured white Cadillac to take them to performances. For the Cook family, music provided the potential for both spiritual fulfillment and material advancement, an intertwining of religion and commerce that would dominate Sam Cooke's entire musical career and his posthumous legacy.

In 1949, during his senior year at Wendell Phillips High School in Chicago, Cook joined a fledgling gospel quartet called the Highway QCs. The group quickly achieved considerable regional success, and the following year Cook was asked to audition for the Soul Stirrers. Formed in Trinity, Texas, in 1926 by Senior Roy (S. R.) Crain, the Soul Stirrers rose to national stardom with the addition of tenor R. H. Harris in 1937.[27] In 1950, the Soul Stirrers were named the country's "Top Gospel Group" by an *Ebony* magazine writer who noted that the Stirrers "employ the revival-type of spirituals which appeal to emotions."[28] That very year, Harris abruptly quit after tiring of the group's grueling tour schedule, and a replacement needed to be found quickly.

Crain and the other Soul Stirrers were impressed by Cook's voice and developing talent for songwriting, and at the age of nineteen, Sam Cook was named to replace one of the most famous gospel singers in the United States. After several months of rehearsals and occasional performances, Cook accompanied the Soul Stirrers to Los Angeles, where the group was scheduled to have a recording session with Specialty Records. Specialty was an independent label run by a white ex-Pennsylvanian named Art Rupe. Rupe had founded the label in 1946 with the aim of producing gospel and rhythm and blues music.[29] Rupe had initially been hesitant to record the Stirrers without Harris, but when Specialty finally released "Jesus Gave Me Water," the first single featuring Sam Cook on lead vocal, the record became the group's highest-selling in history and established Cook as a star.

The Stirrers remained one of the nation's most successful gospel acts through much of the 1950s, during which time they produced a vast and brilliant recorded legacy for Art Rupe's label. The livelihood of a national gospel group, however, was not determined by the studio but by the road, and Cook and his fellow group members toured constantly. While many of these performances went unrecorded, an exception is the 1955 First Annual Summer Festival of Gospel Music, held at Los Angeles's Shrine Auditorium. This recording features three numbers by the Soul Stirrers and culminates in an eight-and-a-half-minute, show-stopping rendition of "Nearer to Thee," an original composition by Cook that is a refashioning of the hymn "Nearer My God to Thee."[30]

The performance at the Shrine is a vocal showcase for Cook: his voice is more full-throated and dynamically spectacular than on Soul Stirrers studio recordings as he dramatically plays with time, phrasing, and volume. His performance is impassioned yet controlled, and even at twenty-four he is a clearly seasoned showman: as the performance reaches its climax, the audience continuously erupts as he moves off the microphone for his loudest cries, a shrewd technique that creates the effect of a power almost unbearable. Baritone Paul Foster echoes each word of Cook's "Nearer My God to Thee" refrain with antiphonal shouts, and the guitarist, Leroy Crume, plays propulsive triplets reminiscent of Sister Rosetta Tharpe. The world of professional gospel stardom—and male gospel stardom in particular—was one in which spiritual charisma and sexual charisma were often deftly melded together, and the ecstasy elicited by Cook's performance on this recording seems not entirely theological.[31]

The Shrine concert sounds a representative triumph of Cooke's time with the Soul Stirrers, and yet one can already hear him beginning to exceed the group's stage. Specialty, well aware of Cooke's tremendous potential, began sending Bumps Blackwell, an A&R man who had recently signed a charismatic Georgian named Little Richard, out on tour with the Soul Stirrers to scout their lead singer's performances. In the mid-1950s Specialty was, in many ways, the perfect incubator for Cooke's growing ambitions. In 1952 the label had released Lloyd Price's "Lawdy Miss Clawdy," the biggest R&B hit in Specialty's history and a record whose "white under-the-counter sales" were a crucial predecessor to the coming commercial explosion of rock and roll.[32]

In 1956, Sam Cooke sent a letter to Art Rupe in which he informed his label head that "a friend I've been knowing for quite a while asked me if I would consider recording some popular ballads for one of the major recording companies if he could arrange it. I told him yes."[33] Rupe told Cooke that under no circumstances could he record for a label other than Specialty, but that Specialty would happily record him singing popular material. Cooke's first foray into pop singing was a song called "Lovable," a secularized rewrite of the Soul Stirrers' "Wonderful." The record, released under the pseudonym "Dale Cook," did not sell. Frustrated, Cooke redoubled his commitment to songwriting and in April 1957 sent Bumps Blackwell a sketch for a song called "You Send Me." Cooke recorded "You Send Me" in the basement studio at Specialty Records' Los Angeles office, and Cooke and Blackwell chose to bring in big-band arranger Rene Hall to give the proceedings an air of pop sophistication. Art Rupe arrived to the session late and flew into a rage over Hall's arrangement, causing Cooke and Blackwell to surreptitiously bring the song across town to a label called Keen Records. Keen agreed to record Cooke's pop material and to give Blackwell and Cooke more artistic and economic independence than Rupe had ever conceded, although the circumvention of Specialty later led to a costly legal dispute.[34]

"You Send Me" is a catchy and straightforward piece of pop music. The verse section relies on a simple I-vi-ii-V chord progression and consists of repetitions of "darling, you send me" and "darling, you thrill me." The bridge, which occurs twice in the single's two minutes and forty-five seconds, contains the closest approximation of a narrative: "At first I thought it was infatuation / But oh, it's lasted so long / And now I find myself wanting / To marry you and take you home."

In a 1958 interview conducted after the breakthrough of "You Send Me," Cooke explicitly credited his pop success to his gospel experience: "I think singing spirituals is the best training for a singer. That's how I developed my easy style from singing spirituals."[35] Nonetheless, "You Send Me" was both a commercial and artistic experiment for the singer: the song's arrangement is decidedly different than anything attempted by the Soul Stirrers, and harmonically the song's chord changes are more reminiscent of Tin Pan Alley than a hymn (the song's chord progression borrows the opening bars of George Gershwin's "I've Got Rhythm," among the most well-worn chord changes in American popular music).[36] Perhaps the most startling difference between "You Send Me" and Cooke's earlier material—and the element of the arrangement that apparently most enraged Rupe—is the presence of white female backup singers: this is the first time in Cooke's recorded career that he is singing with anyone besides an all-male supporting cast, a facet of the recording that both softens and subtly sexualizes the young star. When the song was released by Keen in 1957 (under the name "Sam Cooke") it began a startling rise up the *Billboard* Pop charts, eventually reaching number one and selling more than two and a half million copies.[37]

"You Send Me" made Sam Cooke a star and a watershed figure in American musical history, a position that did not come without its complications. By the time Cooke departed from the Soul Stirrers in the wake of his shocking pop breakthrough, black gospel music had long been big business in the United States. Thomas A. Dorsey had begun his career as a jazz and blues pianist, started writing gospel songs in the early 1930s, and became one of the most successful American songwriters of his generation, owner of his own publishing company, and author of standards such as "Take My Hand, Precious Lord" and "Peace in the Valley." The Soul Stirrers and their contemporaries, like the Golden Gate Quartet, the Swan Silvertones, and Mahalia Jackson, were successful by nearly any industry standard, and the idea that African American religious music was divorced from commercial markets had been false since at least the late nineteenth century, when the Fisk Jubilee Singers of Fisk University achieved great success for their fledgling university by performing arranged spirituals on concert stages for paying audiences.[38] Still, the idea of religious music as being the artistically "purest" form of black musical expression has deep roots: W. E. B. Du Bois, James Weldon Johnson, and Alain Locke are just a few prominent intellectuals who held the spirituals to be the pinnacle of black art in the United States during the first part of the twentieth century, with Johnson describing them as "a record and a revelation of the deeper thoughts and experiences of the Negro in this country," Locke as "the most characteristic product of the race genius as yet in America," and Du Bois, most memorably, as "the most beautiful expression of human experience, born this side of the seas . . . the singular spiritual heritage of the nation and the greatest gift of the Negro people."[39] Much more recently, Radano has argued that this legacy stretches back at least as far as the early writings of white "collectors" of the spirituals in the 1860s, writing that "in images at once Godlike and heathen, the slave songs represented the height of spiritual perfection. . . . References to the slave songs as spirituals epitomized the new alignment of blackness and the sacred."[40]

The elevation of religious music to the epitome of authentic black musicality also speaks to a broader tendency noted by Karl Hagstrom Miller: the urge for critics and historians to describe black music making in terms that are inherently *collective*.[41] This has extended to nonmusical contexts, in which the call-and-response dynamic, the "ring shout," and jazz-derived metaphors of collective interaction have been highly influential in discussions of African American culture more generally.[42] While certainly useful, Miller points out that the abundance of metaphors about music making as a collective experience "has a tendency to trap individuals within a racial collectivity, naturalizing music as an outgrowth of one's life rather than a cultivated talent and obscuring the meaning and uses of art that falls outside of racially defined cultural borders."[43] In other words, individuating traits such as technique, ambition, and stylistic diversity become subordinated to one's role within a group, and his or her imagined obligations to that group.

The presumed aesthetic primacy of black religious music—what Burford names as "gospel triumphalism"—and that presumption's connection to an overarching constellation of ideas about anticommercialism, collectivity, and racial authenticity, is crucial to understanding the dynamics of Sam Cooke's transition from gospel to pop, both in the context of Cooke's initial crossover and in the discourse surrounding it since. When Sam Cooke departed gospel for pop this notion of collective obligation was violated, and in a way that also ran afoul of beliefs that the most "authentic" black music was that which was farthest from the market, the white market in particular.

Gospel finding its way into the secular mainstream was, of course, by no means unprecedented before Cooke. In 1954, Ray Charles scored a massive hit with a song called "I Got a Woman," which reached number one on the *Billboard* R&B charts and paved the way for Charles to become one of the most important recording artists of the twentieth century. "I Got a Woman" was essentially a secular rewrite of the hymn "It Must Be Jesus," one that anyone familiar with the Golden Tones' recording of the hymn that same year would have recognized, and that some would have surely found blasphemous. Charles, however, had never been a gospel star and had been in the business of making secular music his entire adult life—in other words, whatever transgressions he may have committed, he could not be accused of being a musical apostate. Furthermore, "I Got a Woman" did not cross over from *Billboard*'s black music (R&B) chart to its white (Pop) one, as "You Send Me" did.

After the success of "You Send Me," Cooke seized upon the lucrative potential of a mixed-race teenaged audience by writing and recording hits such as "Only Sixteen" (1959) and "Wonderful World" (1960). The singer also started to assume increasing control over his own destiny as both a performer and a businessman. In 1959 Cooke struck a deal with RCA, who would now record and release Cooke's own material. In 1960, Cooke and his associate S. R. Crain founded SAR Records, a label distributed by RCA that recorded an impressive roster of gospel and R&B artists and made Cooke the rare African American recording star who was also a record executive.

Cooke's songwriting began to change as well, showing a growing interest in social concerns. In 1960, he released the song "Chain Gang," stemming from an encounter that Cooke and his brother Charles had with a prison work crew while traveling in the South. While not an explicitly political piece of music, with its emphasis on hardship, pain, and uncertainty "Chain Gang" contained a deeper severity and urgency than any pop material that Cooke had written previously. Despite its bleak subject matter—the song is a lament sung by a prisoner, pining for his "baby" while the other prisoners "moan their lives away"—it reached number two on the Pop charts and became Cooke's biggest hit since "You Send Me." As an RCA artist bio of Cooke from this period proudly declared, "Cooke's musical voicings abound with deep spiritual feeling—or 'soul' as it is labeled in the vernacular. With him, it's a natural way to sing."[44] This description neatly reflects the way Cooke's gospel background productively melded with his pop appeal, in both his music and his marketing.

By the early 1960s Cooke's career was a study in versatility. He was a successful pop idol and gospel producer, a man who could perform both in American living rooms on the *Ed Sullivan Show* and before fervent young audiences at the Town Hill Club in Brooklyn. He had emerged as a study in musical cosmopolitanism, and his talent and breadth of interests led him to challenge numerous musical and cultural borders, implicitly and explicitly. He became a musical leader, helping other musicians that were attempting to transition from sacred to secular music, or from R&B to pop. In 1961 Cooke went on tour with the daughter of his friend the Reverend C. L. Franklin, a shy nineteen-year-old named Aretha, who later recalled that she "deeply appreciated Sam's friendship" and the inspiration she derived from knowing that "if Sam could make it, perhaps I could too."[45]

In April of 1962 Cooke went into a Los Angeles recording studio to record "Bring It on Home to Me," a new composition credited to Cooke that was a loose rewrite of his friend Charles Brown's "I Wanna Go Home." "Bring It on Home to Me" is a fascinating moment in Cooke's musical development. Performed as a duet with backup singer Lou Rawls, Cooke and Rawls sing the entire song in tandem, with Rawls providing gruff baritone harmony to Cooke's lead. The song's refrain—"Bring it to me, bring your sweet loving / Bring it on home to me"—is followed by a call-

and-response pattern, with Cooke singing a simple "yeah" and Rawls, J. W. Alexander, and associate Fred Smith echoing back the same word. From a performance standpoint "Bring It on Home" was reminiscent of Cooke's work with the Soul Stirrers, and it was perhaps the most overtly gospel-influenced recording of his pop career to date.

But the song's lyrics indicate an aesthetic engagement with another contemporary musical happening, one with strong ties to the ongoing civil rights movement: the folk revival of the early 1960s. The final couplet of "Bring It on Home to Me," "You know I'll always be your slave / Until I'm buried, buried in my grave," is an audacious revision of the nineteenth-century antislavery song "Oh, Freedom!," the refrain of which contains the line, "and before I'd be a slave, I'll be buried in my grave." In 1956, African American folksinger Odetta had recorded "Oh, Freedom!" on her debut album, *Odetta Sings Blues and Ballads*, and by the early 1960s the song had become a staple of the folk revival and the civil rights movement. In August of 1963 Joan Baez performed "Oh, Freedom!" at the March on Washington, an event that also featured a young Bob Dylan, who only a few years prior had quit his high school rock-and-roll band to take up folk music. (Notably, the artist whom Dylan later credited with inspiring this musical epiphany was Odetta herself, citing her performances from *Odetta Sings Blues and Ballads* specifically.[46]) That same day, hundreds of thousands of marchers were also treated to Peter, Paul and Mary's rendition of Dylan's "Blowin' in the Wind," the song that would soon inspire what is widely considered Cooke's masterpiece, "A Change Is Gonna Come."

Liveness, Politics, and "A Change Is Gonna Come"

In January of 1963 Sam Cooke recorded a live performance at Miami's predominantly black Harlem Square Club. RCA intended to release the album under the somewhat salacious title *One Night Stand,* although the recording ultimately didn't appear in stores until 1985, now titled *Live at the Harlem Square Club, 1963.* Eighteen months after the Square Club performance, in July of 1964, Cooke recorded another live performance at New York's prestigious (and predominantly white) Copacabana nightclub, released later that year under the title *Live at the Copa.* *Live at the Harlem Square Club, 1963* and *Live at the Copa* are the two most well-preserved documents of Sam Cooke's live performances in the 1960s, and the recordings are a fascinating study in contrasts and versatility. *Harlem Square Club* finds Cooke performing in full gospel fury, inciting the crowd to a frenzy and racking his voice to the edge of oblivion. *Live at the Copa,* on the other hand, is debonair and refined: after a notoriously unsuccessful engagement at the nightclub as a callow teen idol in 1958, Cooke was intent on proving himself to a new audience. "You know these old cats," he told an interviewer before the show, "they don't go out much. A lot of them are lonely. They *need* records. They need them worse than anybody. I'm going to sell them."[47]

The choice of repertoire on *Live at the Harlem Square Club, 1963* and *Live at the Copa* is quite different, perhaps unsurprising given the demographics of each venue, and in the space of this difference we hear the formation of the aesthetic that would birth "A Change Is Gonna Come." In the Square Club recording, Cooke mostly performs his own material in a set heavy with contemporary hits such as "Chain Gang," "Cupid," and "Bring It on Home to Me," while the Copa set is largely made up of standards. An instructive contrast between the two performances can be heard in the difference between the renditions of "You Send Me," which on the Square Club recording lasts only a moment, as a quick tease during a lengthy introduction to "Bring It on Home to Me."

The brief Square Club "You Send Me" features dramatic stop-time accompaniment from the band while Cooke weaves a half-sung, half-spoken narrative about the collapse of a relationship and his desire to get his "baby" back. Cooke works the crowd with precision, inviting and acknowledging their interjections and addressing his audience as "children," a secularized rendition of the gospel tradition of "testifying." Cooke goes on to describe a phone call between him and his baby, which leads to the payoff line, the instantly recognizable "darling, you send me" refrain, released to a deluge of shrieks from his audience. Cooke's vocal here is sung with desperate urgency; the "oh" that precedes the ubiquitous "you send me" refrain on the original recording is elongated into an anguished cry, while the "you" cascades melismatically, dripping with carnal implication. He repeats the refrain three times, then goes into two repetitions of his famous "whoa-oh-oh-oh" yodel—separated by a devious and playful laugh—finally landing on the long-anticipated "honest you do," at which point the band breaks into "Bring It on Home to Me."[48]

Cooke's performance of "You Send Me" at the Copa is hugely different. He performs the song as part of a medley, alongside the standards "Try a Little Tenderness" and "For Sentimental Reasons." Gone is the testifying and stop-time arrangement from the Square Club. Cooke's vocal at the Copa is not furious and ravaged, but subtle and mellifluous. He toys with his phrasing, makes playful asides to his audience, and while his churlish laughter from the Square Club performance is heard as well, here it has a more debonair affect. The arrangement is lush and stately: as opposed to the small group heard on the Square Club recording, the Copa performance includes full horns, a gently swinging rhythm section, and a light electric guitar playing fills and flourishes. By the close of the performance, his Copa crowd is won, and Cooke's return to the club has proved triumphant. "He has dignity, humility and feeling to go with a strong voice,"

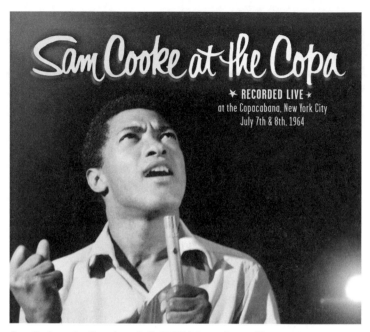

Sam Cooke at the Copa (1964). © ABKCO Records. Used by permission.

wrote a reviewer for the *New York Times,* gently tempering praise with racial platitudes.[49]

It is tempting to hear Cooke's fiery performance before the black audience in Miami as more "authentic" than his more subdued performance on the Copa stage. Indeed, by the time the *Square Club* LP finally appeared in stores this was certainly the line RCA was pushing: according to a 1985 press release, "This album will enhance Sam Cooke's reputation as a founding father of soul music. It presents him in a setting in which he has never before been heard on record, one a world apart from his only previously released live album, *Sam Cooke Live at the Copa.*"[50] The implication is that *Live at the Harlem Square Club, 1963* offers us a window into the "real" Sam Cooke, the version of the singer who can be more easily retroactively slotted into the genre story of soul music.

But a closer listen to both LPs hears Cooke using his own versatility to disrupt various dichotomies and constraints. The Square Club recording finds Cooke overtly applying gospel performance practices to secular and outwardly lustful material, a thrilling transgression that is manifested both in the ferocity of his performance and the titillation of the audience's response. On the other hand, the Copa performance finds a young, black pop star playing before an upper-class, white, and relatively conservative audience, winning them over on his own terms.

Cooke's Copa set features another moment that contradicts the claim that Cooke "continued to tiptoe around the sensibilities of his mainstream white audience," as one writer has it: an upbeat and swinging cover of Bob Dylan's "Blowin' in the Wind."[51] The inclusion of Dylan's civil rights anthem is not merely an unusual song choice in a set largely made up of standards, but it is also a clear political gesture from Cooke, who by the time of the Copa recording had grown increasingly engaged with the movement. In late 1963, Cooke had been arrested in Shreveport, Louisiana, for refusing to leave a hotel that would not allow him and his wife to register, and by 1964 he had established a friendship with Malcolm X, whom he had met through their mutual friend Cassius Clay.

Cooke's decision to bring "Blowin' in the Wind" to the crowd at the Copa was both a politically and culturally transgressive act. While many in his audience surely knew the song—Peter, Paul and Mary's hit version, released in June of 1963, had reached number two on the Pop charts—in mid-1964 Bob Dylan was still a liminal figure in American life, poet-troubadour to a rising New Left whose behavior and artistic persona were viewed by many as overly radical. Dylan was assuredly famous, but his music was perceived as oppositional to mainstream American society, and many of his most publicized moments reflected this, such as his ban from television's *Ed Sullivan Show* for refusing to remove the satirical "Talking John Birch Society Blues" from his act in 1963.[52] Although Cooke was black and Dylan was white, Cooke still had entry into levels of "establishment" America that the young folksinger did not—as the Copa engagement itself illustrates—and the decision to introduce one of Dylan's most politically pointed compositions into the Copa context is not one Cooke would have made casually.

As noted at the start of this chapter, "Blowin' in the Wind" had a profound impact on Cooke and was a primary inspiration for what is arguably his most famous composition, "A Change Is Gonna Come." Cooke biographer Daniel Wolff has also written that partial inspiration for "A Change Is Gonna Come" came from Martin Luther King's "I Have a Dream" speech, while Cooke's fellow Soul Stirrer S. R. Crain claimed that the song was rooted in Cooke's gospel past: "If you ever listen to a Soul Stirrer Song, you'd recognize it."[53] By the time Cooke recorded "A Change Is Gonna Come" in early 1964, the song was a unification of the divergent styles heard on the *Harlem Square Club* and *Copa* recordings, a striking blend of sacred and secular, pop and protest, elegance and urgency.

"A Change Is Gonna Come" opens with a bombastic orchestral introduction, replete with strings, tympani, and a mournful French horn that leads into Cooke's vocal. On the song's opening couplet, "I was born by the river, in a little tent," Cooke's voice soars to a high B-flat on the word "born," then drops the final "r" on the word "river," a clearly deliberate move from a singer who prided himself on diction. "Oh, and just like the river, I've been running ever since," completes the first verse, and we hear the song's refrain: "It's been a long time coming, but I know / a change gonna come." While the musical arrangement and backdrop—strings, lush horns, and a drummer playing brushes— resembles the Copacabana far more than the Harlem Square Club, Cooke's vocal draws from the gospel tradition while his lyrical text culls its imagery from spirituals. The song's third verse, excised from the initial single release, is its most explicitly and immediately political—"I go to the movies, and I go downtown / somebody keeps telling me, don't hang around"— while the bridge is despairing and angry: "I go to my brother / and I say brother, help me please / But he winds up knocking me / Back down on my knees." Harmonically, the song's chord changes weave between major and minor, its refrain featuring a G-minor chord on the line "a change gonna come" that resolves to B-flat major on the final affirmation, "Oh yes it will."

The grandeur of "A Change Is Gonna Come" is stylistically inverse to the stripped directness of "Blowin' in the Wind" as it appears on *The Freewheelin' Bob Dylan.* If one listens closely, however, one can hear "Blowin' in the Wind" in "A Change Is Gonna Come." "I was born by the river, in a little tent / and like that river I've been runnin' ever since" contains the same pastoralism as the roads, mountains, and doves of "Blowin' in the Wind," and both songs include ruminations on death. The closing verse of "Blowin' in the Wind' opens with the question "How many times must a man look up / before he can see the sky?" and ends asking "How many deaths will it take till he knows / That too many people have died?" The second verse of "A Change Is Gonna Come" proclaims "It's been too hard livin', but I'm afraid to die / 'cause I don't know what's up there beyond the sky," a striking ambivalence toward the afterlife that seems to refute Cooke's own gospel background while imbuing the song with earthly immediacy.

"A Change Is Gonna Come" can be heard as an emphatic response to the questions of "Blowin' in the Wind," which unfolds as a litany of interrogatives answered by the refrain "The answer, my friend / is blowin' in the wind." "A Change Is Gonna Come" asks no questions and instead is a series of declarative statements. Moreover, "A Change Is Gonna Come" corrects the indeterminate ambiguity invoked by the "Blowin' in the Wind" refrain, declaring that, in fact, a change *is* going to come. While "Blowin' in the Wind" exists in a premodern bucolic folk landscape, Cooke invokes modern imagery of material deprivation through his explicit mention of being turned away from stores and movie theaters. As Barry Shank writes of "A Change Is Gonna Come," "The not-quite-present violence quietly hides behind the authority of the voice that simply says, don't hang around. . . . Threats did not have to be spoken aloud. They were part of the social order."[54] Here racism and segregation are questions not only of existential morality but also of real, lived oppression and inequality.

In January of 1964—the same month Sam Cooke recorded "A Change Is Gonna Come"—Ralph Ellison gave a lecture at the Library of Congress in which he discussed the power of "technique" in the practice of writing, arguing that the process of mastering a form allows artists to forge an identity and self that transcend boundaries of racial category. "Perhaps the writer's greatest freedom, as artist, lies precisely in his possession of technique," declared Ellison, and then added, "it is *technique* which transforms the individual before he is able to transform it."[55]

"A Change Is Gonna Come" is a triumph of technique and a tribute to its potential freedoms. Cooke marshals a wide array of musical and lyrical devices in a statement of artistic liberation and racial justice, a direct product of Cooke's ongoing project of expanding notions of what black music could or should be. "A Change Is Gonna Come" is an ambitious and audacious piece of music, an orchestral "answer record" from one of the most powerful black entertainers in America to a young white folk-singer, one that stretches from the gospel circuit to the bright lights of Los Angeles, from the Shrine Concert to the Copacabana. Cooke's vision of black music, as evidenced in "Change," held race as a terrain of political struggle rather than a basis for prescribed aesthetic criteria; the notion that one's skin color must necessarily correlate with the content of one's character, musical or otherwise, was to be fiercely resisted.

To argue that "A Change Is Gonna Come" exceeds "Blowin' in the Wind" in political power isn't intended to diminish the latter. Dylan wrote the song when he was only twenty years old, and by the time Sam Cooke recorded his revision, Dylan was already wary of the extent to which "Blowin' in the Wind" had come to define him. Like Cooke, Dylan would soon take the growing pressures he was facing—both interior and exterior—and emerge with a new piece of music, drastically different than his earlier work, that would alter the trajectory of rock and roll music: "Like a Rolling Stone." Sam Cooke, tragically, would not live to hear it.

"Like a Rolling Stone" would also place Dylan at the center of an emergent genre discourse that he would in many senses come to embody, first that of "folk rock" and then simply "rock" music. This discourse did not openly concern itself with discussions of racial authenticity or group obligation. Rather, rock music conceived of musical creativity in fiercely individualist terms, as matters of personal transcendence that could hardly be more starkly opposed to collectivist notions of black musical authenticity. And yet the music nonetheless crucially relied on those notions in crafting its own self-understanding.

Rock music constructed an ideology of authenticity based on an ideal of heroic genius and resistant rebellion that rendered its racial qualifications implicit rather than explicit. By adopting its individualist ethos, rock ideology was able to deny outwardly race's salience, even proclaim its own affinity for and indebtedness to black musical forms, while constructing an expressive ideal increasingly defined by an exclusionary white masculinity. And through no fault of his own, the figure who most enabled this was Bob Dylan, an artist whose mythic "break" from folk to rock was far more of a connective move than both communities might have been inclined to admit.

"It Matters Less Where He Has Been Than Where He Is Going": The Folk Revival and the Making of Bob Dylan

The famed ethnomusicologist Charles Seeger once remarked that "the folk song is, by definition, and, as far we can tell, by reality, entirely a product of plagiarism."[56] It's fitting, then, that it was reportedly Seeger's son, the eminent folksinger Pete Seeger, who first pointed out that the melody to Bob Dylan's "Blowin' in the Wind" was borrowed from the nineteenth-century antislavery song "No More Auction Block for Me" (sometimes titled "Many Thousands Gone").[57] Dylan never made a studio recording of "No More Auction Block for Me," but buried amid the Dylanalia collected on 1991's *The Bootleg Series, Vol. 1* is a 1962 recording of a twenty-one-year-old Dylan playing the song at the Gaslight coffee shop in Greenwich Village.

It's a terrific performance, one whose musical triumph is surpassed only by its strangeness. Dylan accompanies himself on acoustic guitar, his instrumental backdrop marked by sparse, single-string melodic figures cushioned by chorded, thirty-second-note tremolos. The vocal performance carries an affected agedness, a boyish voice rendered world-weary, occasionally venturing to intone the repeated "no more, no more" with a clipped melisma. The song's famous "many thousands gone" refrain is carefully elongated, its severity and sorrow palpable. On the recording Dylan is only a few years younger than Sam Cooke was when he sang "Nearer To Thee" at the Shrine, and while Dylan lacks the soaring virtuosity of Cooke's performance his precociousness is nearly as remarkable, his sense of time and phrasing already well formed. As opposed to the frenzied ecstasy of the Shrine concert, at the Gaslight there is little crowd noise audible outside of the occasional clinking of glasses, as the small audience hangs raptly on the young singer's every word.

There is, of course, something uncanny and perhaps even unsettling in hearing a young white Minnesotan intone a song explicitly about the horrors of chattel slavery, replete with imagery of pints of salt and drivers' lashes, all rendered in the first person. Dylan's performance is remarkably powerful, but deciphering what exactly lies behind this power begs a number of difficult questions. Is the solemnity of this performance, and the audience's response to it, a remnant of what Radano identifies as white inscription of unknowable difference upon black music, traceable to the initial collection of the slave spirituals?[58] Is the imaginative elision of angst-ridden white identity with the historical reality of black slavery, even in such a serious context, simply another iteration of blackface minstrelsy? Or does the intercultural repurposing of this song for a progressive political project represent a harnessing of black music by white performers to a vastly different end, where the envisioned utopia is not the racial subjugation of minstrelsy, but a world made from integration and equality?

The underlying and unresolvable tension of these questions speaks to the strange mix of history, nostalgia, and racial ideology

that permeated the early 1960s folk revival, a musical movement that sought to reconcile a nostalgic American populism
with a progressive political ideology of material redistribution,
Cold War demilitarization, and desegregation. Like all folk
revivals, the revival of the early 1960s was necessarily and
explicitly derived from historical lineage but it was also unique
to its own time, and the revival that produced Dylan's performance of "No More Auction Block" carried its own unique set of
artistic stakes and political motivations.

In the remainder of this chapter, I will argue that the racial
imagination of the folk revival is the clearest intellectual
and ideological antecedent to the racial imagination of rock
music that took shape in the 1960s and has extended far past it.
I'll also argue that the vision of black music that permeated the
folk revival and was transferred to white rock music is strikingly similar, if not even identical, to that which haunts discussions of Sam Cooke. As previously mentioned, the key vessel
through which this transference took place was Bob Dylan.
It was through Dylan that the mass culture of rock and roll
was able to selectively appropriate certain philosophies of the
early 1960s folk revival, a musical culture whose anticommercialism and antimodernism were seemingly antithetical, if not
outwardly antagonistic, toward rock and roll itself. Dylan's
departure from folk music has been recorded in myth as pre-
cipitating both the "end" of the folk revival and the "beginning" of serious rock music, his famously controversial performance at the 1965 Newport Folk Festival and subsequent
release of "Like a Rolling Stone" being held as turning points.
Much in the way that Sam Cooke fled gospel for the world of pop,
helping to create the genre of soul music through sacrilege and
sacrifice, Dylan has carried the burden of genre formation and

musical epoch-making in rock music upon his shoulders since the mid-1960s.

The critic Lee Marshall writes that "the gravitas Dylan attained from being a 'serious' folk artist is important for the ideology of rock," and Simon Frith has argued that Dylan's move from folk to rock and roll gave rock ideology its first legitimate "individual genius" figure.[59] I would go further and argue that Dylan's symbolic significance brought to rock music a way of thinking about African American music that was remarkably similar to that espoused by certain corners of the folk revival. This racial imagination was rooted in deep historical fantasies about the purity and power of black performance that had adapted themselves to various historical circumstances and would again, in transmission from the folk revival to rock music.

The details of Bob Dylan's biography have been recounted exhaustively and frequently elsewhere, so my recounting here will be relatively brief.[60] Born Robert Zimmerman in Duluth, Minnesota, the first of Abraham and Beatrice Zimmerman's two sons, on May 24, 1941, his family moved seventy-five miles northwest to the town of Hibbing in 1947, where Dylan would spend the remainder of his childhood and adolescence. The young Dylan was a musical sponge: in his 2004 memoir, in the same discussion of his first exposure to the folk songs of the Kingston Trio and Brothers Four, Dylan writes effusively of Roy Orbison, who "transcended all the genres—folk, country, rock and roll or just about anything. His stuff mixed all the styles and some that hadn't even been invented yet. He could sound mean and nasty on one line and then sing in a falsetto voice like Frankie Valli in the next."[61] Dylan—then still Zimmerman—joined his first rock and roll band at the age of fourteen, first playing rhythm guitar but soon switching to piano and vocals. As one of his former bandmates recalled, "It was Bob being pretty much of a personality. He was Little Richard, with rhythm in the background. This was strictly Little Richard."[62]

Indeed, one of the most formative musical influences on Dylan's teenaged years in Minnesota was Little Richard, label mate to Sam Cooke at Specialty, who had burst into stardom in 1955 and then abruptly abandoned rock and roll in a fit of religious guilt only two years later. The period from 1955 to 1957 during which Little Richard first unleashed his ferocious brand of music on the American public was extraordinarily significant for Dylan, who briefly played piano professionally in Bobby Vee's band in 1959.[63] Robert Zimmerman's 1959 Hibbing High School yearbook listed the graduating senior's ambition as "to join 'Little Richard,'" and while Dylan also played guitar in this period, Elijah Wald notes that "piano was more distinctive and percussive, a pounding accompaniment to his shouted vocals."[64] In a 1961 interview conducted in advance of his first album, Dylan informed a Columbia Records publicist, "I used to play great, great piano. Very great—I used to play the piano like Little Richard style. . . . You ever heard Little Richard? Ah, Little Richard, he was something else."[65]

Dylan's turn away from the piano was occasioned by his burgeoning interest in folk music, which took shape while living in Minneapolis, where he briefly enrolled at the University of Minnesota before dropping out after a semester. Minneapolis had a vibrant folk scene, and it was here that Bobby Zimmerman began calling himself Bob Dylan and became increasingly drawn to the music of Woody Guthrie. Dylan's fascination with Guthrie would be part of his motivation for leaving Minneapolis for New York City in January of 1961, having learned Guthrie was slowly dying of Huntington's disease in Greystone Park Psychiatric Hospital in Morristown, New Jersey.

Dylan's time as an obscure folksinger in Greenwich Village was strikingly brief; on September 29, 1961, he was the subject of an article entitled "Bob Dylan: A Distinctive Folk-Song Stylist" in the *New York Times* by the folk critic Robert Shelton. Describing Dylan as a "cross between a choir boy and a beatnik" and conceding that "Mr. Dylan's voice is anything but pretty," Shelton nonetheless closed his review with one of the most famous predictions in the annals of music journalism: "But if not for every taste, his music-making has the mark of originality and inspiration, all the more noteworthy for his youth. Mr. Dylan is vague about his antecedents and birthplace, but it matters less where he has been than where he is going, and that would seem to be straight up."[66]

Dylan soon attracted the attention of the legendary Columbia Records talent scout John Hammond, who signed him the following month. Hammond had previously been responsible for "discovering" or otherwise advancing the careers of Benny Goodman, Billie Holiday, and Robert Johnson, and just one year prior to signing Dylan, Hammond had signed an eighteen-year-old vocal prodigy named Aretha Franklin. Dylan's eponymous first album was recorded over two days in November of 1961 and released in March of 1962, and although the album failed to sell particularly well, with his youth, talent, and the energies of Columbia behind him, Dylan was poised to break through.[67] His folk stardom would grow full-fledged the next year with the release of *The Freewheelin' Bob Dylan* in March of 1963, and the enormous success of Peter, Paul and Mary's cover of "Blowin' in the Wind" that summer.

Dylan's rise from obscure Minnesotan to national folk star unfolded remarkably rapidly, nearly as rapidly as Sam Cooke's rise from Chicago High School student to national gospel star. In the early 1960s there was considerable money in folksinging, and Dylan had the commercial folk "craze" of the late 1950s and early 1960s to thank for Columbia's almost instantaneous interest in him, and probably for his own initial exposure to folk music as well, as his own recollections of hearing the Kingston Trio on the radio indicate.[68]

The commercial folk craze was an offshoot of a larger folk revival of the same period; as the folk historian Neil Rosenberg points out, the folk revival was both anticommercial and anticapitalist while also enabled by the commercial and capitalist recording industry.[69] The Kingston Trio sold more than three million copies of the single "Tom Dooley" in 1958 and made the cover of *Life* magazine, Harry Belafonte was a fixture on the *Billboard* charts, and young Joan Baez's debut album reached the Top 10 in 1960. Folk music was big business, and the revival at large was unmistakably implicated in this, if often uneasily.

In the folklorist David Evans's influential formulation, the folk revival of the late 1950s that stretched well into the 1960s was in fact the fourth "stage" of a broader twentieth-century fascination with folk music.[70] According to Evans, the first stage of this was the early twentieth-century interest in folk music that led to concert-hall performances of "folk" music and the rise of folk forms as an object of academic study. The second stage was the Popular Front era of the 1930s and 1940s that saw performers such as Woody Guthrie, Leadbelly, and Josh White using folk music as a tool for social critique and protest. The third stage came with the postwar "reissues" of the 1950s, most famously in the form of Harry Smith's Smithsonian Folkways *Anthology of American Folk Music* (1952), the widespread appeal of which begot the fourth stage, which found young Americans, inspired by the Smith anthology and other recordings, reviving the actual practice of folk song for themselves.

A constant throughout all four stages of the twentieth-century folk revival was an abiding concern with authenticity, the specific stakes and criteria of which fluctuated but the existence and centrality of which was taken for granted. The hermetic authenticity claims of folk revivals and other folkloric movements are generally somewhat fantastic: as Robin D. G. Kelley has argued, "the boundaries erected around 'folk' culture are as socially constructed and contingent and permeable as the dividing line between high and low or, for that matter, black and white."[71] Furthermore, Karl Hagstrom Miller's work on the business and study of folk music in the early twentieth century suggests that the "purity" of folk music was far more central to the recording industry and intellectuals than it was to the music's actual practitioners, and much of this thinking on white and black folk culture derived from the openly inauthentic practice of minstrelsy. Writes Miller: "The folkloric paradigm ascended, in part, by inheriting and perpetuating some of the qualities of minstrel authenticity: folklorists invested minstrel and hillbilly stereotypes with scientific authority."[72]

Of course, each stage of the twentieth-century folk revival took the authenticity of its music for granted and framed it as central, and the fourth stage was no exception to this, although its authenticity ideals were perhaps the most complicated. A crucial distinction between the third and fourth stages of the revival was the reclamation of a left-political ideology for American folk song; in the case of the early 1950s Folkways reissues, the leftist associations of the 1930s folk boom had to be downplayed in the context of the Red Scare. The revival of the late 1950s and early 1960s resuscitated the notion of the folk song as a political tool, and as Ronald Cohen's history of the revival argues, while the political ideology of the late 1950s revival was characterized by a pro-peace, antimilitary stance, by the early

1960s concerns over the bomb were being supplanted by a growing interest in the Southern struggle of the civil rights movement.[73]

The revival of the late 1950s and early 1960s was largely clustered around colleges, undoubtedly helped along by an unprecedented boom of students who now had the means and proclivity to pursue higher education. Much like the early stages of the 1960s New Left—many of whose progenitors were folk enthusiasts themselves—the folk revival of this period was largely a product of middle-class, educated, young white people, the Woody Guthries and Leadbellys replaced by Joan Baez and Bob Dylan, both of whom had grown up in relative comfort (Baez's father was a prominent physicist). The youthful adherents of the fourth-stage revival couldn't claim the lived "folk" hardship of past heroes, so instead they embraced a more personal and flexible notion of authenticity, a curious mixture of metaphysical vagueness, exhaustive study, and a profound veneration of forebears such as Guthrie, Leadbelly, and, perhaps most significantly, Pete Seeger.

A figure of boundless energy and enthusiasm, Seeger was both an inspiration to the fourth-stage folk revival and a key participant in it. British folk historian Georgina Boyes writes that "a revival is inherently both revolutionary and conservative. It simultaneously comprehends a demand for a change in an existing situation and a requirement of reversion to an older form."[74] Seeger himself embodied these contradictions. A Harvard-educated Northeasterner who would freely affect down-home grammatical inaccuracies into his speech, Seeger was a staunch political progressive who refused to name names when called before the House Un-American Activities Committee in 1955, a stance that led to a contempt-of-court conviction and blacklisting. Musically, he was a protective conservationist: the oft-told story of his attempt to take an axe to Bob Dylan's electric cables at the Newport Folk Festival in 1965 is nothing short of mythic. (It is, in fact, a myth, although Seeger did express bitterness at Dylan's performance for years after the fateful evening.)[75]

Seeger exerted considerable intellectual and ideological influence on the fourth-stage folk revival. He was extraordinarily generous to the younger revivalists, encouraging their music and serving as a living example that musical expression and personal politics could intertwine even when the folksinger hadn't emerged from a dust bowl homestead or sharecropper's shack. Seeger's rhetoric was marked by self-making and rebirth, and the suggestion that the authenticity inherent to folksinging was a volunteerist proposition rather than a strictly socioeconomic one held tremendous appeal to young revivalists. In Seeger's telling, self-invention (or self-reinvention) could become its own authenticity, illustrating one's commitment to an identity that one has chosen, rather than what one has simply been born into. It was a vision of authenticity rooted in the personal and political rather than the social or historical, one in which performance and identity were so intertwined as to be nearly indistinguishable.[76]

The folk revival also boasted a typically fierce disdain for commercialism, and rock and roll music was often a target of scorn; in 1959, Alan Lomax organized a concert at Carnegie Hall called "Folksong '59" at which he brought a female doo-wop group from Detroit onstage. "The time has come for Americans not to be ashamed of what we go for, musically, from primitive ballads to rock 'n' roll songs," Lomax told the *New York Times*. His audience seemed less convinced, and the Detroit outfit was widely booed.[77] Despite the fact that performers such as Elvis Presley and Jerry Lee Lewis probably came from backgrounds more similar to the musicians the revivalists revered than many revivalists themselves did, rock and roll's proximity to modernity and the market rendered it deeply suspect.

Many Thousands Gone: Race and Black Music in the Folk Revival

By the early 1960s the revival was becoming more clearly defined in its musical and ideological stances, and more confident and emboldened in articulating these stances. A prominent outlet for this was a small publication entitled the *Little Sandy Review*, which was started in Minneapolis in 1960 by Jon Pankake and Paul Nelson, the latter of whom would go on to become an influential rock critic at the *Village Voice* and *Rolling Stone*, in another small but notable instance of the folk revival following Dylan into rock music.

Spanning thirty issues in total and running from 1960 to 1965, *Little Sandy Review* in many ways anticipates the modern fanzine: its earliest issues were typed and mimeographed, often rife with typographical errors. The writing itself was passionate and fiercely opinionated—an early issue derided Paul Robeson as "pretensious [*sic*]" and declared that the "impression of the Negro spiritual which Robeson (and alas, that fine singer Marian Anderson) have given to the American urban public" was "erroneous."[78] These are brash declarations from an anonymous (but likely young and white) Minnesotan that were themselves rooted in authenticity concerns, as Robeson and Anderson were famous for their concert arrangements of folk spirituals. Such a transgression of musical and cultural spheres would surely violate a purist's sense of folk hermeticism.

Bob Dylan and the *Little Sandy Review* emerged from Minneapolis during the same period, and Dylan was friendly with the
magazine's editors and contributors. As Wald writes, "Dylan was
hanging out with Pankake and Nelson and had access not only
to their reviews but to all the LPs they were writing about."[79]
Little Sandy Review was a publication dedicated to the fourth-
stage revival that was actually spawned by said revivalists itself, which set it apart from *Sing Out!*, the most prominent
national folk music publication, which had been founded in 1950
by Irwin Silber. Although the age difference between the two
publications was only ten years, the tonal gap was vast, and the
opinionated passion of *Little Sandy Review* carried with it a
sense of upstart energy and impatience, particularly when contrasted with the more measured style of *Sing Out! Little Sandy
Review* was argumentative, iconoclastic, and obsessed with
authenticity: early issues derided the music of the Kingston Trio
as "Ivy League Folkum" and characterized Harry Belafonte as
"AWFUL," going so far as to declare that the latter's Carnegie
Hall album failed to contain "even one honest folk song."[80]

Little Sandy Review's youthful impetuousness mixed with its
purist devotion to the past in curious ways, a contradiction
that was more broadly reflected in the early stages of 1960s progressive political counterculture. The language of the Port
Huron Statement—the widely disseminated 1962 political man-
ifesto of Students for a Democratic Society (SDS), and a bed-
rock document of the New Left—is rife with mystical idealism,
lamenting "the decline of utopia and hope" as its authors declared
that "we regard men as infinitely precious and possessed of
unfulfilled capacities for reason, freedom, and love."[81] The language of declension is elegiac and nostalgic, while the language
of unfulfilled potential is hopeful and forward-looking.

The New Left was steeped in an ideology that linked political activism to self-actualization—what the historian Doug Rossinow has called a "politics of authenticity"—an ideology broadly analogous to the folk revival's notion of self-making through musical practice and performance.[82] The most overwhelming area in need of attention was the civil rights movement; the Port Huron Statement cited "the Southern struggle against racial bigotry" in its opening paragraphs as the first concern of SDS, ahead of the Cold War and nuclear escalation.[83] Identification with African American culture and struggle became linked to political activism, which was in turn held as a way to remedy the "unfulfilled capacities" of the individuals lamented above.[84]

In the early 1960s this interest in civil rights was paralleled in the folk revival, where the movement was becoming an increasing focus and the performance of black music was seen as a mode of aligning oneself with the struggles of black people more generally. In 1962, the *New York Times* ran a lengthy article by Robert Shelton entitled "Songs a Weapon in Rights Battle" that noted that "there have been many echoes in the North of the freedom songs among white and Negro singers. . . . Bob Dylan, a young professional songwriter, has penned 'The Ballad of Emmett Till' about a slaying in Mississippi, and 'Blowin' in the Wind' about patience and dignity."[85] The next year Shelton wrote another article entitled "'Freedom Songs' Sweep North" that included a photograph of Dylan, and he noted that "new songs on this theme [the Southern civil rights struggle] are not only weapons in the civil rights arsenal, but are also developing into valuable commodities in the music industry." Shelton declared that "the new anti-segregation lyricists are the descendants of the Hutchinson Family of New Hampshire," a reference to the famed abolitionist singing group of the 1840s and 1850s and a comparison that perfectly encapsulates the potent mix of nostalgia and progressive politics that permeated the music in this period.[86]

For the folk revival the performance of African American music offered a powerful entry into a worldview in which proximity to black culture was linked to political progress, which was in turn linked to self-fulfillment and personal authenticity. In many cases the link between black music and white youth progressive politics was made explicit, such as Baez's frequent performances of "My Lord What a Morning," "Kumbaya," and of course, "We Shall Overcome," which, while popularized by Pete Seeger years earlier, by the early 1960s had become indelibly associated with the Southern freedom struggle.

And yet the folk revival's mixture of political progress with a nostalgic yearning for a more "authentic" past became more complicated with its increasing focus on the civil rights movement. When its political focus had been Cold War demilitarization, protests against the bomb could be easily enfolded into an antimodernism, but looking to the past for solutions to racial inequity was a more troublesome proposition. Furthermore, a parallel problem emerged of how to reconcile investment in African American music with the belief in musical authenticity through performative self-invention. After all, the notion of a white folksinger inhabiting the spirit of Woody Guthrie presented fewer complications than the notion of a white folksinger inhabiting the spirit of Leadbelly or Blind Lemon Jefferson.

The solution to these quandaries was partly worked out in a profoundly imaginative relationship to black music, one that held black music and musicians to be engines of raw and unknowable power that existed almost exclusively in the past. Modernity and "authentic" African American music were implicitly, and sometimes explicitly, held to be irreconcilable to one another. This belief coexisted easily with the revival's generally ambivalent relationship to the present, although it left the current status of black music and musicians in a precarious position. There are scores of stories of young folk revivalists being shocked to learn that heroes from the Harry Smith *Anthology* were not only alive but still performing music. In an article on legendary gospel-blues guitarist Reverend Gary Davis, for example, the *Little Sandy Review* noted that Davis's "territory is the streets and store-front missions of New York City's Harlem, where he has provided free music for twenty years while, just a couple of miles down the Island, his old records were sold for fabulous prices to collectors unaware of his existence."[87] In their history of the Cambridge folk revival, former revivalists Jim Rooney and Eric Von Schmidt recalled their surprise when Mississippi John Hurt turned up alive and well at the Newport Folk Festival in 1963: "John Hurt was dead. *Had* to be."[88]

Proximity to African American culture was key to both political conscience and musical purity, untrammeled as it was by the bourgeois commercialism of whiteness. What many white revivalists could not accommodate was a vision of black music as fluid and present: to do so would have exposed the contradictions of their intermingled musical and political ideology. The notion of black music being a product of the same market system as white music might suggest that Mississippi John Hurt had more in common with Elvis Presley or Frank Sinatra than he did with the anonymous authors of the spirituals, and such a suggestion did not conform to certain expectations of authenticity.

The anthropologist Johannes Fabian famously argued that the discipline of anthropology rests on the assumption that its objects of study are always in the past or otherwise outside of time, and that it is by way of this assumption that anthropological knowledge produces and protects its own authority.[89] Folk revivals are fundamentally anthropological undertakings, and by insisting that authentic black music was on the brink of extinction, the fourth stage of the folk revival produced its authority of knowledge while simultaneously validating its own musical practices. "Real" black music was always believed to be vanished or vanishing and thus in need of preservation by revivalists. This was consistent with the revival's view of folk music of all kinds, although the notion of disappearance was particularly affixed to black music, and necessarily so, as it muted any problems attendant to appropriation and identity transference.

Again, this idea is made resoundingly clear in the pages of the *Little Sandy Review*. In a 1963 review of *Blues, Rags, and Hollers* by "Spider" John Koerner, Dave "Snaker" Ray, and Tony "Little Sun" Glover, a trio of white blues musicians who had formed while students at the University of Minnesota, the writer Barry Hansen opened his review with the following statement: "It seems inevitable that by 1970 most of the blues worth hearing will be sung by white men. For years, the younger Negroes have been losing interest in this 'old-fashioned' form; no really significant young Negro blues singer has emerged since 1953. As the older singers pass their prime, the Negro blues seem doomed to certain extinction."[90]

There is a youthful presumptuousness and perhaps even odd prescience here, although likely not as its author intended—after all, it's hard to imagine that Led Zeppelin circa 1970 would have fit Hansen's definition of "blues worth hearing," or even one-time folkie Janis Joplin, who is excluded a priori by the phrase "white men." The passage also indicates the extent to which its author felt comfortable making claims on what was or wasn't authentic black music, and similar statements abound in the *LSR*. An album called *Negro Folk Rhythms* was criticized for being "a purposeful attempt by educated Negroes to remove the white stereotype of Negro music as something 'barbaric' and to show these whites that negro music is noble and good, *in the whites' own image,*" a strange and not particularly self-aware accusation for a white writer to make.[91] A review of a John Lee Hooker album praised the guitarist for returning to his "primitive and harsh" style and complained about his recent, "more sophisticated" recordings: "Hooker [has] deliberately turned to an older blues style—he plays alone with a non-electric guitar. The result is his best recording to date AND his emergence as a fine folk artist."[92] Finally, a review of an album by Robert Pete Williams, a penitentiary inmate in Louisiana, praised the artist as "a singer who has developed to a fabulous level of artistry in an all-Negro environment completely free of any reason or desire to 'refine' for a sophisticated folkum market," a celebration of authenticity-through-incarceration to which we might imagine Williams himself objecting rather vehemently.[93]

By constructing a worldview in which "real" black music was on the verge of disappearance, and casting themselves as the last line of defense in this disappearance, revivalists added a new dimension to the concept of playing black music as an ethical act—it now came from not only a political impulse, but a preservationist one—while also boxing the potentials of black music into an impossible position. Deriding "more sophisticated" recordings by black artists as "inauthentic" reinforced the anti-modernism and anti-intellectualism of the revival, but it also allowed no forward-looking concept of black music that wasn't determined by white stereotypes.[94]

Dylan's emergence as a major figure in the folk revival of the early 1960s complicated this construction, and sooner than many would notice. As previously noted, Dylan's early musical years had been steeped in rock and roll music, a fact that surely did not make him unique among many of his fellow revivalists. However, unlike many of his contemporaries, Dylan appears to have never fully cast off the legacy and influence of rock and roll, and in certain of his early performances he even seems to embrace it. An example of this can be heard on Dylan's frenetic and stirring version of Blind Lemon Jefferson's classic "See That My Grave Is Kept Clean," the last track on his 1962 self-titled debut album for Columbia Records.[95] "See That My Grave Is Kept Clean" was first recorded in 1927—two years before Jefferson froze to death during a visit to Chicago—and rereleased on Smith's influential *Anthology* in 1952, attracting the attention of revivalists to Jefferson's music and both his nimble, flamenco-inflected guitar playing and his gruff and powerful singing voice. Dylan's performance of "See That My Grave Is Kept Clean" is, as one might expect, vastly different than Jefferson's: the guitar lacks the percussiveness, rhythmic nuance, and melodic precision of Jefferson's, and while the tempo on Dylan's version is quicker, his vocal performance is boyish and reedy, bearing little resemblance to Jefferson's deep baritone.

Dylan's blues performances have attracted a considerable amount of critical and scholarly attention. Keith Negus has written that "the blues had a profound and enduring impact on Bob Dylan, as they did on many musicians and listeners of his generation. Dylan acquired a means of expression from the blues voice . . . over time it has become clear that Dylan is far more part of a blues tradition than any modern-day rock tradition."[96] This argument makes generic sense with regards to Dylan's performance of Jefferson, although it seems overly broad, given the differences in musical, social, and historical context between the two performers. Furthermore, partitioning Dylan off for the "blues tradition" rather than the "modern-day rock tradition" obscures the intense connectedness between these two traditions—Dylan himself is exemplary of this. Barry Shank has also pointed out that Dylan sings the melody of "See That

My Grave Is Kept Clean" nearly a full octave higher than Jefferson (Jefferson's recording of "Grave" is in E-flat, Dylan's is in D), and he argues that "this shift to an upper range of either basic notes or overtones is common in white appropriations of black musical forms and styles," which leads Shank to suggest that "this upward tonal shift characterizes the historical performance practice of blackface minstrelsy."[97] This is a provocative claim but hard to confirm, since no real sonic evidence exists of what early blackface minstrels actually sounded like. Furthermore, Blind Lemon Jefferson himself had a famously deep voice, far more so than other folk blues heroes like Mississippi John Hurt, Son House, or Robert Johnson.

Rather than the blues or minstrelsy, I would instead suggest that the most pressing influence heard on Dylan's version of "See That My Grave Is Kept Clean" is rock and roll music. Dylan's 2004 memoir contains an evocative description of early rock and rollers as "singers who sang like they were navigating burning ships," and it is this frantic, desperate intensity that pulsates through Dylan's performance of Jefferson on his first record. There is more Little Richard than Blind Lemon Jefferson to be found here, and considering Dylan's background, why shouldn't there be? The differentness of Dylan's performance of "See That My Grave Is Kept Clean" becomes particularly evident when contrasted with Dave Van Ronk's version from 1961, titled "Please See That My Grave Is Kept Clean." Like Dylan, Van Ronk was a young white transplant to Greenwich Village, although his journey was considerably shorter (Van Ronk was born and raised in Brooklyn). Van Ronk became one of the most highly regarded musicians of the folk revival, widely admired for his fingerpicking guitar techniques and vocal ability. He was also more of a traditionalist than Dylan, so it's not surprising that Van Ronk's rendition of "Grave" is closer to Jefferson's version than Dylan's in most respects, from tempo to arrangement to performance style.[98]

Dylan was certainly familiar with Van Ronk's performance of "Grave." The two had become friends shortly after Dylan's arrival in Greenwich Village, and Van Ronk was one of the members of the revival with whom Dylan maintained a friendship after his perceived defection.[99] The fact that he strays from Van Ronk's performance and arrangement and into the propulsive rhythms and vocal style associated with early rock and roll suggests that even at this early stage in his career Dylan was cut from a different musical and ideological cloth from many of the folk revival's progenitors and adherents. Dylan's performance of "See That My Grave Is Kept Clean" weds the sound of rock and rollers like Little Richard and Johnny Burnette to the music of Blind Lemon Jefferson.

The same year he released his debut album Dylan recorded what would become his first single for Columbia Records, "Mixed-Up Confusion." (Columbia had not released any of the tracks from *Bob Dylan* as singles.)[100] The song featured guitar, piano, bass, and drums and is unmistakably a rockabilly-infused rock and roll track, squarely in the vein of Carl Perkins and early Elvis Presley. Two other tracks were recorded during these sessions with a similar full-band lineup—"Rocks and Gravel" and a version of Arthur Crudup's "That's Alright, Mama," most widely known as Elvis Presley's 1954 debut single—though neither were released. "Mixed-Up Confusion" hit shelves in mid-December of 1962 but didn't sell, and yet the existence of these recordings shows Dylan's comfort playing within a rock and roll idiom, a vision of black music in which Little Richard and Chuck Berry remained as relevant as Robert Johnson and Blind Willie McTell. It also suggests that Columbia Records and producer Tom Wilson, who produced these sessions and Dylan's other

Columbia material through "Like a Rolling Stone," were nearly as flexible in their vision of the singer's future as Dylan himself was.

Despite the fame he achieved from "Blowin' in the Wind," Dylan was never exclusively a political or protest songwriter, and by the release of *Another Side of Bob Dylan* in 1964, he had all but purged his songwriting of overtly topical material.[101] As Tom Wilson put it to the *New Yorker*'s Nat Hentoff in 1964, "He's not a singer of protest so much as he is a singer of *concern* about people. He doesn't have to be talking about Medgar Evers. . . . He can just tell a simple little story of a guy who ran off from a woman."[102] In the same article Dylan spoke of his determination to stop writing "finger-pointing songs," "pointing to all the things that are wrong. Me, I don't want to write *for* people anymore. You know, be a spokesman. Like I once wrote about Emmett Till in the first person, pretending I was him. From now on, I want to write from inside me."[103] The choice of words is telling, as Dylan seems to obliquely critique the widely held folk-revival belief that by singing songs written by or about African American people—and specifically dead people—one might come closer to spiritually inhabiting an African American experience.

A Different Kind of Bag: The Invention of "Folk Rock"

In late 1964 Irwin Silber, the editor of *Sing Out!* magazine, published an infamous "Open Letter to Bob Dylan," in which Silber expressed his worry that Dylan seemed "to be in a different kind of bag now": "Your new songs seem to be all inner-directed now, innerprobing, self-conscious—maybe even a little maudlin or a little cruel on occasion. . . . Now, that's all okay—if that's the way you want it. But then you're a different Bob Dylan from the one we knew. The old one never wasted our precious time."[104] The letter reads as an ill-advised mix of hand-wringing and entitlement, and the phrase "the old one never wasted our precious time"—a reference to the closing lines of Dylan's "Don't Think Twice, It's All Right"—lands as a particularly barbed attack. If Dylan was feeling unduly confined by the ideological pressures of the folk revival, Silber's decision to use his own lyrics to shame him in such a public forum was unlikely to alleviate his growing sense of constriction.

In early 1965 Dylan released the single "Subterranean Homesick Blues," an homage to Chuck Berry's 1956 hit "Too Much Monkey Business" and his first release with an electric band since "Mixed-Up Confusion." The single became Dylan's biggest chart hit to date, and his first entry into the Top 40.[105] In March of 1965 Dylan released his fifth studio album for Columbia Records, *Bringing It All Back Home*.[106] The first side of *Bringing It All Back Home* featured electric guitars and a rhythm section and included a song called "Maggie's Farm," Dylan's most disdainful swipe at the folk community yet. "They say 'sing while you slave' / and I just get bored," sneered Dylan, and the potential meanings embedded in the imagery of slavery are notable— Dylan as "enslaved" by the confines of folk music, but also the revival's equation of black hardship with musical authenticity. The phrase even recall Sam Cooke's similarly audacious invocation of slavery on "Bring It on Home to Me," the title of which bears obvious similarity to Dylan's own LP. The second side of *Bringing It All Back Home* consisted of more traditional acoustic material, including "Mr. Tambourine Man," which would soon become a number one *Billboard* Pop hit for the California rock and roll band the Byrds.[107]

If "Subterranean Homesick Blues," *Bringing It All Back Home,* and the Byrds' version of "Mr. Tambourine Man" all brought

Dylan to the precipice of mainstream stardom and a profound shift in his genre association, "Like a Rolling Stone" would be his decisive and irreversible breakthrough. Recorded at New York's Studio A on June 16, 1965, with a band made up of session musicians, including pianist Paul Griffin, drummer Bobby Gregg, guitarist Mike Bloomfield, and organist Al Kooper, "Like a Rolling Stone" was released in late July of 1965 and reached number two on the *Billboard* charts, kept from the top spot only by the Beatles' "Help!"[108]

"Like a Rolling Stone" was a landmark recording in both Dylan's career and popular music more generally. At over six minutes long, it far outlasted any prior hit rock and roll single. As Greil Marcus notes, longer records such as Ray Charles's "What'd I Say" (1959) had previously been hits but were usually partitioned into two parts, with the first side getting the overwhelming majority of radio play.[109] From almost the moment of its release, DJs played "Like a Rolling Stone" in its entirety.

The song turned Dylan into a full-on rock and roll star, and it also changed the way that people talked about rock and roll music. By the end of 1965 the music press buzzed with a new phrase, "folk rock." Such a concept had certainly floated around before Dylan: as Elijah Wald notes, at Newport in 1965 the Chambers Brothers had been referred to as "folk 'n' roll," and Donovan and the Byrds had occasionally received similar neologisms.[110] But Dylan and "Like a Rolling Stone" soon came to embody and exemplify the concept.

"Folk rock" was a strange piece of terminology—after all, it was hard to tell what precisely about "Like a Rolling Stone" was folk-related, other than that its author had been previously identified as a folksinger. Still, a *Los Angeles Times* article from September of 1965 (which described the phenomenon as "rock-folk") suggested that "the new songs are called rock-folk because they

Bob Dylan and Tom Wilson, 1965. © Don Hunstein and Sony Music Entertainment combine the rock beat, tunes and performers with the 'message words' of one branch of folk music," and a few months later the *New York Times* described folk rock as "a folk song sung to a rock 'n' roll big-beat background."[111] For his part Dylan often bristled at the term, telling an interviewer, "We're not playing rock music. . . . These people call it folk rock—if they want to call it that, something that simple, it's good for selling the records. I can't call it folk rock. I have a whole way of doing things that's been on every single record I ever made, a certain feeling. And I know that it's real."[112]

By the time the *Los Angeles Times* covered the "folk rock" phenomenon again in 1966, a consensus had emerged that whatever this music was, it was more serious, thoughtful, and artistically high-minded than previous rock and roll music. "Let's face it, folk rock is big because the teens love it," wrote the *Times*. "And the teens love it because it has the rhythm that is theirs, and has something to say—something besides 'I love you' and 'moon, June, spoon.'" The article also noted that "it all started with Bob Dylan—the original poet of protest, a writer of contemporary folk songs, a rebel with many causes—some personal, some social."[113] And in a 1967 essay, the rock critic Ellen Willis declared that "as composer, interpreter, most of all as lyricist, Dylan has made a revolution. . . . Since then rock-and-roll, which was already in the midst of a creative flowering dominated by British rock and Motown, has been transformed."[114]

"Like a Rolling Stone" is an extraordinary piece of music.[115] From Gregg's snare hit that opens the song, to Bloomfield's gorgeous guitar fills coming out its choruses, to Griffin's dancing barrelhouse piano and Kooper's indelible, on-the-fly organ part, the recording is a work of tremendous invention by any measure. Dylan's vocal performance is assured and mature, as intricate and dazzlingly wordy phrases like "you never turned around /

to see the frowns on the jugglers and the clowns / when they all did tricks for you" pour forth with both feeling and precision, his voice rising to a high G on the wordless "aaahhh" that sets up the song's final verse. The text is a mélange of strange and evocative imagery—Napoleons in rags, diplomats on "chrome horses," soon-to-be pawned diamond rings—in the service of what is finally nothing more or less than a jilted love song. Its mixture of timely and timeless is announced in its first four words, only the most famous phrase in storytelling: "once upon a time."

"Like a Rolling Stone" exceeds the sum of its parts but its legacy has outstripped even its own considerable ambitions. Much like the Beatles' music of this same period, in the years since its release "Like a Rolling Stone" has been claimed by many as a moment rock and roll music became "serious," a suggestion we begin to see emerging in the "folk rock" discussions that surrounded it. If, as critics at the time argued, the seriousness of "folk rock" was derived from its partial roots in the folk song, this is by no means the only ideological vestige of the folk revival that crossed over into rock and roll music on June 14, 1965, when Dylan and his bandmates finally nailed "Like a Rolling Stone" on the fourth take of their second day of trying.

Once upon a Time: "Like a Rolling Stone" and Rock Ideology

The release of "Like a Rolling Stone" has frequently been spoken of in terms of a rapture. Inducting Dylan into the Rock and Roll Hall of Fame in 1988, Bruce Springsteen recalled the snare-drum hit that opens "Like a Rolling Stone" as sounding "like somebody kicked open the door to your mind," a lovely piece of imagery whose hyperbole mirrors the level to which the song's importance has been elevated in criticism and historiography.[116]

"Like a Rolling Stone" has been positioned as a foundational text of rock ideology, its authentic creativity and individual expression unimpeachable, a notion that was both informed and allowed by Dylan's position as the wunderkind auteur of the folk revival.[117]

"Like a Rolling Stone," and the period it marks in Dylan's career, has become a genesis event in the creation myth for the genre of "rock," which takes care to distinguish itself from the earlier, passé sounds of "pop" or "rock and roll." As Keith Negus writes, by 1966 "Bob Dylan seemed the archetypal rock singer, defining the style as an intelligent genre addressed to adults, leaving behind the inarticulate rebellion of rock 'n' roll and the naïve romance of pop."[118] While the Beatles would also bolster the notion of rock music as art in this period with the experimentations of *Rubber Soul* (released in December of 1965), *Revolver,* and *Sgt. Pepper's Lonely Hearts Club Band,* Dylan's status as both a white American male and an artist whose *individual* intellect and seriousness had already been confirmed by his position in folk music made him a uniquely appealing figure for an emergent ideology of rock music.

As I noted in the Introduction, rock ideology is, at its core, profoundly concerned with authenticity. The epistemological break that holds earlier rock and roll trivial and "rock" as serious and enduring is located around this concept of authenticity: as Theodore Gracyk has argued, more than simply being "fun" or "enjoyable," rock music takes itself seriously as a vehicle for personal expression.[119] This preoccupation with authenticity largely derives from a tension between the music's aspirations to art and its reality of being a mass, commercial culture: by clinging to a notion of rock stars being driven entirely by personal expression and self-actualization through music, rock ideology is able to excuse away the fact that its heroes have made millions of dollars by seeing this as a happy by-product of their art, rather than a driving force behind it. The phenomenal success of "Like a Rolling Stone"—the piece of authentic self-expression that achieves the coincidence of commercial success—becomes an ideal moment of transference.

Through Dylan's move from folk to rock (at the time seen as the creation of "folk rock," later as simply the creation of rock), rock's emergent genre ideology was able to selectively appropriate certain remnants of the folk revival—its anxieties over commerce, its notion of authenticity through self-expression, its blurry obsession with originalism—while leaving others behind, perhaps most centrally the revival's political concerns. Also transferred, crucially and incompletely, was the racial imagination of the folk revival, a legacy that helps explain what a generosity of attention paid to Bob Dylan might have to tell us about a paucity of attention paid to Sam Cooke.

Bringing It All Back Home: Bob Dylan, Sam Cooke, and Race

As both history and ideology there are numerous problems with positioning "Like a Rolling Stone" as a Big Bang moment for serious rock music. For starters, by casting Dylan as a progenitor of individual rock genius, the contributions of others are written out. In the case of "Like a Rolling Stone" this could include Bobby Gregg, Paul Griffin, or producer Tom Wilson, each of whom made formative contributions to one of the most famous records ever made (and the latter two of whom are African American), but none of whom are household names. By extension, it also writes out other practitioners of rock and roll with whom Dylan heard himself in conversation, such as Little Richard, Chuck Berry, or

Phil Spector's famed "Wall of Sound" productions with such groups as the Ronettes and the Crystals.[120]

One glaring injustice of such erasures is that the origin story of "Like a Rolling Stone" has been used to buttress an image of rock music as a fundamentally white enterprise, one that outwardly denies the salience of race in its ideal of individual authenticity while silently confirming the centrality of whiteness. This is the most striking ideological remnant of the folk revival in rock ideology: by deciding that "Like a Rolling Stone" is a formative moment for when rock music turned serious, black music becomes something to be admired but at the same time kept at a remove. The consensus emerges that while Little Richard and Chuck Berry and the Crystals were important influences on Dylan, Dylan took what they did and made something more significant. As Simon Frith writes, "Deeply embedded in rock ideology is the assumption that while black music is valuable as an expression of vitality and excitement, is in other words 'good to dance to,' it lacks the qualities needed for individual expression."[121] Through no fault of his own, we can see this notion in rock music starting to solidify around Bob Dylan and "Like a Rolling Stone."

In critical literature on Bob Dylan there is a long-standing and persistent tendency to describe the singer through metaphors of racial indeterminacy. A number of writers have linked Dylan to the history of minstrelsy, and Todd Haynes's celebrated 2007 biopic *I'm Not There* featured a segment in which a young "Dylan" is played by a young African American boy.[122] This is not a new development, and since early in his career much has been made of Dylan's supposed ease within nonwhite musical traditions: Nat Hentoff's 1964 profile of Dylan in the *New Yorker* characterized his singing as "strongly influenced by such Negro folk interpreters as Leadbelly and Big Joe Williams."[123] A year later, in a lengthy *New York Times* piece on Dylan, Thomas Meehan argued that Dylan's songs "mix for the first time the sounds of Negro blues with the twang of country music."[124] (One imagines Elvis Presley canceling his subscription.) Biographer Paul Williams has argued that Dylan's "seemingly authentic spiritual awareness" in his early music derived from "a direct transmission through black music, through the records he'd been listening to,"[125] while another critic writes that "this skinny white boy seemed to be singing from the soul of a black man who had seen it all."[126]

It is noteworthy that all of these passages rely on a notion of black music as predecessor, as something old. The racial imagination that was transferred from the folk revival to rock ideology was one that held black music on a mystified pedestal, viewing it as raw, powerful, and important but at the same time denying it as presently viable. As the 1960s progressed, older black blues performers such as Howlin' Wolf, Muddy Waters, and Robert Johnson became elevated to heroic status among white rock stars, American and British, but these performers were thought to be of a bygone era, and in cases such as Johnson they were long dead.[127] When Muddy Waters released an album entitled *Fathers and Sons* in 1969 featuring young members of the Paul Butterfield Blues Band, the album's cover depicted a revision of Michelangelo's famous image of God reaching down to Adam: in the album cover God is depicted as an old black man, Adam a young white man wearing sunglasses.[128] The message was unmistakable: the aging black "god" Waters passing the secrets of the blues down to his white disciples.

The ideological concept of black music that emerged in rock music around the mid-1960s, a view largely derived from the folk revival and partially enabled by the figure of Bob Dylan, is remarkably similar to the concept of black music that haunts discussions of Sam Cooke. The idea that black music is the product of a race while white music is the product of individuals has led to a cultural shorthand in which black music and black people are imagined to be one and the same. Such a notion is not merely conducive to but required by a racial imagination such as that embraced by certain corners of the folk revival and then transferred over to rock music, which rested on both a denial of heterogeneity within black music as well as a denial of its present vitality, a disavowal that black musicians might be afforded the same capacity for identity transcendence afforded to white folksingers and, later, white rock stars.

Sam Cooke's music has been marginalized by critical discussions in which its worth has been judged by its adherence to a predetermined racial-cum-musical authenticity, a construct based around an intertwining of anticommercialism, political uses, aesthetic "raw"-ness, and hermetic blackness. It cannot be overemphasized that all of these criteria might as well be ripped from the pages of the *Little Sandy Review*. What has been disallowed in considerations of Sam Cooke is the notion that a black artist pushing boundaries of form and genre might achieve a liberatory identity transcendence *through* music, that his pop-chart triumphs and orchestral performances at the Copacabana might in fact be his own attempts to reconfigure the possibilities of what black music could be, where it could go, what sorts of music black people could make. In short, he has been denied access to the same notions of identity transcendence that the folk revival was predicated on, and which Dylan brought with him to the emergent ideology of rock music. The notion of white performers sonically transcending racial category had been part of rock and roll music at least since Elvis Presley, and it was a shared tenet of the folk revival through its linkage of political authenticity to the performance of black music. When this formulation traveled from the folk revival to rock music, the "political" element disappeared, and not particularly gradually.

By placing the burden of "serious" rock music squarely on Dylan's shoulders, the music thus became naturalized as the birthright of white men, a development that radically reracialized rock and roll as a cultural form. Heard from this context, the snare hit that opens "Like a Rolling Stone" in 1965 sounds less like an explosion into possibility than the opening sounds of a reactionary ideology of white heroism and intellectual supremacy, a move that was no fault of Dylan's own but was enabled by his symbolic capacity as a young American white male in this period. After all, to talk about the singular Promethean genius of "Like a Rolling Stone"; to speak of identity fluidity—both personal and musical—as a badge of creativity rather than a mark of betrayal; to incessantly remark upon someone's exceptional, precocious comfort within black musical forms: all of these are just ways of talking about someone being white while pretending to talk about something else. The folk revival claimed itself as the preserver of a black musical culture that it assumed had already vanished; rock music took this notion of interracial transference and made it the stakes of white creativity. In the ideology of both, casting off the shackles of one's whiteness through musical performance was central to musical and personal authenticity. But in order to cast off the shackles of whiteness, one must be white to begin with.

CHAPTER 2

The White Atlantic

Cultural Origins of the "British Invasion"

THE OCTOBER 27, 1962, issue of *Melody Maker*—
England's most venerable weekly periodical for the coverage
of jazz and popular music—featured a letter in its "Mailbag"
column entitled "Why Must We Copy?" Penned by one Mervyn
Wilmington of Nelson, Lancashire, the missive reads as follows:

> The American influence on our popular music personalities
> strengthens every day. Even the speech of many singers is
> becoming slovenly and tainted with an American accent.
>
> I fail to understand the tendency for the pop music industry
> in Britain to constantly adopt the current American music
> trends without question.

Of course America is the home of rock and Twist, but why must we try to make cheap copies of American styles of music—many of which are shocking to start with?

Let's have a little more home enterprise, a few more people of the caliber of Anthony Newley, people who realize that good, original work is what we need.

Newley is successful here and has sold his work to the Americans.

American young people I have met have been amazed at the way in which we have adopted their music unquestionably. They laugh at our foolishness.

I long for something more pure and unadulterated.[1]

At first glance there is little in this letter to distinguish it from similar complaints that appear frequently in the reader correspondence and editorial content of *Melody Maker* during this period.[2] The lack of originality in British popular music in the 1950s and early 1960s is a popular and hopelessly overdetermined lament: as Mr. Wilmington's letter illustrates, jeremiads over musical mediocrity and copyism barely conceal broader worries over the scandal that rock and roll had recently unleashed on both sides of the Atlantic, to say nothing of the rise of postwar Americanization more generally. Wilmington's concluding flourish—"I long for something more pure and unadulterated"—is almost breathless in its romanticism.

The significance of this particular letter lies not so much in its content but in the date of its publication. The October 27, 1962, issue of *Melody Maker* also boasted its weekly "Top Fifty" listing, and appearing at number forty-eight that week was "Love Me Do," the first EMI/Parlophone release from a quartet called the Beatles.[3] It's unknowable whether Mr. Wilmington would have his yearnings for purity satisfied by this single—it's quite possible that to his ears the Liverpudlian Beatles' "Scouse" accents would be as "tainted" as American ones—but the Beatles' emergence would soon render the lack of a "home enterprise" in British popular music a quaint notion.

In 1963 the Beatles dominated the British music scene, placing four singles atop the pop charts; in February of 1964 they arrived at John F. Kennedy Airport in New York City, where two nights later they played before an estimated seventy-three million Americans on CBS's *Ed Sullivan Show,* the largest television audience in history at the time.[4] This performance and its attendant fanfare have widely come to be seen as the opening salvo in a happening known colloquially as the "British Invasion," as the Beatles' runaway success would soon open America to what fans and detractors alike perceived as an unrelenting onslaught of British musicians with ambitions fixed on the *Billboard* charts. The Beatles gave way to the Dave Clark Five, Gerry and the Pacemakers, the Animals, and the Rolling Stones, who in turn gave way to the Kinks, Manfred Mann, the Zombies, and the Who.

The British Invasion concept has cut a powerful swath in retellings of popular-music history and the cultural history of the 1960s more broadly. It has spawned a cottage industry of books, music compilations, television documentaries, and radio theme weekends, and it fits nicely with a long-standing American attraction to English culture that well predates the Beatles.[5] This chapter examines this construct from a transatlantic perspective, through its prehistory, its points of emergence, and in its relation to a broader historical landscape, with specific attention to the ways in which musical and racial imaginations were intertwined, broadcast, and re-broadcast in the period before the Beatles' legendary touchdown at JFK. Specifically, I want to explore the foundational role of postwar British youth sub-

cultures, musical and otherwise, in the development and international emergence of the generation of musicians that would form
the British Invasion. Most infamous among these subcultures
are the "teddy boys," young working-class men defined by their
Edwardian dress and perceived proclivity for violence, spectacularly demonstrated in the 1958 Notting Hill race riots. The
teds also loved rock and roll, which, I argue, makes them among
the earliest fans of the music to sever the imaginative power of
black music from its connection to actual black people. Even
more notable were two nascent musical cultures that emerged
in the 1950s: the brief but significant moment known as the
"skiffle craze" of the mid-1950s, and the emergence of the British
blues subculture shortly thereafter. Both British skiffle and
British blues had sprung from the preexisting musical movement known as "trad" (short for "traditional") jazz, itself a
curious form that was both obsessively American and uniquely
British. Toward the end of this chapter, I'll examine the residue
of these subcultural legacies in the Rolling Stones' "Not Fade
Away," the band's Bo Diddley–inflected cover of a Buddy Holly
song that gave the up-and-coming Stones the biggest hit of their
young careers.

Through all this I will show not only that the monolithic concept of the British Invasion is rife with historical inaccuracy
and confusion, but also that, when a vast network of British musicians were enfolded into a single construct, what emerged was
a perceived "rebirth" of rock and roll music produced by new
imaginings of white male musicality that came bundled with the
otherness of British musicians. As *Time* magazine pithily declared in a 1965 cover story on the state of rock and roll: "The
Beatles made it all right to be white."[6] Indeed, no artists aside
from Bob Dylan were more central to the creation of rock
ideology during this period than the Beatles and the Rolling

Stones, bands whose foreignness made them immensely exotic to Americans and whose British origins easily lent themselves to the belief that they were the progenitors of a new creative tradition. As British historian Charlie Gillett wrote in his seminal 1970 volume *The Sound of the City: The Rise of Rock and Roll,* "A major source of this new music [rock] was Britain. . . . Britain served the useful function of re-establishing popular music as a medium for personal expression rather than as the raw material for mass-produced entertainment, which it once again had become."[7]

In the years since, the unilateral nature of the "Invasion" metaphor has helped buttress and justify a vision of rock tradition structured around white men—as Raymond Williams famously argued, dominant cultural "traditions" are combinations of historical fantasy and presentist ideology, "a version of the past which is intended to connect with and ratify the present . . . a sense of *predisposed continuity.*"[8] What seemed to American audiences and media to be a unified assault of shaggy-haired and accented young men was actually a diverse mixture of aspirations, localities, performance ideologies, and, of course, musical abilities: despite the breathless hype of interested parties on both sides of the Atlantic, none of the bands that followed the original Invaders would prove to be the "next Beatles." The sense of mystery conjured by various iterations of the British Invasion idea has often obscured how profoundly transatlantic the aesthetics of the British Invasion were, and specifically how creatively dependent these bands were on African American artists—often far more so than they were upon each other.

This chapter's title is an ironic homage to Paul Gilroy's classic study *The Black Atlantic,* in which Gilroy argues that "examining the place of music in the black Atlantic world means surveying the self-understanding articulated by the musicians who have made it . . . the social relations which have produced and reproduced the unique expressive culture in which music comprises a central and even foundational element." [9] Given the centrality of this world to twentieth-century popular culture, this chapter submits that such an examination should also extend to the skiffle cellars of Liverpool and jazz and blues clubs of London during the long epilogues of World War II and British colonialism, where white English youth performed their own negotiations of black musical cultures and ultimately redirected global popular music in the process. [10]

The British Invasion Myth

The most common version of the British Invasion narrative is that in the early 1960s American rock and roll was in the doldrums. The music's early history had been thrilling but had grown increasingly beset by crises: the untimely deaths of stars like Buddy Holly, Ritchie Valens, and Eddie Cochran; the military conscription of Elvis Presley and his subsequent move to Hollywood; the imprisonment of Chuck Berry on Mann Act charges; the departure of Little Richard from secular music; the public stain of payola. Into this void stepped a dubious industry of white bread, white-skinned teen stars like Frankie Avalon, Fabian, and the hated Pat Boone. In this telling, rock and roll was on the verge of dying until the Beatles "invaded," along with their countrymen, and heroically rescued the music from the very Americans who had created it and then neglected it. In the words of the influential rock critic Lester Bangs, who paired the significance of the Beatles' arrival with that of the Kennedy assassination in an essay from *The Rolling Stone Illustrated History of Rock and Roll*:

The British accomplished this in part by resurrecting music we had ignored, forgotten or discarded, recycling it in a shinier, more feckless, and yet more raucous form. The fact that much of this music had originally been written and performed by American blacks made it that much more of a sure thing, but this was not quite a replay of Pat Boone rendering Little Richard palatable to a white audience.[11]

This narrative isn't totally faulty, and like many myths it contains kernels of truth: there can be no question that the Beatles reshaped popular music, and little of the music that immediately preceded their arrival has held up to critical scrutiny nearly as well as theirs (although little music made since has, either). What's more, there was certainly a shocking suddenness to the way Beatlemania exploded in the United States, much as there had been in the United Kingdom. Rarely before or since has a cultural happening commanded so much undivided attention, and the moment of popular "consensus" that the group managed to achieve remains startling: the record viewership on *Ed Sullivan*, for instance, or the week of April 4, 1964, when the *Billboard* Top 5 was made up entirely of Beatles songs.[12]

However, the British Invasion idea is also deeply flawed, and four problems stand out. First, and most obviously, the concept contains a deeply American bias—even in its more self-flagellating forms the narrative enacts its own sort of parochial exceptionalism, with America at the center and the "invaders," heroic as they may be, as irreducibly alien. Since its beginnings, the British Invasion wasn't so much a way for Americans to understand a transatlantic musical movement as it was a way to understand something they perceived as happening *to them*, and much of the early press coverage of the impending British "invaders" betrays isolationist alarmism. In 1963 the *Boston Globe* ran a dispatch from England entitled "Beatle Scourge Spreads" that called for the creation of "A National Society for the Extinction of Beatles," and on the eve of the band's *Ed Sullivan* appearance *Newsweek* suggested their impending arrival was "Old Testament retribution for all the rock 'n' roll America had sent to Britain."[13]

Second, the myth suggests a strange simultaneity and "all-at-once"-ness that's simply incorrect. The British Invasion did *not* happen overnight, as the Beatles and Rolling Stones would be the first to concede, both having suffered numerous and painful stateside failures before finally breaking through. In 1963, Vee-Jay Records released two Beatles singles stateside ("Please Please Me" and "From Me to You") and an album (*Introducing . . . The Beatles)*, and Philadelphia's tiny Swan Records had even acquired the rights to "She Loves You" for American pressing.[14] None of these early releases sold well, derailed by circumstance, audience indifference, and poor promotion.[15] The delay in American recognition was enough to cause a British reporter to interrogate a visiting Roy Orbison about the Beatles' stateside viability in 1963, prompting Orbison to predict that "these boys have enough originality to storm our charts in the U.S. with the same effect as they have already done here, but it will need careful handling."[16]

The Rolling Stones took even longer to find sustained American success: their first U.S. number one hit, "(I Can't Get No) Satisfaction," came in June 1965, by which point the Beatles had already charted eight American number ones.[17] Despite occasional stateside newspaper stories with titles like "New British Invaders Outdo Beatles" that warned readers that the Stones were "hard to describe without seeming offensive," the suggestion that the Rolling Stones simply sailed triumphantly across the Atlantic on the Beatles' coattails is inaccurate.[18] In fact, after the Stones' initial 1964 trip to the States, Mick Jagger himself acknowledged to a British reporter that "we bombed in some parts but so have all the other British groups, with the exception of the Beatles."[19]

Third, the British Invasion idea has tended to lump together a variety of artists who had little in common with one another outside of nationality, to invent connections where there are none and to ignore difference in favor of false unity. For instance, American coverage of the Beatles tended to broadly focus on their Englishness and downplay the fact that they were from Liverpool, a port city that offered a vastly distinct musical and cultural context than London (birthplace of the Rolling Stones), Manchester (Herman's Hermits), or Newcastle upon Tyne (the Animals). This national flattening has persisted, and again nowhere more than in the recurring tendency to hear and analyze the Beatles and the Rolling Stones in tandem. The differences between the early careers of the Beatles and the Rolling Stones are vast and significant, but rock history has still tended to view the Beatles and the Stones as a duality, or dichotomy, with the Beatles as the music's Apollonian ego and the Stones its Dionysian id.[20] This has been a powerfully persistent formation, one that again took its roots from an "outsider" view of England as a distant land from which new ideas about music as art, hedonism, or both were bequeathed to rock and roll.

Finally, and most importantly, the British Invasion myth is faulty for the denial of porosity implicit in its central metaphor. Not only does the language of "invasion" give an adversarial tinge to the musical happenings of this period, but it also neglects the fact that the British music press had been using the language of "invasion" for years before Americans took it up, in reference to popular touring acts such as Buddy Holly, Jerry Lee Lewis, and Sam Cooke.[21] Moreover, the British Invasion myth obscures the avenues of exchange that existed in these early years between British musicians and their American, and especially African American, counterparts. The Beatles, the Rolling Stones, the Animals, and other British bands name-checked black musical heroes with obsessive frequency in interviews, and they sometimes spoke openly of their discomfort with the fact that their music had reached heights of popularity in England that their American idols had never achieved. As a young Mick Jagger declared to *Melody Maker* in 1964: "To those who listen to groups like ours, and think we are originators, we say—don't listen to us. Listen to the men who inspire us. Buy their records. Why get your information second hand when it's fairly easy to buy it new?"[22]

For many of his listeners, this question remained unanswered, and in years going forward it would increasingly go unasked, lost in the haze of Invasion mythology. In order to best understand the meaning of February 1964 and all that came after it, we must return to the contexts that produced that moment, contexts that suggest the British Invasion was really a sustained flash of unprecedented visibility for an ongoing transatlantic musical exchange that stretched back far longer than the onset of Beatlemania. The remainder of this chapter examines the peculiar intermingling of youth, music, and racial imagination in England in the long moment before four young Liverpudlians touched down at JFK.

Teenage Dreams and American Slouches: Young England and the Long Boom

> I got off my stool and went and stood by the glass of that tottering old department store, pressed up so close it was like I was out there in the air, suspended over space above the city,

and I swore by Elvis and all the saints that this last teenage year of mine was going to be a real rave. Yes, man, come whatever, this last year of the teenage dream I was out for kicks and fantasy.[23]

The above passage appears in the opening pages of *Absolute Beginners*, Colin MacInnes's novel of late 1950s disaffected British youth, a first-person account of four months in the life of a working-class teenaged photographer in a multicultural London cityscape. Published in 1959, *Absolute Beginners* quickly became an influential text of postwar England, cherished by some for its unflinching portrayal of teenaged angst, reviled by others for its alleged endorsement of delinquency and nihilism.[24] While predating the international breakthrough of British rock and roll by nearly five years, *Absolute Beginners* offered a glimpse into a changing England, where the nationalistic pride of past generations had given way to a stark awareness of encroaching provincialism, rendered in a teenaged voice that articulated insecurities of race, class, and sexuality with surprising frankness.

In the years since MacInnes's novel, the youth subcultures of postwar Britain have been a recurring subject of interest to scholars and critics, and numerous classic texts of British cultural studies have taken them as muses.[25] These subcultures, which bore names like teddy boys, rockers, mods, and skinheads, to list just a few, were often clustered around tastes in popular music. MacInnes himself was a frequent if cautious defender of these groups, noting that the groups of young people gathering around jukeboxes in coffee houses and milk bars to the consternation of their elders seemed less determined by England's rigid class structure than any generation in history.[26] Others were less convinced, as indicated by the following extended passage from Richard Hoggart's classic 1957 study *The Uses of Literacy*:

I have in mind rather the kind of milk-bar—there is one in almost every northern town with more than, say, fifteen thousand inhabitants—which has become the regular evening rendezvous for some of the young men. Girls go to some, but most of the customers are boys aged between fifteen and twenty, with drape-suits, picture ties and an American slouch. Many of them cannot afford a succession of milk-shakes, and make cups of tea serve for an hour or two whilst—and this is their main reason for coming—they put copper after copper into the mechanical record player. About a dozen records are available at any time; a numbered button is pressed for the one wanted, which is selected from a key to titles. The records seem to be changed about once a fortnight by the hiring firm; almost all are American . . . all have been doctored for presentation so that they have the kind of beat which is currently popular; much use is made of the "hollow-cosmos" effect which echo-chamber recording gives. . . . The young men waggle one shoulder or stare, as desperately as Humphrey Bogart, across the tubular chairs.[27]

In the years since these writers and others first attempted to glean meaning from youths dressing and behaving in new ways, class has been the primary critical lens through which most commentators have examined postwar British youth cultures. There are a number of reasons why this should not be particularly surprising: first, England has a long history of class rigidity, and as MacInnes and others argued, the emergence of "youth" as a meaningful social category during this period was a real disruption. Second, in the latter half of the twentieth century, England developed a robust left-intellectual tradition drawn to a generally class-based view of historical and cultural processes, from E. P. Thompson's pathbreaking "bottom-up" social history to Raymond Williams's ruminations on the intersection of culture and nation to Hoggart's own work on literature and popular culture.[28] As Gilroy later argued, these scholars tended to embrace a vision of England with class at its core, occasionally to the exclusion of other concerns, race chief among these.[29]

Finally, the emergence of these cultures came at a time in which England was experiencing a dramatic economic realignment. Coming on the heels of austerity the new British youth cultures emerged into what Eric Hobsbawm calls the "long boom," a period of growth and affluence that largely mirrored the preceding American postwar economic explosion.[30] The emergence of the "teenager" as a subject of fascination was directly tied to this, as the new youth cultures seemed crucially united by a recourse to disposable income. In the passages quoted above, Hoggart and MacInnes both suggest that a disproportionate amount of that income was dispensed into jukeboxes and record-store cash registers. A robust economy rife with opportunities for young people had clearly created a vision of British youth with unprecedented purchasing power and social and cultural power soon to follow.

But the overwhelming focus on class has tended to obscure the racial fantasies and ways of racial thinking that ran through British youth cultures. These ideologies, preoccupations, and sometimes obsessions were most nakedly revealed at jukeboxes and record stores, coffee houses and jazz clubs, and by the early 1960s a generation of young Britons had spent considerable time and money feeding their own racial imaginations through music, in modes no less powerful than their young American counterparts and to their own unique ends.

The historian George McKay argues that, at least since the arrival of jazz music in England in the early twentieth century, there has been a tendency among British musicians and writers to strategically avoid discussions of race. "The racial element of the music's origins, its dominant blackness from the United States, is to be lost in translation, or ignored, or considered secondary, while their own ethnic identity, as whites, is barely worth consideration at all," writes McKay.[31] And yet any suggestion that England has enjoyed a markedly less potent relation to interminglings of musical and racial imagination during the twentieth century is readily dispelled, as the long history of black music in England quickly reveals the prominent role of racial ideology in British musical discourse. McKay notes that in 1926 the rector of Exeter College, Oxford, implored his congregation not to "take your music from America or from the niggers," and that same year the founding editor of the jazz periodical *Melody Maker*, Edgar Jackson, penned an editorial in which he declared that "the habit of associating our music with the primitive and barbarous negro derivation shall cease forthwith."[32]

While British audiences filtered their listening through racial imagination to similar degrees as their American counterparts, one must be careful not to graft American understandings and archetypes onto British listeners and performers. Young white Britons' relationships to black music, while surely complicated and profound, were different than Elvis Presley's or Bob Dylan's, and while postwar England harbored a generous mixture of musical and racial fantasies, the specific content of these fantasies was widely varied and distinctly homegrown. In the days of rock and roll's first arrival to the United Kingdom, arguably the most spectacular exhibitor of these fantasies was the teddy boy, among the most fretted-over and enduring subcultural figures in English history.

Rock and Roll, Riots, and Race

Unlike beatniks or rockers, the teddy boy had no real American analogue. His style and worldview were uniquely British, right down to his clothes, the Edwardian formalwear that provided his name. As Tony Jefferson has argued, the teds' "adoption and personal modification of Savile Row Edwardian suits" was their "one contribution to culture . . . their dress represented a symbolic way of expressing and negotiating with their social reality; of giving cultural *meaning* to their social plight."[33] In his 1970 quasi-memoir *Revolt into Style,* George Melly recalled that "the way the Ted 'came on' was no more aesthetic in intention than the scarlet throat of a robin or the identifying smell of a dog's arsehole. It provided, like a dog or robin, a warning, a provocation, a sexual flag, a recognition signal; the interpretation depending entirely on who was exposed to it."[34] The teds' style and attitude were governed by affected indifference to school, the law, and civil society in general, and as a posture it was clearly effective. By the mid-1950s the teds had come to be characterized by the press as violent, nihilistic louts and seen as a general menace to Britain.[35]

Although the teds' emergence in England predated the arrival of American rock and roll by several years, the teds were quick to co-opt the music, one of the reasons that the demarcation between the teddy boy and the slightly later "rocker" subculture is often blurry. It is necessary to emphasize here the fluidity and ever-changing nature of youth subcultures in general: of course, this is partially due to the time-bound nature of "youth" and also to the fact that these cultures never exist in true autonomy. As Stuart Hall and Jefferson wrote, subcultures tend to experience themselves *in terms* of the dominant culture, and youth subcultures in particular inhabit a "double-articulation," simultaneously located in relation to both the "parent culture" and the "dominant culture."[36] A working-class youth subculture such as the teddy boys thus negatively defined itself in terms of both adult working-class culture, with its affected dress and embrace of American rock and roll, and in terms of dominant "British" culture, through violent behavior and rejection of institutions of work and education. This doubly determined nature resulted in constantly shifting and frequently incoherent ideologies, and nowhere was this more evident than in the figure of the teddy boy.

Dick Hebdige, the great theorist of subculture and one of the teds' more unimpressed observers, wrote that "temperamentally detached from the respectable working class," the ted "found himself on the outside in fantasy. He visibly bracketed off the drab routines of school, the job and home by affecting an exaggerated style which juxtaposed two blatantly plundered forms," specifically his Edwardian sartorial preferences and his chosen soundtrack of American rock and roll.[37] By the mid-1950s the teds had fully incorporated rock and roll music into their peculiar aesthetic, and in 1956 a moral panic erupted in Britain at the conjunction of the music itself and the violence of its listeners. The British release of the film *Blackboard Jungle*, with its prominent use of Bill Haley and the Comets' "Rock around the Clock," occasioned riots throughout the country, widely seen as the work of teds run amok.

Several historians have argued that the "rock and roll riots" helped cement a connection between rock and roll and juvenile delinquency in the 1950s British cultural imagination.[38] Even more specifically, I would suggest that a racialized imaginative link between the teddy boys (white English youth), rock and roll (interracial American music), and "riot" violence was forged during this period that would take on even greater proportions in the wake of the Notting Hill riots of 1958, one of postwar England's most destructive outbreaks of racial violence and, like the cinema riots, an event for which the teds were widely blamed.

As the 1950s progressed, many teds were drawn to an insurgent white supremacy pervading certain corners of British culture during a period of racial upheaval in the country, as the decline of colonialism was resulting in a steady influx of East and West Indian immigrants into the United Kingdom.[39] The teds' combustible combination of racial nationalism and anti-social behavior reached a flashpoint during the race riots of August and September of 1958. The demographics of West London's Notting Hill area had grown increasingly Caribbean since World War II, and while relations between blacks and whites in the area had been generally peaceful, in the later part of the 1950s the neighborhood became increasingly targeted by right-wing nationalist groups such as Sir Oswald Mosley's Union Movement, organized under the slogan "Keep Britain White."[40] Rioting began on the evening of August 23rd, died down, then resumed in force on August 30th, ultimately raging for four consecutive days and nights. One historian writes that by September 2nd "Notting Hill looked like a scene from a film set in the American South . . . as it began to get dark gangs of several hundred youths started roaming around the Colville area shouting: 'We want a nigger.' "[41]

All in all 108 people (76 white, 32 "coloured") were arrested during the violence, but the harshest sentences were reserved for nine youths who brutally attacked five Caribbean men in separate incidents on the night of August 24. When apprehended, they informed police that they had been "nigger-hunting," and they received four years a piece from a judge who declared, "It was you men who started the whole of this violence in Notting Hill."[42] The nine young men ranged in age from seventeen to twenty; all were pointedly identified in London's *Times* as either working-class or unemployed. The teddy boy subculture was widely vilified for its overzealous participation in the riots, and in 2002 the *Guardian* revealed confidential police files confirming that "the disturbances were overwhelmingly triggered by 300- to 400-strong 'Keep Britain White' mobs, many of them Teddy boys armed with iron bars, butcher's knives and weighted leather belts, who went 'nigger-hunting' among the West Indian residents of Notting Hill and Notting Dale."[43]

The teddy boys' devotion to rock and roll—a black-derived musical form—and their enthusiastic participation in antiblack violence have been difficult for commentators to reconcile. Hebdige has argued that the teds focused their most intense musical fandom on white rock and rollers such as Elvis and Gene Vincent, leaving them "impervious to any sense of contradiction" in their attacks on West Indian immigrants:

> It was not until black gospel and blues had fused with white country and western to produce a completely new form—rock 'n roll—that the line between the two positions (black and British working-class youth) could be surreptitiously elided. . . . In the face of what was necessarily a somewhat crude and cerebral appropriation, the subtle dialogue between black and white musical forms which framed the trembling vocals was bound to go unheard. The history of rock's construction was, after all, easily concealed.[44]

While this is an interesting argument, I am not sure it tells the whole story. For starters, with regards to the riots themselves, the implication that a teddy boy would infer commonality between black American musicians and West Indian immigrants is a shaky one, as is the general inference that there might be a correlation between the demographics of one's record collection and one's personal commitment to racial justice: after all, the long history of white enjoyment of black music in America would seem to indicate otherwise. Second, the suggestion that the teds simply convinced themselves that rock and roll was white in origin seems unlikely, given the widespread circulation of rock and roll records and the fact that artists such as Berry, Little Richard, and Fats Domino had enjoyed British chart success alongside their white American counterparts.

I would instead suggest that teddy boys took what they wanted from the gateway that rock and roll provided into long-standing white fantasies of blackness—danger, aggression, liminality—and simply discarded its real attachment to black bodies, or at least any political uses of that attachment. In his account of the era Melly describes the position of rock and roll for the teds during this period as "a contemporary incitement to mindless fucking and arbitrary vandalism: screw and smash music."[45] The teddy boys were thus able to reconcile a worldview marked by ethnic nationalism, a desire to "keep Britain white," with an enthusiasm for a music that was neither white nor British. This move seems extraordinarily important, as it positions the teddy boys as among the earliest in a long line of white rock and roll fans who have violently mined the music for racialized fantasies of hypermasculinity while strategically ignoring any real connection to black people—one need only look to the vehement anti-disco rhetoric of the late 1970s or pockets of white supremacy in the 1980s Los Angeles punk and hardcore scenes for other such examples.

The teddy boys' Britishness also complicates suggestions that the "whitening" of rock and roll was simply another iteration of an exceptionally American legacy of racial expropriation. In 1950s America, rock and roll was still an object of hysteria among white supremacists, evidenced by the persistent linkage of the music to miscegenation (and, by theoretical extension, communism) by conservative commentators.[46] The teddy boy, in a rather stunning reversal, was both the youthful face of a reactionary British white supremacy *and* the country's most visible connoisseur of rock and roll records. Through the public panic over the teddy boy in the wake of the "rock and roll riots," a panic that took on graver scope and profile after the Notting Hill riots, in late 1950s England an imaginative link was forged between rock and roll and racial violence. This link would prove long-lasting and deeply consequential for rock music: as Chapter 6 shows, its most spectacular inheritors are the Rolling Stones themselves, a band whose members came of age against this 1950s backdrop.

Trad, Skiffle, and Beatle Beginnings

For all of their significance as England's most visible early rock and roll connoisseurs, by and large the teds were not a music-making subculture, failing to take the crucial step from buying Elvis Presley records to buying an electric guitar. One of the prominent and influential music-*making* subcultures of 1950s England, that of traditional, or "trad," jazz, existed in almost direct opposition to the teddy boy. Musical cousins to the more literary "beatniks," "traddies" tended to be openly intellectual, politically liberal, and musically snobbish.[47] Trad as a form boasted a strangely nostalgic emphasis on what were considered to be the original, or traditional, roots of American jazz music, specifically the acoustic, duple-meter-driven New Orleans jazz combo. Trad was also far more enduring than a simple fad, lasting into the 1960s and even still persisting in England to this day, albeit in niche form.[48]

Historians and critics have rightfully treated trad as part of the larger transatlantic interest in "folk" music during this period (discussed in Chapter 1), although in the United States this interest did not encompass traditional New Orleans jazz to nearly such strong degrees.[49] Like other folk revivalists, many in the trad community saw themselves as the last bastion of "true" jazz music, as evidenced by a 1961 *Melody Maker* editorial by bandleader Chris Barber that claimed "there's no U.S. jazz scene; it's our job to teach the Americans about jazz."[50] McKay suggests that the traddie's avowed disinterest in bebop and other more modern styles had sprung from an acute awareness of the technical difficulties of these forms, and that "bebop was understood as an avowedly racialized cultural form. . . . Its complexities, secrets, language, and semiotics of style were expressions of black masculine authority, originality, exclusivity."[51] This would partly explain the traddie's embrace of earlier forms of jazz music that featured relatively simple rhythmic and harmonic structures, less emphasis on individual virtuosity, and, crucially, more potential for dancing. Trad offered a music that was relatively accessible for both musicians and listeners on a variety of levels, and it could be learned and performed by homegrown players without endless practice or immersion.

Trad as a musical and cultural movement began shortly after World War II but reached its apex in the 1950s. Among its more significant figures were trumpeter Humphrey Lyttelton, trombonist Barber, clarinetist Acker Bilk, and, perhaps most centrally, trumpeter and cornetist Ken Colyer. In 1952, Colyer joined the merchant marines with the sole purpose of making his way to New Orleans, where he jumped ship and played in a band with African American clarinetist George Lewis, his adventures catalogued in a series of widely read, foreign-correspondent missives to *Melody Maker*. When he was ultimately deported back to England in 1953, rumors circulated that his return was occasioned by his courageous and flagrant violations of the city's segregationist racial mores.[52]

Racial imagination and musical ideology were intertwined to dizzying extremes in trad jazz. On one hand, and much to their credit, traddies tended to be attuned to issues of racial justice:

these concerns were initially focused abroad, toward black-white relations in South Africa and the United States, but throughout the 1950s they would become increasingly germane to racial strife within England as well.[53] The flip side of the traddies' enthusiasm for racial equality was a naked fetishization of black musicianship. In his 1989 autobiography, Ken Colyer confessed his belief that he "was born about sixty years too late, the wrong colour, and in the wrong country."[54] Others may have taken this wish to more literal extremes, such as a widely circulated tale about a man who went into Charing Cross Hospital "to see if they had injections to turn his white skin black."[55]

Traddies shared many of the contradictions of American folk revivalists: they were politically progressive (Colyer was a vocal supporter of the Campaign for Nuclear Disarmament) yet aesthetically reactionary; they were self-appointed white protectors of decades-old black American music; and they embraced a fiercely antimodern stance while cobbling together a musical subculture that was uniquely enabled by circumstances of modernity (the transatlantic circulation of records, the postwar economic boom). And like the folk revival, when rock and roll began to invade England in the mid-1950s, trad had little use for it.

If trads and teds offered competing racial imaginations through which they filtered their musical tastes—the trads by placing black music and musicians on an exalted pedestal, the teds by selectively and incompletely re-racializing their music in service of a white supremacist worldview—both subcultures came to their music secondhand, its authenticity bound in no small part to its Americanness. The most significant "home-grown" musical subculture in 1950s England, skiffle, emerged out of trad but would have a far greater impact on British rock and roll than any other jazz- or folk-based musical form.

In early 1956, the singer and guitarist Lonnie Donegan shot up the British charts with a frenetic version of Leadbelly's classic

"Rock Island Line." Thus began what would soon come to be known in England as the "skiffle craze," a brief and strange musical moment that would prove to have resounding implications for global popular music in the next decade. A skiffle musician and historian, Chas McDevitt, notes that the word "skiffle" is most likely Scottish in origin and appears frequently in Ulster dialect; its slang meaning is simply "in a hurry."[56] As a musical term, the word first appears in association with African American musicians: in 1925, clarinetist Jimmy O'Bryant recorded with a group called "Chicago Skifflers," and in 1928 Paramount Records released a recording entitled "Hometown Skiffle" by a six-person all-star blues group that was purported to feature Blind Lemon Jefferson. In its American contexts the word is curiously amorphous, loosely applied to energetic, improvisatory music that could range from jazz to downhome country blues. The Scots-Irish origins of the term suggest a significant degree of white (and quite possibly rural) involvement as well, although the few American recordings that bear the term tend to feature African American performers.[57]

Perhaps unsurprisingly, the impetus for "reviving" skiffle came from the trad scene, though it must be stressed that, unlike trad itself, skiffle was less a revival than a complete reimagination. As the writer Harry Shapiro describes it, skiffle "was essentially a jazz-band rhythm section with the voice carrying the melody instead of the brass frontline," and British skiffle supposedly originated from the rhythm section "breaks" featured in Ken Colyer's band, which at various points included musicians such as bassist/trombonist Chris Barber, guitarist Alexis Korner, and Lonnie Donegan himself.[58]

Skiffle was a passing if intense fad in England—Donegan, the music's longest-lasting star, had his last British chart hit in 1962, perhaps fittingly departing the charts as the Beatles' "Love Me Do" was entering.[59] The cultural impact of the skiffle craze in the United Kingdom, however, was enormous: if trad had appealed to young musicians for its relative simplicity of performance, skiffle was even easier. The typical skiffle performance contained three or four chords, an easily accessible vocal melody, minimal dynamic variation, and a simple, driving rhythmic feel. In its emphasis on speed and energy it was undeniably effective dance music, and during the mid-1950s "skiffle cellars" throughout the British Isles were populated with young people. In the words of British pop singer Adam Faith, "Anyone who could afford to buy a guitar and learn three chords was in business as a skiffler. It grew in cellars, nice dark cellars, and it shot up like mushrooms."[60]

The legacy of the skiffle craze as introducing young Britons to the *practice* of music—and particularly a guitar-based, American-derived, aurally transmitted music—is hugely significant. McDevitt suggests that by 1957 there were between 30,000 and 50,000 skiffle groups throughout the United Kingdom; while this number is impossible to confirm and might be astronomically high, that same year a major British retailer estimated selling *250,000* guitars, as opposed to just 6,000 in 1950.[61] A notable side effect of this popularity was a tendency among musicians, promoters, and record companies to label nearly any record made by young English people as "skiffle" for the duration of the craze, and such fluidity makes the ideological components of skiffle as a genre, already remarkably diffuse, difficult to pin down.

The racial imagination of skiffle was less foregrounded than that of trad, where the presumed correlation of skin color to musical ability was sometimes explicitly stated. Because of the preexistence of traditional British folk music that bore an understandable resemblance to American folk music, and which would itself be the subject of a revival in late 1950s England, skiffle was far more easily reconciled with Englishness than trad, even if many of skiffle's figures of admiration, such as Leadbelly, Josh White, and Big Bill Broonzy, were African American, and Donegan's own repertoire included minstrel-ish folk songs such as "Pick a Bale of Cotton."[62]

Skiffle's import lay neither in its aesthetic achievements nor in its ideology of authenticity, both of which were modest, but rather in its availability. It was easy to play, and it was sufficiently hybrid enough to welcome amateur performers from London to Liverpool who might have previously balked at playing "American" music. Major British musicians who began their amateur careers in skiffle bands during this period include Van Morrison, Roger Daltry (later of the Who), David Gilmour (later of Pink Floyd), and, most famously, John Lennon and Paul McCartney, whose musical collaboration began in a Lennon-founded skiffle group called the Quarrymen. As McCartney later remembered, "Once Lonnie Donegan came along, we got the feeling we could actually be part of it. We could actually do it."[63] The influence of skiffle can be heard in the Beatles' music on such recordings as "I've Just Seen a Face," McCartney's lovely composition from *Help!* that features driving acoustic guitar and a stomping, two-beat rhythm, and "Maggie Mae" from *Let It Be,* a traditional Liverpool folk song that Lennon and McCartney first performed in their Quarrymen days.

Despite its enormous, if indirect, impact on global popular music in the coming decade, the skiffle craze barely touched the American charts, although Lonnie Donegan did make the Top 10 stateside twice, once for "Rock Island Line" and again in 1961 with the novelty song, "Does Your Chewing-Gum Lose Its Flavor on the Bedpost Overnight?" By this time skiffle was foundering in England, partly run aground by its own limitations and partly supplanted by a new musical culture that was also drawn from the trad community. This was the movement of British blues, or "rhythm and blues" (the terms were used more or less interchangeably), and as the 1960s unfolded, it would emerge as one of England's most significant subcultural musical movements.

Blues, the Rolling Stones, and Bo Diddley's Buddy Holly

If Lonnie Donegan was the towering influence of British skiffle, his equivalent in British blues may have been guitarist and bandleader Alexis Korner, though Korner never achieved Donegan's level of commercial success and popular recognition. Korner was a musician, bandleader, disc jockey, critic, and collector, and by the early 1960s British blues and R&B essentially ran through him and his band, Alexis Korner's Blues Incorporated. While perhaps most famous for his role in the early career of the Rolling Stones—Mick Jagger and Charlie Watts had previously played together in Korner's band, and Korner secured the Stones some of their earliest bookings—Korner was a mentor figure to countless other young British musicians and blues enthusiasts. Born in 1928 in London to immigrant parents (his mother Greek, his father an Austrian Jew), Korner endured a somewhat speckled childhood, part of which was spent in a quasi-reformatory called Finchden Manor where he'd been sentenced after stealing 78s from a record store in Shepherd's Bush. In 1947 Korner joined the British Army, where his growing knowledge of music and fluent German secured him a position at a radio station in Hamburg, the same city that would play host to the young Beatles years later.[64]

Like Donegan, Korner had strong links to trad jazz—his first major gig as a performer was as a banjo player in Chris Barber's band—yet Korner never embraced the rigid purism of certain other trad devotees. Korner was an avid bebop fan at a time when many traddies scorned the music; conversely, despite a friendship with Donegan he despised the skiffle craze, writing in the pages of *Melody Maker* that "British skiffle is, most certainly, a commercial success, but musically it rarely exceeds the mediocre and is, in general, so abysmally low that it defies proper musical judgment."[65] As skiffle exploded and trad continued to thrive, Korner found himself increasingly drawn to American blues music. In 1955 he had been instrumental in bringing bluesman Big Bill Broonzy to England, and shortly thereafter Korner and Barber arranged for Muddy Waters's first British visit. By 1957 Korner had left his job at the BBC to become a full-time musician and blues evangelist, and by early 1958 he had made his first recordings with Blues Incorporated.

Korner was a self-made intellectual who published prolifically as a writer, both in magazines and in liner notes that he frequently wrote for U.K. reissues of classic American blues recordings. He was also, by all accounts, extraordinarily generous to younger musicians. Although born a short but crucial generation earlier than apostles such as Jagger and Eric Clapton, his musical and intellectual impact on these musicians makes him an enormously important figure in the early history of British rock and roll.

If skiffle had been a brief but powerful fad, British blues was a true subcultural movement: oppositional, anticommercial, and passionately high-minded. The subculture of British blues was obsessed with authenticity, but whereas trad had placed a premium on meticulous imitation, British blues was not as outwardly concerned with attempting to *replicate* the sounds of Robert Johnson, Big Bill Broonzy, or Muddy Waters. Korner viewed himself as more promoter than protectionist: whereas trad saw itself as the last bastion of "true" jazz music, Korner, prodigious in his efforts to bring American blues musicians to England, made no such claims. Black American performers such as Sonny Terry and Brownie McGhee, who toured England frequently in this period, were undoubtedly revered, but their living presence dulled impulses toward obsessive conservationism among young British musicians. In his 2010 memoir *Life,* Keith Richards recounts the tensions between older preservationists (whom Richards explicitly associates with trad) and younger practitioners like himself, in the context of an electrified Muddy Waters concert in the early 1960s:

> But for this audience, blues was only blues if somebody got up there in a pair of old blue dungarees and sang about how his old lady left him. None of these blues purists could play anything. But their Negroes had to be dressed in overalls and go "Yes'm, boss." . . . They wanted a frozen frame, not knowing that what they were listening to was only part of the process; something had gone before and it was going to move on.[66]

British blues also lacked the explicit ties to political causes that many trad musicians had cultivated, and the political conscience of British blues tended to be more vague and introspective. As Shapiro argues, the "communal" elements of trad, specifically its emphasis on collective improvisation, were conducive to politicizing, and the generation of musicians who came under Korner's tutelage were more interested in the blues as a vehicle for personal liberation rather than social or political. It was, in Shapiro's words, "their own sense of 'otherness' as much as social commentary" that attracted bored or otherwise-disaffected British youth to the music, a yearning to express a sense of *personal* authenticity rather than replicating the authenticity of those who, to paraphrase Colyer, had been born sixty years earlier and another color.[67]

British blues was as much an intellectual subculture of "angry young men" as it was a musical one, and it tended to attract poised, self-serious, and ambitious followers. Mick Jagger's time as a student at the London School of Economics is a frequently remarked-upon piece of trivia, as though it is ironic that one of the world's most recognizable rock stars came from such a lofty intellectual background. Considered in terms of Jagger's beginnings as a singer and harmonica player on the London blues scene, it might be more remarkable if he came from anything else.

While an impressive number of devotees of the scene would later ascend to rock stardom, in its early years British blues' relationship to much rock and roll ranged from ambivalence to outright contempt. Consider, for instance, the Rolling Stones' repeated insistence on *not* being called a rock and roll group in their early career: "if you call them rock 'n' roll, they positively glower," reported *New Musical Express* in 1963.[68] Even in 1964, when the Stones were on top of the *Melody Maker* charts with a cover of the Valentinos' "It's All Over Now" (a song first released on Sam Cooke's SAR Records, and written by a young Bobby Womack), a column appeared in *Melody Maker* under Jagger's byline in which he wrote disparagingly of Motown, calling the Temptations and Marvelettes "boring" and praising only Marvin Gaye's "Can I Get a Witness" (a song the Stones would soon cover, and which is, probably not coincidentally, a double-time twelve-bar blues).[69]

Some have argued that as the British blues scene progressed into the 1960s, the cults of exaltation that surrounded its musicians relied increasingly on a European romantic tradition of the intellectual and artistic hero—the legendary "Clapton is God" graffiti that appeared near the Islington underground station in 1967, for instance—a troubling development given the African American background of their source material.[70] While this may be true, I would suggest that the potential for white male co-optation was present in British blues since its inception: by conflating fantasies of racial authenticity with fantasies of personal authenticity, British blues had already radically de-racialized itself. The British blues community embraced a notion of the blues as a deeply democratic form: if one were compelled to sing the blues, then by all means one should, regardless of skin color, provided one treated the music with the respect and rigor it deserved.

Taken on its surface this was a bold idea, one that would allow for a premium on creativity unafforded by trad or skiffle. As Chicago-based harmonica player Sonny Boy Williamson put it to a *Melody Maker* interviewer in 1963, "I enjoy hearing them sing blues here; it makes me feel good. In the States, you don't have no white boys sing the blues."[71] Of course, this dual move to simultaneously democratize and rarify the blues did not mean that the British blues community was less obsessed with racial imagination than the trad community had been; if anything, the move away from more overtly political engagements of racial justice made the blues community's emphasis on the more fantastical side of racial thinking even more pronounced.

Young British engagement with the blues was romantic and mystical, and while the still-living American forebears of this music became figures of intense adulation, deceased performers such as Robert Johnson were elevated to truly mythic heights.[72] The ambivalences—personal, social, and musical—aroused by this confrontation may account for the racial imagination that British blues adopted, one that was obsessed with authenticity but which could not allow that authenticity to become racialized to the point that it negated the practices of its members. The prioritizing of personal "authenticity" over racial identity may have been a problematic move by the nascent British blues subculture but it was also necessary for the subculture's survival, the only way to reconcile its expressive ideals with the whiteness of its idealists.

These complexities can be heard in raw form in the early music of the Rolling Stones, and they are perhaps most productively exemplified in the band's 1963 cover of Buddy Holly's "Not Fade Away," which became their most successful U.K. release to date, reaching number three on the charts.[73] Holly's original version of "Not Fade Away" employs a figure commonly known as the "Bo Diddley beat," named for the musician who popularized it on his eponymous 1955 hit, "Bo Diddley."[74] The "Bo Diddley beat" is itself an iteration of the 3/2 clave beat that is commonly found in Cuban music and which is almost certainly West African in origin.[75]

The original recording of "Not Fade Away" is a tangled black Atlantic web indeed, one that finds a white musician from Lubbock, Texas (Holly), paying homage to a Chicago rhythm and blues musician (Diddley), who was in turn largely responsible for introducing an Afro-Cuban rhythm to rhythm and blues, and consequently rock and roll, in the mid-1950s. Holly's version of "Not Fade Away," released in 1957, is performed in the singer's own inimitable, hiccupping vocal style—aside from the beat, absolutely no one would mistake Holly's performance for Bo Diddleys. "Bo Diddley" is marked by a pulsing, reverb-drenched, electric guitar, driving tom-toms, and a wash of maracas at the front of the mix; "Not Fade Away," while employing an identical rhythmic figure, has a clean electric guitar, understated percussion, and doo-wop-style backing vocals. Holly's vocal style was famously distinctive, and long after his death in 1959 the singer and songwriter would remain an exceedingly influential figure for many young British rock and rollers; one of the earliest Quarrymen recordings, released as part of the 1995 Beatles *Anthology* series, is a performance of Holly's "That'll Be the Day" from 1958.

The Rolling Stones were, of course, exceptions to this: for Mick Jagger and Keith Richards, music was meant to be played like Chuck Berry or Muddy Waters, or it ought not to be played at all. In his memoir Richards describes a diary he kept from January to March of 1963, less than a year before the band recorded "Not Fade Away." "Inside the cover of the pocket diary are the heavily inked words 'Chuck,' 'Reed,' 'Diddley.' There you have it. That was all we listened to at the time. Just American blues or rhythm and blues or country blues."[76]

In many senses "Not Fade Away" was thus a perfect match for the Stones: far more avid Bo Diddley fans than they were Buddy Holly fans, the Stones' version of "Not Fade Away" sounds remarkably as one might imagine Diddley's own version of the song would, or at least as the young Stones might imagine it would. Richards's overdriven guitar jangles at the front of the mix, Brian Jones plays blues harmonica fills to punctuate Jagger's vocal phrases, and the "Bo Diddley beat" is even more exaggerated than it is on "Bo Diddley," courtesy of hand claps, maracas, a tambourine, and Charlie Watts's pounding tom-toms. The Stones also ratchet up the tempo considerably from Holly's original version of "Not Fade Away"—the cover clocks in at a cool one minute and forty-eight seconds, nearly forty seconds shorter than Holly's version.

But the most remarkable aspect of "Not Fade Away" is Jagger's vocal performance: unlike the band's previous single releases, on which the young singer sounds affected and stilted,

"Not Fade Away" carries an air of comfort and confidence with the material that is absent on the band's first single, a cover of Chuck Berry's "Come On."[77] Jagger culls a darkness from "Not Fade Away" that's embedded in the song's lyrics but largely missing from the original version, awash as it is in Holly's playful phrasing and trademark hiccups. "I'm gonna tell you how it's gonna be / You're gonna give your love to me," sings Jagger in the song's opening couplet, the second line delivered with a sneering force.

The significance of "Not Fade Away" being a Buddy Holly song is crucial to this. The Stones' obsessive relation to older African American music may have been most fraught for Jagger, and the distractingly dogged efforts of a young white Englishman to avoid sounding either young, white, or English—what critic Michael Coyle has described as "a merely antic authenticity"—are a common feature of many early Rolling Stones records.[78] "Not Fade Away" finds these more blatant affectations at a minimum. By accentuating the Bo Diddley beat and blues cadences of Holly's original, the Stones positioned themselves to make a "blacker" version of the song than the original, and by tackling a revision of the distinctly Caucasian-sounding Holly, Jagger temporarily freed himself from preoccupations with "authentic" verisimilitude.

For all that would later be made of Jagger's iconic rock-star panache, as a vocalist his most enduring contribution to rock and roll music may be his sheer earnestness: from a technical standpoint he was deficient to Lennon or McCartney, lacking either's intonation, range, or harmonic acuity. Jagger's most significant musical act was to recognize these deficiencies and proceed anyways, carving out a vocal style that relied on blues-derived phrasing techniques and on the dramatic flair of American R&B stars such as James Brown and Solomon Burke. Jagger's is a voice steeped in the radically democratic ideology of British blues, in which the will and desire to perform black music was seen as self-justifying and worthy on its own terms. "Not Fade Away" is the first sound of this voice reaching something like fruition, and this development would have massive ramifications for rock and roll in the years going forward.

In late 1964 the Rolling Stones finally had their first Top 10 U.S. hit with a cover of the Jerry Ragovoy composition, "Time Is on My Side," which had first been a hit for the New Orleanian rhythm and blues star Irma Thomas. The band would reach the American Top 10 again in early 1965 with "The Last Time," an original composition based loosely around the Staple Singers' 1955 gospel classic, "This May Be the Last Time," but it was not until summer of that year that the Stones would have their first international number one hit, "(I Can't Get No) Satisfaction," a Jagger-Richards composition that firmly established the group as one of the most important musical acts of the 1960s.

When the subculture of British blues was wedded to the mass culture of rock and roll, most significantly through the Rolling Stones, it altered both the musical and racial imagination of the music, and triggered a chain reaction marked by dialectical flickerings of expropriation and homage, fetishization and appreciation, opportunism and guilt. As Chapter 6 shows, the Rolling Stones' relationship to racialized fantasies of musical authenticity—and attendant ideas of masculinity, sexuality, violence, and desire—would inform both popular conceptions of the band and the band's conceptions of themselves throughout the 1960s and beyond. These imaginings, and the aesthetic responses they triggered, can all, in some way, be traced back to England and the constellation of musical and racial imagination that percolated in British youth culture in the long moment before the "Invasion."

The British Invasion did not happen suddenly, simultaneously, or unilaterally. Nor did it happen "to" America; by the time the Beatles arrived at JFK in early 1964, the degree to which they and their countrymen had been steeped in American music was so profound that it might be more accurate to say that the British Invasion happened to England long before it came home to roost in the United States, and that the transatlantic crossing of Beatlemania was just one particularly prominent leg of a multidirectional and ongoing journey of black Atlantic musical activity. Nor was it by any means the termination of this journey: as Chapter 3 shows, the Beatles continued to engage with black American music well after their stateside arrival in 1964, even if these engagements were sometimes obscured by the various forms of mania the band inspired.

"Friends across the Sea"

Motown, the Beatles, and Sites and
Sounds of Crossover

> *When I think about the Sixties, I think of two things:*
> *I think of Motown, and I think of the Beatles. Those*
> *are the major influences . . . we all really influenced*
> *each other. That's really what it's all about.*
>
> —Stevie Wonder, 1987

TO EXAMINE THE RUN of *Billboard* magazine, that
frenetic weathervane of the American music industry, from late
1963 into the middle of the 1960s is to behold two stories un-
folding simultaneously: one dramatically, the other less percep-
tibly. The first of these is the North American breakthrough of
the Beatles, a happening that remapped the commercial, artistic,
and geographic landscape of popular music. In early November
of 1963 there was a small item in the well-buried "Britain"

portion of the magazine entitled "Beatles Soar to Success" that called the group "the sensation of the [British] nation."[1] In mid-December *Billboard* noted that the band's latest single had already sold almost a million copies in England a week in advance of its release, and reported that "the group flies to New York on February 7 to make its debut on the 'Ed Sullivan Show' two nights later."[2] The band was still nowhere to be found on the magazine's Pop charts, however, which were topped that week by the Singing Nun's "Dominique."[3]

A few issues later *Billboard* published a review of "I Want to Hold Your Hand," the Beatles' first stateside Capitol Records single. The write-up, in its jargon-ridden entirety: "This is the hot British group that has struck gold overseas. Side is driving rocker with surf on the Thames sound and strong vocal work from the group. The flip is 'I Saw Her Standing There.'"[4] "Surf on the Thames" proved to be a popular sound in the United States. Only a month later *Billboard*'s front page boasted five stories on the Beatles and the British music industry in advance of the *Ed Sullivan Show* performance.[5] By the time the April 4, 1964, issue of *Billboard* arrived on stands, the band had twelve songs in the *Billboard* Hot 100, including one in each of the top five slots. Just like that, one band from Liverpool had ensured that England would never again be an afterthought to the American record industry.[6]

The second and more gradual story during this same period concerned the changing position of African American music with regards to the American popular music industry. In late November of 1963 *Billboard* discontinued its black music chart, which had existed in some form since 1942.[7] *Billboard*'s decision to discontinue the chart—later reinstated in January 1965—was never officially explained by the magazine, but historians speculate that it is because *Billboard* was convinced that its R&B chart was no longer accurately reflecting what R&B audiences were listening to. *Billboard*'s black music chart, in the mind of the magazine, had become too white.[8]

It is ironic, then, that while *Billboard*'s R&B chart was missing, a lucrative revolution was taking place at the intersection of black American music production and white American musical consumership, spearheaded by Berry Gordy, Jr., president of the Motown Record Corporation and its various holdings. Gordy had founded his operation in 1959, financed by an $800 family loan. He festooned its headquarters with the name "Hitsville, U.S.A." and would soon adorn its records with the slogan "The Sound of Young America." Motown had a breakthrough year in 1963, with Gordy's company scoring nine Top 10 Pop hits; his company would soon grow to become the most successful African American-owned business in the country, dominating American popular music through artists such as the Supremes, the Temptations, the Miracles, and the Four Tops.[9] In 1965 *Billboard* reported that "the firm's batting average is the envy of the record industry,"[10] and the following year 75 percent of Motown's single releases entered the *Billboard* charts, compared to an industrywide average of 10 percent, and for the entire period between 1960 and 1969 the label put a new single onto the charts at a rate of once every week and a half.[11]

In the heat of American Beatlemania Motown was often singled out as the Fab Four's primary rival: "Next to the Mersey sound, the 'Motown sound' currently dominates the rock 'n' roll market," *Time* reported.[12] "Knowledgeable persons in pop music think the strongest element of American rock 'n' roll now, musically and financially, is the 'Detroit sound," wrote the *New York Times* in 1965, in an article about the Beatles' ongoing dominance.[13] For significant swaths of the 1960s, Motown appeared to be the primary force keeping the American pop industry afloat against unrelenting waves of British imports.

In early 1964, in a fawning interview the likes of which routinely dominated the pages of the British music press at the height of Beatlemania, Beatles guitarist George Harrison was asked by a *Melody Maker* reporter about his favorite group in the world. He listed the Miracles and Martha and the Vandellas, then proceeded to read aloud a telegram the band had received that had been signed by Marvin Gaye, Stevie Wonder, and Smokey Robinson: "Hi, George, Paul, John and Ringo. Congratulations on your fantastically successful trip to our country. You took our country by storm and we all love you. . . . We are looking forward to visiting England in the near future and recording some tracks together with you for an album like 'Friends across the sea.' "[14]

This chapter explores the vibrant, complex, and productive transatlantic relationship between the Beatles and Motown Records during the 1960s. In this long and vital relationship we can hear a hidden history of 1960s music unbounded by genre anxieties and ideological mythmaking. There has been a long-standing tendency to hear these two entities as leading protagonists in two separate stories—that of white music and black music in the 1960s, specifically—and it is overdue that we hear them together, as "friends across the sea," as the artists themselves once hoped we would.

The Beatles' reputation in popular-music discourse is unimpeachable—aside from Bob Dylan, no other artist of their era has received the level of critical and scholarly attention that the Beatles have, and any attacks against the band's cultural significance and artistic legitimacy would be flatly dismissed today. Motown's position in critical discourse is more complicated, and the label has long held a precarious position in the historiography of R&B music. Similarly to what we have seen with Sam Cooke in Chapter 1, Motown's "crossover" aesthetic and proximity to the white market have frequently led critics to claim that the label was insufficiently or inauthentically black. As later chapters show, in the late 1960s a number of prominent critics assailed Motown for diluting black music for the market, valuations that often rendered Motown's aesthetic virtues lacking in comparison to Southern rhythm and blues studios in Memphis and Muscle Shoals.

This trend has continued in decades since, as historians of rhythm and blues have found many occasions to wring their hands over Motown's legitimacy or illegitimacy as a properly "black" musical entity. Peter Guralnick excluded Motown from his otherwise excellent history of 1960s R&B, *Sweet Soul Music,* on the grounds that it is not "soul music" because it "appeal[ed] far more to a pop, white, and industry-slanted kind of audience."[15] Nelson George, one of the earliest and most thorough chroniclers of Motown, delivered perhaps the harshest assessment when he wrote that Gordy presented himself to white America on the terms of "don't worry; I want to be just like you," attacked the label for harboring "powerful feelings of black inadequacy," and all but accused Gordy of treachery in his dealings with other parties in the black music industry.[16]

The musicologist and Motown historian Andrew Flory argues that "due largely to crossover success, historical representation of Motown and its music often suffer from being branded as 'inauthentic' black music."[17] Flory sees this in largely socioeconomic terms, tied to a broader continuum of anxieties over the black middle class and Gordy's roots and fluency within that community. Flory traces this discomfort back to influential texts like E. Franklin Frazier's *Black Bourgeoisie* and LeRoi Jones's *Blues People,* which were both published roughly contemporaneously with Motown's rise.

But I would suggest that attacks on Motown's authenticity are more directly rooted in the general denial of porosity endemic to discussions of black music such as those described in Chapter 1, discourses in which success within and proximity to a white market renders musical blackness suspect. Nowhere is this more evident than the persistent critical tendency to wield unflattering comparisons to a romanticized vision of Memphis's Stax Records against Motown like a cudgel of racial authenticity.[18] Leaving aside the fact that Stax was a white-owned company for most of the 1960s, such comparisons don't acknowledge the fact that Berry Gordy did not set out to be Stax. In fact, it is far more accurate to suggest he set out to be the Beatles, though long before anyone knew who the Beatles were. Gordy did not found Motown on the goal of being the most successful black record label in America, but rather on the goal of being the most successful record label anywhere, period. Gordy and Motown were after the same integrated teenaged market that the Beatles so spectacularly attracted, and throughout the 1960s only the Beatles would prove to be as adept at attracting it.

When Gordy opened Motown in 1959 he did so with the conviction that with the proper mix of craft and marketing, black music and musicians could be successfully packaged to white America, and his vision succeeded beyond anyone's wildest dreams. While much of this was due to the talent he assembled and the famously regimented "quality control" standards that his label employed throughout the 1960s, Motown's triumph was also one of messaging, marketing, and media. The famous "finishing school" overseen at the label by Maxine Powell prepped artists for television and prestigious supper-club engagements, and by the mid-1960s all this had paid extraordinary dividends. As *Billboard* noted in 1966, "Berry Gordy's Detroit finishing school . . . graduates nothing but polished entertainers."[19]

Nowhere was this more evident than in the case of Diana Ross and the Supremes, the most successful American recording act of the 1960s. The Supremes were media darlings, a group whose appeal appeared to transcend gender, age, and race. Their squeaky-clean, youthfully sophisticated image was carefully maintained: a Motown press release from around the time of the group's first hit, "Where Did Our Love Go," trumpeted them as "three young ladies—in every sense of the word" and reported that the group "say[s] that they felt that a contemporary performer did not have to utilize sex as a means of putting across a musical number."[20] The *Boston Globe* described them as "good looking, bright sounding, hard working, constantly improving, and we think you'll enjoy them whether you're a member of the Coke set or voted for Calvin Coolidge."[21] The *Chicago Tribune* published a lengthy profile of the group that noted "Diana studies modeling, make-up, 'visual poise,' etiquette, independently of the others, and Motown plans to teach her German and French, using records."[22] More trenchantly, the critic Richard Goldstein wrote in 1967, "The Supremes are a tribute to an ever-assimilating pop market of adults, eager for the 'with it' drive of youth without its radicalism. . . . The Supremes concede just enough in their material and approach to be understood without a teen-slang code book."[23] If Gordy's dream was to transform his performers into a perfect vehicles for lucrative middle-American acceptance, Motown's artist development was that dream realized.

In doing so Gordy's label changed the cultural perception of African American popular music and also the cultural perception of rock and roll music more generally. Indeed, during the 1960s only the Beatles themselves were more responsible for changing rock and roll's image from that of a teenaged fad to that of a serious business, in every sense. But while the Beatles' perceived transformation from teen sensations to highbrow art musicians has been cause for veneration by most critics, Motown's careful transformation of black rhythm and blues into the dominant force in American pop—"the Sound of Young America"—has been treated with suspicion.

This disparity may be one reason that critics rarely discuss the vast expanse of the relationship between the Beatles and Motown. In Beatles historiography, consideration of Motown's influence on the band tends to be confined to their early years, focusing on the obvious example of the three Motown covers on *With the Beatles* while paying vague lip service to the "formative" impact of Motown on the band in its early days. There are several problems with this, the most glaring being that it neglects the ongoing influence of Motown on the Beatles' later music. More insidiously, it falls back on a tendency in rock discourse to view black music as strictly precursory, which I've discussed in earlier chapters and which Fred Moten describes as "an active forgetting of black performances or a relegation of them to mere source material."[24] This also results in simply bad history, such as when one Beatles biographer lumps Smokey Robinson and the Miracles in with "early innovators" and implies that Lennon and McCartney were listening to the Miracles as early as 1957. John Lennon and Smokey Robinson were born the same year, and in 1957 both were still in high school.[25]

The Beatles and Motown remade popular music in the 1960s and they did not do so in isolation from each other, but rather in tandem. Rather than taking on the entire, vast history of either or both of these entities—a task that has been ably undertaken elsewhere—this chapter focuses on three distinct historical episodes to demonstrate the multilayered and extraordinarily productive relationship between the Beatles and Motown throughout the decade.[26] I begin with a reading of the historical significance and musical meaning of the three Motown covers on *With the Beatles,* recordings that were made as both Gordy's label and Epstein's band were in ascendance. I'll discuss how the nature of these recordings speaks to the unprecedented nature of the moment from which they emerge, and how the versions of "Please Mr. Postman," "You've Really Got a Hold on Me" and "Money (That's What I Want)" on the Beatles' second album complicate traditionally held ideas about white-on-black song covers. I'll then explore the ongoing impact of Motown music on the Beatles in the period spanning the releases of *Rubber Soul* and *Revolver,* paying particular attention to the influence of Motown session bassist James Jamerson on the band's music in this era. In doing so I'll show that a moment long heard as the Beatles turning away from pop into the avant-garde of (white) rock was still marked by a deep engagement with contemporary black music, particularly that which was coming out of Detroit.

Finally, this chapter concludes in the aftermath of the Beatles' breakup, when two Motown artists approaching their own career crossroads remade iconic Beatles songs at the close of the 1960s. Marvin Gaye's "Yesterday" and Stevie Wonder's "We Can Work It Out" arrived at the twilight of Motown's dominance, as the label was leaving Detroit, and foretold a moment when both Gaye and Wonder would win unprecedented autonomy from Gordy's once-monolithic operation. If the Beatles' covers of Motown songs at the dawn of Beatlemania had sounded the arrival of something new in 1960s popular music, Gaye's and Wonder's covers of Beatles songs at the decade's close sound something ending, and something else beginning.

Detroit to Liverpool: Covers, Commerce, and Beatlemania

The Beatles had already transformed British popular music well before their first appearance on American television in February of 1964. In October of 1962 the band's debut single, "Love Me Do," was released in the United Kingdom and reached number twenty-one on the *Melody Maker* charts; by the time they appeared on *Val*

Parnell's Sunday Night at the London Palladium a year later, their three follow-ups to "Love Me Do"—"Please Please Me," "From Me to You," and "She Loves You"—had all hit number one, and their performance on the variety show was watched by an estimated audience of fifteen million.[27] By fall of 1963 the band's extraordinary chart performance, their blinding rate of success, and the rabidity of their fanbase were perfectly bundled into a neologism that blared from the headlines of British newspapers: "BEATLEMANIA!"

The Beatles' first British LP, *Please Please Me,* a famously rushed piece of work, had been recorded in just over twelve hours on February 11, 1963.[28] Producer George Martin formulated *Please Please Me* as essentially an in-studio version of the band's live act, well honed from countless hours on club stages in Hamburg, Liverpool, and elsewhere. The album contained an eclectic mix of Lennon-McCartney originals plus a diverse array of American pop covers, from Arthur Alexander's "Anna" to a rendition of Phil Medley and Bert Russell's "Twist and Shout" (popularized by the Isley Brothers) that closed the album. When recording commenced on a follow-up album in July of 1963, EMI allotted the band considerably more time and resources. *With the Beatles* was finished in October and released in the United Kingdom on November 22, 1963. The album's black-and-white cover photo, featuring all four Beatles in black turtlenecks against a black background, remains one of the most famous images in rock and roll and would also grace the cover of the band's first U.S. LP, *Meet the Beatles!,* released in late January of 1964.[29]

On *With the Beatles* Lennon and McCartney's songwriting had tightened and matured, as immediately evidenced by the album's roaring opener, "It Won't Be Long," which boasted cheeky lyrics snuggled against inventive chord changes and a wealth of melodic ideas. "Hold Me Tight" and "I Wanna Be Your

Man" were rollicking crowd-pleasers, and the album's high point may have been its third track, "All My Loving," which would quickly become one of the group's most beloved compositions. The album also featured numerous covers, including a version of Chuck Berry's "Roll over Beethoven" and a gender-inverted rendition of the Donays' obscure 1962 girl-group record, "Devil in His Heart," re-fashioned as "Devil in Her Heart."

With the Beatles also contained three covers of Motown songs, a remarkable percentage of the fourteen-track LP. These tracks were "Please Mr. Postman" (originally recorded by the Marvelettes in 1961), "You've Really Got a Hold on Me" (The Miracles, 1962), and "Money (That's What I Want)" (Barrett Strong, 1959); all three are sung by John Lennon on lead vocals.[30] The original versions of "Please Mr. Postman" and "You've Really Got a Hold on Me" had been hugely successful in the United States, with the former reaching number one on the *Billboard* Pop charts (Motown's first chart-topper) and the latter reaching number eight. "Money" was the first single ever released by Berry Gordy's operation, and in 1960 peaked at numbers two and twenty-three on the R&B and Pop charts, respectively.[31] These singles had not been hits in England, however, where Motown would not achieve widespread success until the aftermath of its 1965 U.K. tour.[32]

"Please Mr. Postman" was the first Motown track heard on *With the Beatles*, coming at the end of the LP's first side. "Please Mr. Postman" is an exceedingly straightforward piece of music, consisting of a repeating I-vi-IV-V chord progression and a simple story of a lovelorn female who misses her boyfriend. The backing vocals play an active role, from the opening "wait!" (answered by the lead singer's "oh, yes, wait a minute, Mr. Postman") to the incessant "ooh–wah–doos" on the song's verse. The Marvelettes' 1961 version of "Please Mr. Postman" features a drum part played by Marvin Gaye, and the song's stuttering hand claps and cascading piano lines lend a vaguely calypso feel that evokes a more up-tempo version of Maurice Williams and the Zodiacs' "Stay," a number one *Billboard* hit in 1960.[33] This is reinforced when lead singer Gladys Horton intones "de-liver de letter / de sooner de better" in a faux Caribbean accent over the song's out-chorus, a charming if incongruous bit of islands-meet-Detroit. While the single became Motown's first national number one pop hit, the "picture sleeve" of the 45 pointedly declined to show the group's faces, instead boasting a cartoonish drawing of an empty mailbox, as if to preemptively calm the nerves of anyone reluctant to embrace the idea that the sound of young America might look like three young black women.

The Beatles' version of "Please Mr. Postman" is louder, faster, and generally more raucous than the Marvelettes' original. The drums are mixed louder, effectively supplanting the hand claps so integral to the Motown recording. The piano part that drives the original is gone, replaced by jangling guitars. The backup vocals have a more exclamatory quality, and John Lennon's lead is hoarse and devoid of the sultry sweetness of Horton's performance. The gender inversion is notable: the song's narrative, sparse as it is, fits more snugly with early 1960s stereotypes of teenage femininity—the protagonist sitting at home while her boyfriend is "so far away," waiting to hear from him, a vague implication that perhaps he is up to no good. It is a song that is superficially about romantic disempowerment, although as the music historian Jacqueline Warwick suggests, its presentation is subtly affirming: with the "boyfriend" of the song absent, the singer is left with the solidarity of her bandmates.[34] The Beatles' version plays upon the song's undercurrents of frustration and disillusion, the gathering desperation of Lennon's vocal hinting at someone aware of being taken for granted. The group's reworking might also have held particular appeal to young female fans, riffing off the love letters that were already inundating the group.[35]

The Miracles' "You've Really Got a Hold on Me," released a year after "Please Mr. Postman," is a more sophisticated piece of music than the latter by most measures. The Miracles' original recording is in a lilting 12/8 time signature, with a piano playing triplet triads while an electric guitar plucks a memorable, six-note phrase into the I-to-vi chord change. This device of a repeated, earworm guitar hook leading into a harmonic change was often employed by the Beatles during this period as well, with "She Loves You," "Please Please Me," and "I Want to Hold Your Hand" featuring prominent examples. Unlike "Please Mr. Postman," which cycles through its four-chord progression for the entirety of the song, "You've Really Got a Hold on Me" features considerable harmonic variation, stop-time segments, and a climactic bridge. Lyrically the song is one of Robinson's earliest masterpieces, full of the evocative imagery and brilliant wordplay that would later be heard on compositions like "My Girl," "The Tracks of My Tears," and "I Second That Emotion." Similarly to "Please Mr. Postman," the song is about a romantic power imbalance, being in thrall to someone who might not reciprocate one's own devotion. The word "hold" becoming the perfect lyrical pivot for this masochistic dynamic, as "you've really got a hold on me" becomes "hold me, tighter," and "hold me, please, hold me." Robinson's vocal performance is controlled and assured, his mellifluous tenor carrying a preternaturally mature bluesiness.

The Beatles' version (retitled "You Really Got a Hold on Me") features a swaying rhythm guitar in lieu of the piano triads heard in the original. Like "Please Mr. Postman," the performance feels louder, more dominated by guitar and drums. Lennon's vocal is hoarser and fiercer than the original recording but his performance is still clearly influenced by Robinson's, even co-opting some of the latter's melodic flourishes and falsetto swoops.[36] All in all the Beatles' "You Really Got a Hold on Me" is a remarkably faithful rendering of the original: the Beatles make almost no significant alterations to either the form or the lyrics, and unlike "Please Mr. Postman" there is no need for a gender inversion.

If "Please Mr. Postman" and "You Really Got a Hold on Me" are relatively straightforward reinterpretations of the originals, "Money," the third Motown track on *With the Beatles,* is a different story entirely. Barrett Strong's original version of "Money" is structured around a repeating, churning piano riff. It is a simple and immensely clever piece of music, a twelve-bar blues whose verse sections are simply the first four bars of the form in stop-time, the chorus the last eight. As Dave Marsh has written, " 'Money,' which revolves around the idea of avarice as a substitute for love, has come to seem almost too paradigmatic of Motown's greed," and the song is in many senses the perfect distillation of Gordy's musical worldview, one that heard the sound of rock and roll songcraft and cash registers in perfect harmony. [37] Even the song's first line, "The best things in life are free / but you can keep them for the birds and bees," is a terrific bit of writing, opening with a reference to Ray Henderson's Tin Pan Alley standard "The Best Things in Life Are Free," then parrying it back with playful, irreverent defiance.

"Money" is also a crucial symbol in Gordy's personal mythology, a love song to success whose catchiness ensures its own fulfillment. The song was mostly written by Gordy, but in his own telling, then-receptionist Janie Bradford came up with the line "your love gives me such a thrill / but your love don't pay my bills." According to Gordy, the small contribution so completed the song that he insisted upon giving Bradford a cowriter credit, a story he has been fond of repeating over the years.[38] If the "Money" origin story isn't precisely the Motown origin story, it's at least a snug symbolic fit for propaganda purposes, a perfect way for Gordy to demonstrate his ear for pop success while also highlighting his own generosity to underlings, a characterization essential to the corporate paternalism that undergirded his company's operations.

The Beatles' version of "Money," released four years after Strong's original, shatters the song and rebuilds it in the Liverpool quartet's image. The song drops a half-step from F (the key of Strong's original) to E, and its iconic piano riff, played here by George Martin, is loud and overdriven. The riff features a minor musical variant that betrays the new British context of "Money": the upper voicing of Martin's piano part moves from a fifth to a flatted sixth atop the lower voicing of flatted third to major third, while the upper voicing of the Motown version remains on the fifth over both the minor and the major third. It's a small change that transforms a bluesy passing tone into a more pronounced chromaticism and gives the harmonic character of the riff an angular abrasiveness, particularly when played over the V chord in the song's ninth bar, when the C-natural becomes the flatted second of the B chord's root, a harmonic clash normally anathema to pop songwriting. Given Martin's classical training it's quite possible that this tiny but notable alteration was unintentional, as he would have been less accustomed to the fluidity between minor and major thirds so common in American blues-derived music.

The Beatles' version is even more notable for Lennon's vocal, which is snarling and nasal, dripping with the avaricious contempt that's only latent in Strong's original performance. The Beatles' first album, *Please Please Me,* had ended with a frenetic version of "Twist and Shout" that Lennon sang with such force that, according to legend, it caused his throat to bleed, and "Money," the final track on *With the Beatles,* carries a similar intensity. But as opposed to the mad exuberance of "Twist and Shout," the effect on "Money" is that of an angry young man at the end of his rope. The entirety of the Beatles' version has a shouted quality, from Lennon's performance to McCartney's and Harrison's backup parts. Indeed, if there is one shared quality between the three covers of Motown songs heard on *With the Beatles* it is the change in their volume: while the Motown versions of "Please Mr. Postman," "You've Really Got a Hold On Me," and "Money" are primarily piano-driven affairs with light guitars and modestly mixed drums, the Beatles' versions are guitar-driven, background and lead vocals are more exclamatory and emphatic, and drums are mixed higher and played harder.

The likely reason for this is the context in which the Beatles first came to perform these songs: on concert stages. A major difference between the early Beatles and most early Motown groups is the extensive experience that the Beatles had as a live act. The Marvelettes' Gladys Horton was fifteen when she recorded "Please Mr. Postman," plucked from a high school talent show, and Smokey Robinson also met Gordy while still in high school. In fact, a relative lack of show business experience was seen as a plus at Motown, as it meant artists were more malleable in any number of ways. Gordy saw himself first and foremost as a "record man" and saw his company's performance talent as just one stop in a successful production line, along with songwriting, recording, distribution, and promotion. For Motown, record sales were paramount, and live performances and tours were seen as vehicles for singles promotion.

In the Beatles' early years this situation was effectively reversed. In a British pop industry largely dominated by American imports but where visa restrictions made it difficult for American acts to tour, live performance was a necessity for British rock and roll bands. The Beatles had played hundreds of shows before obtaining their contract with EMI, and the loudness of the Beatles' versions of Motown songs clearly reflects this. The Beatles had played "Please Mr. Postman" frequently in concert, "Money" was one of the songs they had chosen to perform in their failed audition for Decca Records that same year, and they had introduced "You Really Got a Hold on Me" into their live shows by early 1963, only a few months after the song's American release.[39] The difference in performance style on *With the Beatles* can be at least partially attributed to the foursome taking Motown songs imagined for the medium of the 45rpm recording, adapting them for live performance, and then committing these adaptations to record, a complex cycle of mediation and re-mediation.

This cycle also subverts the traditional trajectories of white-on-black song covers in several ways unique to this historical moment. First, these covers represent an inversion of media patterns and ideas of how black and white music was thought to circulate. In his work on black sound and modernity, Alex Weheliye writes of "the assumption that black cultures are somehow pre- or antitechnological," an assumption that has widely proliferated in American culture at least since the days of minstrelsy, when white performers often claimed to be re-creating performances that they had "heard" on trips to the South.[40] While these claims were often false, they encoded a notion of black music as being local, premodern, and unmediated that would later be rehearsed in the fetishized regionalism of the early folk and blues industry in the 1920s, the institutional and commercial obstacles to black jazz bands touring during the 1930s and World War II, and the 1950s racist radio practices that saw white versions of black rock and roll songs receive disproportionately more widespread airplay than the originals.[41] The Beatles' covers of Motown speak specifically to the extraordinary circulation of Motown music even in this early period, and they are an early indication of the extent to which Motown's global aspirations were being realized.

Second, in discourses of white-on-black musical appropriation there has been a long-standing tendency to view black music as foundational, even primordial. And yet the Beatles' relationship to Motown was not a preservationist or nostalgic one, à la American folk revivalists or British devotees of traditional jazz and blues: rather, they were drawn to Motown *because* it was current and already successful.[42]

Which brings us to a third way that the Beatles' covers of Motown invert prior trajectories of white-on-black song covers: namely, their relation to commerce. The phenomenon of white performers receiving market compensation for performances of black music vastly disproportionate to the originators of that music is one of the oldest in modern popular song: only a few years before the Beatles' breakthrough, white performers like Gale Storm and Pat Boone had profited handsomely from bowdlerized covers of black rock and roll songs. Boone's music in particular, including his bloodless reworkings of Fats Domino's "Ain't That a Shame" and Little Richard's "Tutti Frutti," has become a sort of limit-case exemplar of white-on-black appropriation in rock and roll music.[43]

One of Motown's signature accomplishments was to flout that very segregation, refusing to accept that "pop" meant necessarily "white." As Berry Gordy wrote emphatically in his own autobiography years later, "In the music business there had long been the distinction between black and white music, the assumption being that R&B was black and Pop was white. . . .

'Pop' means popular and if [a million-selling record] ain't, I don't know what is. I never gave a damn what else it was called."[44] The *Billboard* chart success of the three Motown covers on *With the Beatles* reflects this: the Beatles did not sell more copies of "Please Mr. Postman" than the Marvelettes, nor were they in a position of advantage over Gordy's label when they recorded "Please Mr. Postman," "You've Really Got a Hold on Me," and "Money" for *With the Beatles*. In fact, according to Motown lore, when the Beatles' manager Brian Epstein first approached Motown about securing the rights to record the songs, Gordy tried to shake him down for an astronomical fee, firmly convinced that his musical properties were worth far more to Epstein's clients than said clients were worth to his company's royalty statements.[45] Several of Gordy's Motown employees, already aware of the Beatles' British success, convinced him this wasn't an opportunity to risk losing, an intervention their boss surely appreciated when *With the Beatles* became the fastest-selling LP in British history.

Gordy saw himself in a position of power, and for good reason. Against the long-standing historical backdrop of an endless pattern of black musicians being grossly undercompensated by an inequitable music industry, then seeing their material taken up by white musicians with access to an off-limits commercial mainstream, Gordy and his label had already begun to disrupt this historical trend. If, in 1963, Motown and *With the Beatles* represented different visions of "crossover" aspiration—Motown from R&B to pop, the Beatles from England to America—the former was farther along in its quest than the latter.

Which brings us back again to "Money," the anthem of aspiration that sounds the opening of Motown Records and the closing of *With the Beatles*. Heard in 1959 from Barrett Strong the song is exuberant, awash in catchiness, as magnetic as its

titular subject. Gordy endeavored to make songs that you'd remember forever, and it is this ambition that Barrett Strong's
version of "Money" embodies, the youngest sounds of "The
Sound of Young America." The Beatles' version is the sound of
something else, something similarly unprecedented at a similarly formative stage: by the time the Beatles recorded "Money"
in late June of 1963 they had already released two U.K. smashes,
"Please Please Me" and "From Me to You," and a third—"She
Loves You"—was on the way. They were huge and getting huger:
the June 22, 1963, issue of *Melody Maker* contained an amused
report of two seventeen-year-olds who were fined two pounds
each by a magistrate court for "walk[ing] round town singing the
Beatles' hit 'From Me to You' at the tops of their voices."[46] For the
four young men from Liverpool, things were beginning to get
strange.

"Money" is this strangeness rendered into musical form, particularly Lennon's vocal performance, which takes an unbridled
anthem of capitalist exultation and renders it into something
much more ambivalent. Lennon was always the member of the
band who seemed least comfortable with the level of fame they
ultimately achieved, and "Money" is one of the earliest sounds
of this discomfort: his vocal is sneering and desperate, alive
with the paranoia that invariably accompanies the unrepen-
tant greed of the song's subject. Nowhere is this more evident
than in Lennon's most notable revision to Strong's original, the
snarling statement "I wanna be free" on the song's out-chorus.
The ad lib inverts the song's moral universe, ambiguously perched
between a cynical suggestion of money as the way to freedom
and a desperate desire to throw off its shackles.

The Beatles never released another Motown cover after *With
the Beatles;* their next album, *A Hard Day's Night,* was their first
LP that consisted entirely of original compositions.[47] And yet

Motown's influence never left the band, and often remained profound. I will now turn my attention to 1965 and 1966, a period that spans the LPs *Rubber Soul* through *Revolver* and that is generally thought to be one of the most significant in the band's history, notably coinciding with the most commercially dominant period of Motown's own history. During this period many commentators heard the Beatles as moving away from African American musical influences and toward "folk rock," classical, and avant-garde art music, genres generally associated with whiteness.

But the Beatles' music during this period still found them engaging with and absorbing contemporary black music—and specifically Motown—in new and inventive ways. The fact that these connections were missed is perhaps unsurprising, since one of the greatest musical influences on the Beatles in this period was also one of the most important, yet anonymous, musicians of the 1960s: Motown house bass player James Jamerson.

Low End Theories: James Jamerson and Paul McCartney in the Mid-1960s

"There was only one James Jamerson. All the rest were imitators—just like there was only one Charlie Parker," Motown arranger Gil Askey once said of the legendary Motown session bassist.[48] In the words of Nelson George, "The invention, technique, and drama that emanated from James Jamerson's 1962 Fender Precision bass made him one of the most influential musicians of the sixties."[49] "There is hardly a successful pop band in the world that doesn't owe homage to James Jamerson," Gordy himself remarked. "His influence is omnipotent."[50]

Outside of circles of musicians and fervent R&B aficionados, James Jamerson has never been a household name. When he died in 1983 at the age of forty-seven, the *New York Times* printed a seven-sentence wire story five days after his passing that misreported his age.[51] *Rolling Stone*'s obituary, which declared him "one of the greatest and most influential musicians of our time," still ran nearly two months after Jamerson's death and was buried sixty pages into the magazine.[52] In the years since, Jamerson has been the main subject of a single, self-published book, Allan "Dr. Licks" Slutsky's invaluable *Standing in the Shadows of Motown: The Life and Music of Legendary Bassist James Jamerson*. While most histories of Motown praise the bassist reverently, they do so in passing. Jamerson may have been, in Marvin Gaye's words, "a genius," but he was never a star, and his name did not appear on a Motown release until 1971.[53] Crediting session musicians on singles and albums during the 1960s was generally not common practice, but the anonymity of the "Funk Brothers," the in-house nickname for Motown's studio band, was also a strategic move on Gordy's part: by keeping its session musicians unknown, Motown could avoid other labels luring them away with promises of more money.

James Lee Jamerson was born on Edisto Island, South Carolina, on January 29, 1936, seven years later than Berry Gordy and six years earlier than Paul McCartney.[54] He moved to Detroit in 1954 and started playing the upright bass while a student at Northwestern High School on West Grand Boulevard, only blocks away from the two-story house that would soon bear the moniker "Hitsville, U.S.A." By the time he graduated, Jamerson had already become a fixture on the Detroit jazz scene, where he occasionally played alongside burgeoning legends like Kenny Burrell and Yusef Lateef. Jamerson quickly developed a reputation as a prodigiously talented and versatile player who could play anything from bebop to pop to R&B. By 1958, he was, according to Slutsky, "one of the biggest fish in the small pond that was Detroit's studio scene."[55]

It is unclear exactly when or how James Jamerson first came to Gordy's recording studio at 2648 West Grand Boulevard: he was not the first bassist at Motown, and over the years many ex-Motown musicians would claim to be the one who introduced Jamerson to the label. The earliest Gordy-produced track that Jamerson is thought to have played on is the Miracles' 1959 single, "Way over There," released a year prior to the group's breakthrough, "Shop Around." Through the early 1960s he played on a majority of Motown singles while also touring extensively with both Motown and non-Motown artists, but by 1964 the label had come to consider him indispensable. Production teams often refused to record without him in the studio, and Gordy offered him $250 a week to leave the road and become Motown's full-time bass player.

Jamerson did not accompany the Motor Town Revue on its 1965 tour of the United Kingdom, when the Beatles met Gordy at Pinewood Studios and reportedly gushed to him about Motown's bass player's extraordinary abilities.[56] While Jamerson remained anonymous to the listening public, his legend among fellow musicians on both sides of the Atlantic only grew. In terms of technique and ideas Jamerson had always boasted an improvisatory style several cuts above the previous standard for rock and roll bass parts, which were often as simple as the root and fifth played on the two and four.[57] As Slutsky notes, Jamerson's playing in the early 1960s was marked by "chromatic passing tones, Ray Brown style walking bass lines, and syncopated eighth-note figures—all of which had previously been unheard of in popular music of the late fifties and early sixties."[58] An early, widely heard example of Jamerson's dexterity appeared on Mary Wells's number one hit "My Guy," recorded in 1964, a track on which Jamerson plays an acoustic upright bass. As Wells intones variations on the song's refrain over the song's fade, the backing track drops out so that we hear only finger snaps and

Jamerson's bass, playing dancing sixteenth-note runs and funky chromatic flourishes.[59]

In 1964 and 1965 Jamerson recorded classic bass lines for hit recordings like Martha and the Vandellas' "Nowhere to Run," the Four Tops' "It's the Same Old Song," and the Temptations' "Get Ready," all of which featured melodic, driving lines in which Jamerson's bass is effectively positioned as a lead instrument.[60] By 1965 Jamerson's sound had become so iconic that one of the biggest non-Motown hits of that year, Fontella Bass's "Rescue Me," featured a blatant imitation of a mid-1960s Motown bass line, a counterfeit so effective that to this day the song is often confused for Motown. (The bass part was played by Chicago session bassist Louis Satterfield.)[61]

According to Slutsky, Jamerson's bass style dramatically evolved in late 1965: "Sixteenth notes, quarter note triplets, open string techniques, dissonant non-harmonic pitches, and syncopations off the sixteenth seemed to enter into his style almost overnight. . . . Out of nowhere, James started playing almost as if he was the featured soloist."[62] By 1966 Jamerson was laying down iconic lines like "You Can't Hurry Love" (the Supremes) and "Uptight (Everything's Alright)" (Stevie Wonder) while also breaking musical ground on a trio of Four Tops singles: "Reach Out I'll Be There," "Standing in the Shadows of Love," and "Bernadette" (the last of which was released in early 1967). Two of the most common elements of Jamerson's bass playing in this period are heavy uses of octave leaps or drops, often broken up by the insertion of a fifth (which can be heard on "It's the Same Old Song," and with even greater frequency on "Standing in the Shadows of Love" and "Bernadette"), and the anticipation of the downbeat through a tied eighth note on the back end of the previous measure. ("Nowhere to Run" and "Uptight" are just two of many Jamerson performances that feature this device prominently.)

In late 1965, as Motown was dominating the American charts and Jamerson was rewriting the vocabulary of his instrument, the Beatles were approaching their own crossroads. Since their British breakthrough in 1963 the band had released LPs at a rate of two per year, a grueling output in the face of extensive touring and film appearances. By the time the group's fifth studio album, *Help!,* was released as the soundtrack to a movie of the same name in August of 1965, it seemed unlikely the band would maintain the breakneck two-a-year schedule. And yet in December of 1965 a new album managed to arrive. Bearing the title *Rubber Soul,* it was positively received on both sides of the Atlantic: *Variety* called it "a surefire mop-up" and evidence of "an evolving style that is related to but distinctly different from its earlier disks," while England's *New Musical Express* gave the album five stars and declared that "the Beatles are still finding different ways to make us enjoy listening to them."[63]

In the years since, *Rubber Soul* has been widely heralded as an artistic leap for the Beatles.[64] The band's songwriting and musicianship seemed to hurtle forward, from the jangling sitar of "Norwegian Wood" to the sparkling angst of "Girl." Even amid such buoyant moments as "Drive My Car" and "I'm Looking through You," the album seemed more serious and adult: "Michelle," with its francophone lyric, lilting melody, and jazz-infused chord changes, won the Grammy for Song of the Year, the first time a rock and roll act had ever captured the award.

What went largely unnoticed at the time was the considerable influence of contemporary African American popular music, particularly Motown, on *Rubber Soul,* even though the Beatles themselves were so acutely conscious of this that they satirized it in the album's title.[65] The chord progression to "You Won't See Me" is loosely based on the Four Tops' "It's the Same Old Song," and Paul McCartney has confirmed that John Lennon's "In My Life" was inspired by the Miracles.[66] McCartney has also spoken of the influence of James Jamerson on his bass playing on *Rubber Soul*, specifically citing "You Won't See Me" as an example, and indeed McCartney's line on the song is rife with eighth-note syncopations and octave intervals.[67]

Even more striking in this regard is McCartney's bass playing on "Nowhere Man," a composition penned by Lennon that appeared as the fourth track on the British version of *Rubber Soul*. "Nowhere Man" finds McCartney making heavy use of Jamersonian octave intervals and anticipated downbeats: indeed, on the song's verse form nearly every downbeat features an eighth note tied to the eighth note of the previous measure, the same device we can hear Jamerson employ on "Nowhere to Run" and other well-known lines. The effect created is propulsive, the bass leaning into the downbeat a half-beat before the drummer lands on the one.

"Nowhere Man" is often cited as a transitional song in the Beatles' catalogue, one of Lennon's earliest forays into writing about a topic other than simple romance.[68] When critics write of the Beatles elevating popular music above simple boy-meets-girl subject matter, songs like "Nowhere Man" are what they have in mind: as one critic notes, "More than any track on the album, 'Nowhere Man' breaks the unstated rules for pop content. Love, cars, parental constraints—'Nowhere Man' leaves these commonplaces behind."[69] And yet to hear "Nowhere Man" solely as the Beatles separating themselves from other contemporary music is to elevate lyrical content over all other facets of musical performance.

If the influence of Motown and other black pop on *Rubber Soul* went underacknowledged, this was partly a reflection of the way that the album was curated and marketed in the United States. As is well known to American fans of a certain age and to generations of frustrated vinyl collectors, through 1966 the Beatles' LPs

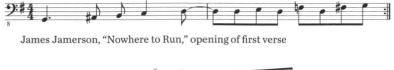

James Jamerson, "Nowhere to Run," opening of first verse

Paul McCartney, "Nowhere Man," opening of first verse

were released in different forms in the United States than they were in the United Kingdom, due to the Byzantine workings of an American music industry that had been astonishingly ill-equipped to handle such success from a British band.[70] The version of *Rubber Soul* that arrived in American stores in December of 1965 was only twelve tracks long instead of fourteen and was missing "Drive My Car," "What Goes On," "If I Needed Someone," and "Nowhere Man."[71] In their places were two tracks that had originally appeared on the U.K. version of the Beatles' previous album, *Help!*: "I've Just Seen a Face" and "It's Only Love."

Capitol Records, the American counterpart to EMI, had many specious reasons for revising the track order and selection of the Beatles' American releases, many of which have been traced back to much-vilified Capitol executive Dave Dexter, the man who oversaw the Beatles' American releases.[72] In the case of *Rubber Soul*, though, the alteration came from a desire to market the Beatles' music as "folk rock," in order to take advantage of the perceived rage for the genre in the wake of "Like a Rolling Stone," the Byrds' version of "Mr. Tambourine Man," Barry Maguire's "Eve of Destruction," and other American hits of that year.[73] As Dave Marsh has written of *Rubber Soul's* American repackaging, "the Beatles had had an intent, and folk rock wasn't it." [74] But the rebranding worked: a *Los Angeles Times* article on folk rock from early 1966 declared that "even those classics the

Beatles have succumbed . . . and their new album, 'Rubber Soul,' has even more influences of this kind of rock folk."[75]

The American packaging of *Rubber Soul* as folk rock is evident from the first track of the U.S. release, the acoustic guitar–driven "I've Just Seen a Face," which appeared in place of the R&B-infused "Drive My Car." "I've Just Seen a Face" had appeared in England months earlier, on the U.K. *Help!* album—an album that, with its Dylanesque "You've Got to Hide Your Love Away," was probably far closer to "folk rock" than *Rubber Soul*. As described in Chapter 1, "folk rock" was seen as a break from previous rock and roll and was seen as more artistically and intellectually serious than its forebears. This was also a way of not so subtly separating a generation of young white rock and roll musicians from black predecessors and contemporaries, and Capitol's American packaging of *Rubber Soul* as a folk rock album would have distanced the band from current black music in the minds of audiences. This was a deeply ironic development, given that, again, the enormous influence of that music was suggested by the album's own title.

The Beatles ended 1965 with *Rubber Soul*, and 1966 would be arguably the most momentous year in their career. It was the year that Beatlemania turned a dark corner, from the "more popular than Jesus" controversy to a bizarrely tense standoff with the Marcos regime in the Philippines, and by the year's end the Beatles announced that they would no longer tour. But it was also a groundbreaking musical year for the band. In late spring they released their first new music since *Rubber Soul*, a single whose A-side, "Paperback Writer," went to number one in the United States and the United Kingdom. Featuring gnashing, distorted guitars and a driving rhythm track, "Paperback Writer" found the Beatles in a louder, edgier mode than anything on *Rubber Soul*.[76]

The B-side, a Lennon composition entitled "Rain," was just as striking. Its lyrics were stark and foreboding, and its haunting melody and chord structure bore traces of the Indian ragas that were increasingly drawing the attention of the band. This influence was particularly evident on the song's bridge, with its densely clustered harmonies and melismatic, descending vocal melody. It also featured a number of innovative studio techniques, including backward vocals on the song's outro, as well as Ringo Starr's adventuresome drum performance that was then slowed down on tape by the engineer, Geoff Emerick, giving a dark and logy texture to the rhythm track.

Equally impressive was McCartney's bass line, which bore the influence of Jamerson more prominently than any prior Beatles track. The bass on "Rain" is the song's most active melodic instrument, providing a similar sort of galloping, driving low end heard on a track like "Nowhere to Run." As opposed to simply being an unobtrusive half of the rhythm section, McCartney's bass is an intricate and active force in the song itself. The musical content of McCartney's bass line is also remarkably Jamersonian, full of leaps and tumbles between octaves and bubbling chromaticisms. Rhythmically McCartney's bass line is a whirl of sixteenth-note syncopations and anticipations of the one and three, nimbly sliding and ricocheting off of Starr's drum track, nestled behind Lennon's vocal and the churning layers of guitars.

The dexterity of McCartney's bass playing on "Rain" shows the extreme to which Jamerson's style had influenced him, although there were, of course, several differences in style between the two players. For starters, as a converted guitarist, McCartney tended to play with a pick whereas Jamerson played with his fingers, a difference in attack that can be heard in the timbre of the instrument and that is also reflected in certain

Paul McCartney, "Rain," opening bars

stylistic flourishes. For instance, McCartney's playing occasionally boasted quick bursts of a single note played repeatedly, a quick "strumming" effect that can be heard prominently on the first notes played by the bass on "Paperback Writer." It is in McCartney's pickwork that one hears prominent traces of another major influence, Los Angeles session bassist Carol Kaye, though Kaye's lines tended to eschew the relentless syncopation and melodic intricacy found in Jamerson's work that carried over to McCartney's playing.

McCartney's playing was also less improvisatory than Jamerson's, his lines tending to be more repetitive cycles of elaborate "riffs" as opposed to Jamerson's more freely developing opuses that occurred with increasing frequency as the 1960s progressed. "Rain" is among the most varied and free-form of McCartney's lines in this period, but it still doesn't begin to approach the improvisational expanses of "Standing in the Shadows of Love" or "Bernadette," to say nothing of later Jamerson performances like his work on Marvin Gaye's "What's Going On" (1971).[77]

Both of these differences—the pickwork versus the fingerwork, the disparity in improvisation—can be chalked up to background: Jamerson had started out as a jazz musician and until the end of his life jazz remained his first love, and his idiosyncratic single-finger playing style was an obvious vestige from his time playing upright bass. Still, in McCartney's bass lines from this period we can hear an attempt to forge a low-end aesthetic for the Beatles rooted in the melodic invention and rhythmic intricacy of Jamerson's style.

In August of 1966 the Beatles released their follow-up LP to *Rubber Soul*, titled *Revolver*.[78] For all of the plaudits that would be garnered by *Sgt. Pepper* a year later, in terms of its historical impact *Revolver* was nearly as foundational in creating the idea of rock music as a serious form. In the introduction to an academic volume on the album, the title of which credits it with nothing less than "the Transformation of Rock and Roll," Russell Reising describes *Revolver* as "a haunting, soothing, confusing, grandly complex and ambitious *statement* about the possibilities of popular music."[79] Similarly, *Rolling Stone* magazine has declared that *Revolver* "signaled that in popular music, anything—any theme, any musical idea—could now be realized."[80]

Statements like these indicate *Revolver*'s status in many critical and historiographical circles as the first major avant-garde rock album. Two tracks in particular, "Eleanor Rigby" and "Tomorrow Never Knows," stand out in this regard. "Eleanor Rigby" was a somber, minor-key meditation on loneliness set to a string octet, the band's most explicit foray yet into the European classical-music tradition. "Tomorrow Never Knows" wedded harmonic and instrumental tropes derived from Indian music to tape loops and other sonic gadgetry associated with electronic art music, while Lennon's double-tracked vocal intoned lyrics, derived from the *Tibetan Book of the Dead,* amplified through a rotating Leslie speaker cabinet. Both "Eleanor Rigby" and "Tomorrow Never Knows" showed the Beatles engaging with musical styles—European concert-hall classical and avant-garde electronic music, respectively—that held considerably higher cultural capital than rock and roll, styles whose artistic and intellectual "significance" was taken for granted. For many listeners, the presence of these tracks stood as evidence that the Beatles were separating themselves from the pack of 1960s popular music.

Surrounding these two performances, though, was an album's worth of tracks that found the Beatles engaging with contemporary African American popular music in newly adventurous ways. From the bluesy snarl of "Taxman" to the propulsive backbeat of "Dr. Robert" to the uptown horn lines of "Got to Get You into My Life," *Revolver* arguably finds the Beatles engaging with contemporary R&B music to even more pronounced degrees than *Rubber Soul*. Despite the overwhelming critical tendency to hear *Revolver* as a groundbreaking avant-garde rock record, it can be just as easily heard as an avant-garde rhythm and blues record.[81] In fact, in April of 1966 both *Billboard* and *Variety* published reports that the Beatles were looking into recording in Memphis, with the latter noting that "the Beatles, according to plans, will cut one album and about sixteen songs at the Stax Recording Studios."[82] According to Stax historian Rob Bowman, the Beatles had initially hoped to employ Stax songwriters to make a "contemporary rhythm and blues" album, although the idea fell through after Brian Epstein grew worried about the studio's ability to provide adequate security for the band.[83]

For all of the counterfactual intrigue of *Revolver*-at-Stax, I would argue that the album is even more influenced by Motown. The cleanly sparkling rhythm guitar and McCartney's lilting, falsetto-infused tenor on the sumptuous ballad "Here, There, and Everywhere" distinctly recall the Miracles' "Tracks of My Tears," released the previous year.[84] The musicologist Walter Everett has also shown that the horn lines on "Got to Get You into My Life" bear strong resemblances to the lines heard on both the Vandellas' "Dancing in the Street" (1964) and Stevie Wonder's "Uptight (Everything's Alright)" (1965).[85]

But the strongest Motown influence on *Revolver* is again that of Jamerson, heard in the bass playing of McCartney and, in one

instance, that of Harrison. "I Want to Tell You" is awash in octave leaps and downbeat anticipations, while the intricate syncopations and skipping sixteenth notes of "She Said She Said" (a
line played by Harrison) clearly bear the distinct mark of Motown's virtuoso bassist. "And Your Bird Can Sing" might be the
most Jamerson-inspired line on *Revolver*, another track on which
McCartney's bass emerges as a primary melodic instrument
against jangling rhythm guitars and Harrison's cascading, har-
monized lead-guitar part, which effectively imitates an R&B
horn section. Particularly on the song's bridge, McCartney's bass
line outlines the voice-leading, chromatically descending harmonic structure (G#m–G#m/G–G#m/F#–C#/F–E) through
octave leaps and syncopated melodic runs much as Jamerson
does in similar harmonic contexts like the Miracles' 1966 hit
"Come 'Round Here (I'm the One You Need)" and the Four Tops'
"Bernadette."[86] "Bernadette" was not released until 1967, but
its similarities to "And Your Bird Can Sing" show the degree to
which McCartney had internalized many of Jamerson's stylistic
proclivities.

In June of 1967 the Beatles released *Sgt. Pepper's Lonely
Hearts Club Band,* an album that prompted an historic shift in
the way people talked about the value of popular music.[87] In one
encomium, the literary critic Richard Poirier wrote in the
Partisan Review that *Sgt. Pepper* represented "an astounding
accomplishment for which no one could have been wholly prepared, and it therefore substantially enlarges and modifies all
the work that preceded it . . . gestations of genius that have now
come to fruition."[88] The *Washington Post* ran two banner stories on the day of the album's release, one of which described
the LP as "a musical infinity through a miraculous metamor-
phosis of dozens of Eastern and Western musical ideas, some
centuries old, others from our own era and more than a few from

James Jamerson, "Bernadette," opening of chorus

Paul McCartney, "And Your Bird Can Sing," opening of bridge

the future."[89] The other opened with the simple declaration, "Music may never be the same again."[90] Only a few years earlier the notion of anyone saying such things about rock and roll music would have been inconceivable.

Sgt. Pepper also struck a decisive blow for the 33 1/3 LP as the premiere format for rock and roll: the album was deliberately released without a single, which to that point had been the dominant vehicle of 1960s popular music. In elevating the full-length LP over the single, the Beatles seemed to embrace a more "adult" medium, one that came with the trappings of prestige previously afforded to album-oriented forms like classical and jazz. What's more, by retiring from touring and reimagining themselves as a collective that existed solely for the production of recorded music, the Beatles definitively severed themselves from screaming hordes of teenagers that had long provoked disbelief and occasional derision from commentators, while also distancing themselves from imaginings of rock and roll as an ephemeral, teenybopper phenomenon.

As Elijah Wald has argued, in the late 1960s the Beatles' music became the new benchmark for "serious" rock music. Writes Wald:

> As rock was vested with more and more importance, both as an art form and as the voice of a young counterculture, its

acolytes began to be bothered by the blatantly commercial, dance-hit mentality that had been taken for granted in the music's early days. And, with increasing frequency, that meant that rock was being separated from black music. Or, more accurately, from recent black styles.[91]

It is perhaps ironic that in the years since *Sgt. Pepper,* it is *Revolver* that has come to now be heard as a birth of avant-garde rock, as positioning *Revolver* in this way occludes its connections to the very "recent black styles" whose disappearance Wald justifiably laments.[92] Hearing *Revolver* as a cutting-edge R&B album—an alternative listening that respects musical fluidity over ideological rigidity—not only acknowledges the ongoing influence of black music on the band's work, but also places the album in the broader context of interracial influence and exchange heard on *With the Beatles* and *Rubber Soul,* rather than as the beginning of a new tradition that subtly denies its connection to black music. What's more, it recognizes the extraordinary contributions of Jamerson, whose anonymity was forced upon him by his employer for many years but who nonetheless transformed the possibilities of his instrument and inspired musicians born an ocean away to push the musical boundaries of rock and roll.

As the late 1960s progressed, the Beatles' commercial domination maintained its intensity in new forms, whereas Motown's gradually began to slip. The advances that the Beatles made in popular music contributed to this: in early 1967 Brian Epstein had renegotiated the band's contract with EMI, giving them new levels of control over their artistic and commercial destinies. The autonomy afforded the Beatles surely did not go unnoticed by other artists, white and black, and the inflexibly top-down, paternalistic system of Motown would become increasingly untenable. Motown also began moving to California, and many of the studio musicians responsible for creating the label's iconic sound were unwilling or unable to transition westward, most notably Jamerson, whose alcoholism was slowly eroding his musicianship. But perhaps the most fundamental and inevitable cause of the label's slow decline was its inability to remain on the cutting edge of popular music as it had for so much of the decade. With the emergence of the psychedelic R&B of Sly and the Family Stone, the pioneering funk of James Brown, and the insurgent Southern soul of Aretha Franklin (who'd grown up in Detroit), black popular music was rapidly changing as it expanded into new directions.

With the possible exception of Diana Ross, no two artists would be more instrumental in bridging the gap between the "golden age" of Motown in the 1960s and the changing landscape it would confront in the next decade than Marvin Gaye and Stevie Wonder. At the end of the 1960s, on the cusp of massive career transitions for both, Gaye and Wonder each released their own renditions of songs by the Beatles. Gaye's 1970 cover of "Yesterday," originally recorded by the Beatles in 1965, appeared on *That's the Way Love Is,* the last album Gaye would release prior to his landmark 1971 LP *What's Going On.* Stevie Wonder's 1970 version of "We Can Work It Out," also recorded by the Beatles in 1965, was released as a single and became a hit at a moment when Wonder was plotting his own career transformation. Much in the way that Motown music informed and enabled a period of transition for the Beatles, these covers of Beatles songs by Motown artists can be heard as informing a period of transition for Wonder, Gaye, and Motown itself.

Liverpool to Detroit: Marvin Gaye and Stevie Wonder at the End of the 1960s

Marvin Gaye was always a reluctant rock and roll star. A mid-1960s Motown press release went out of its way to mention that his idol was Frank Sinatra—"When he's at home in Detroit, he and his wife Anna like nothing better than to listen to the records of their favorite singer, Frank Sinatra"—and shortly before his death Gaye would tell biographer David Ritz that his "dream was to become Frank Sinatra."[93] Gaye was also deeply insecure, torn by a fiercely independent streak on one hand and an equally fierce desire for mainstream acceptance on the other. Gaye held himself on another plane from other Motown singers—aside from Sinatra he also admired Perry Como, Nat King Cole, and particularly Sam Cooke, adding an "e" to his own name in an early stab at imitation of the singer—and yet he was often jealous of younger stars like Stevie Wonder and, later, Michael Jackson.[94]

He was also arguably the most brilliant singer at Berry Gordy's label, bringing a crooner's perfectionism to a voice forged in his father's Washington, D.C., Pentecostal church. In his early career Gaye brought soft charm to confections like "Pride and Joy" and "How Sweet It Is (to Be Loved by You)" and gospel edge to show-stoppers like "Stubborn Kind of Fellow" and "Can I Get a Witness." He was also remarkably handsome and one of the deftest conveyors of male sexuality in the history of popular music. His mid-1960s duets with Mary Wells and Kim Weston were reliable standbys for Motown, but it wasn't until paired with Tammi Terrell that Gaye found his most incomparable musical partner, as the two recorded hits like "Your Precious Love," "Ain't Nothing Like the Real Thing," and "Ain't No Mountain High Enough." In late 1968 Gaye's solo stardom reached new heights when his recording of Norman Whitfield and Barrett Strong's "I Heard It through the Grapevine" became the biggest hit in Motown's history. He followed this up with two more Top 10 hits: "Too Busy Thinking about My Baby" and "That's the Way Love Is."

In a sense Gaye was a microcosm for Motown's own ambitions, the music of black America repackaged and resold to white America, on black Americans' own terms, although always carefully. This had been a lucrative proposition for Gaye's label but one that left the singer increasingly torn: as Gaye recalled, "I remember I was listening to a tune of mine playing on the radio, 'Pretty Little Baby,' when the announcer interrupted with news about the Watts riot. . . . I wanted to throw the radio down and burn all the bullshit songs I'd been singing and get out there and kick ass with the rest of the brothers."[95] As the 1960s progressed and his own political awareness grew more pronounced, Gaye began to chafe against Gordy's deep aversion to any controversial material but also against his own ambitions, as he grappled with how his dream to "sit on a stool and croon" might coexist with his growing urge to speak to the times and world in which he lived.

Gaye's 1970 album *That's the Way Love Is* was produced by Norman Whitfield, the cowriter and producer of "I Heard It through the Grapevine" and a figure widely credited for bringing the cutting-edge sounds of psychedelia—most notably the influence of Sly and the Family Stone—to a label that had found itself increasingly playing musical catch-up.[96] By Whitfield's standards *That's the Way Love Is* is a relatively conservative album: apart from its title track it's mostly a mix of second-tier Whitfield/Strong compositions, first-tier Whitfield/Strong compositions that had already been hits for other artists (such as "I Wish It Would Rain" and "Cloud Nine," both successes for the Temptations), or covers of non-Motown hits, including Dion's "Abraham, Martin and John," the Young Rascals' "Groovin'," and, notably, the Beatles' "Yesterday."

"Yesterday" has one of the most famous origin stories in all of music: by his own account, Paul McCartney awoke from a dream with the melody in his head, then wandered about for weeks asking people to identify it, not believing that he'd actually written it. For a while the working title of the song was "Scrambled Eggs"; after a name change, "Yesterday" was released on the U.K. version of *Help!* in 1965.[97] The original version of the song featured only McCartney, backed by a string quartet, and when the decision was made to release it as a single in the United States, George Martin suggested crediting it simply to "Paul McCartney," a suggestion that McCartney himself quickly dismissed. Credited to "The Beatles," the single went to number one.

By the time Marvin Gaye recorded "Yesterday," McCartney's composition was well on its way to becoming the most-performed song of the twentieth century.[98] The song had already been covered by artists ranging from Marianne Faithfull to Ray Charles, and even Gaye's idol, Frank Sinatra, had released his own version in 1969. By the end of the 1960s "Yesterday" had become a standard in the most classic sense, its melody so instantly recognizable that McCartney himself couldn't believe someone else hadn't written it.

Gaye's version of "Yesterday" takes the song's well-worn familiarity and reworks it into something drastic and unknown. Jonathan Flory has written of what he calls Gaye's process of "vocal composition," "how the singer assembled and developed a musical work by harnessing his vocal talents in the studio," and Gaye's rendition of "Yesterday" serves as an example of the singer rewriting a preexisting standard through vocal technique.[99] Whereas the Beatles' original recording of "Yesterday" was understated and austere, Gaye's recording of "Yesterday" is sweeping and enormous in its range of dynamics. The track opens quietly, with gently strummed guitars, then adds a spare rhythm section and xylophone. The drums are a light heartbeat of kick drum and high hat; an electric guitar bubbles quietly underneath, while a second guitar plays sparse fills.

Gaye's vocal performance immediately announces itself as something new, beginning with an ad-libbed "mm-mm" that tumbles into the song's opening, "ohh, YES-terday," accenting the first syllable. Gaye's rendition is a full fifth higher than the Beatles' version—the original is in the key of F, Gaye's is in C—a considerable leap that forces Gaye to essentially rewrite the song's melody. This is heard as early as the song's first word: in the Beatles' version, the three syllables of "Yes-ter-day" are melodically mapped as II-I-I, whereas in Gaye's version the phrase is I-I-VI, a small difference that subtly changes the texture of the opening phrase and anticipates the harmonic move to the relative minor (vi) chord that occurs in the third bar of the verse.

The drop of two whole steps in Gaye's opening phrase—as opposed to just one in the original version—also foreshadows the immense range that Gaye brings to the melody. One quality of "Yesterday" that has led to its endurance is its relative singability: in the original form the melody for the most part spans a single octave, dropping below the root only once (during the "I believe in yesterday" refrain). Gaye's vocal explodes these parameters: on the song's bridge Gaye's voice breaks into falsetto and soars up to a high D, more than a full octave above the root and nearly an octave and a half above where he lands on the song's opening phrase.

Gaye's vocal pyrotechnics provide style and showmanship but they also transform the texture and impact of the song. By soaring into falsetto on the "why" that opens the bridge, elongating the word tonally and temporally, Gaye transforms the "why she had to go / I don't know" sentiment into something dark and desperate, making a song about loss into a song about paranoia and confusion. Similar effects are achieved at other moments during the song as well: on the second repetition of the opening verse (which comes on the heels of the bridge), Gaye soars up on "*Now* I need a place to hide away" and adds strain on "need," drawing out the song's wishful fantasies of escape and isolation. And on the last verse, a piercing falsetto marks the word "seemed" in the phrase "all my troubles *seemed* so far away," emphasizing the lyrical themes of destabilization and disillusionment. And Gaye does all of this against a lush orchestral backdrop that more closely resembles Sinatra's own version, from his Reprise album *My Way*, than McCartney's original.[100]

Gaye's version of "Yesterday" is an audible fulcrum in the history of Motown at the end of the 1960s: both old-fashioned and new, the illustrious middlebrow tradition of the midcentury pop crooner brought to bear on a new standard, a testament to the versatility of Gaye. By the time Gaye's version of "Yesterday" was recorded, the Beatles were breaking up and Motown was leaving Detroit. In Gaye's rendering the nostalgia embedded in the text of "Yesterday" takes on a vast array of meanings, the sound, to paraphrase another Motown hit of the same period, of whole worlds ending and others beginning.

Gaye would not release any more new music in 1970, a year that found him grappling with the death of Tammi Terrell and questioning his own musical and political directions. During that year Gaye informed Gordy that he wanted to make a protest album. Gordy was hesitant at first: Motown marketed singles, not albums, and Gordy wanted little to do with any music that smacked of protest. Gordy ultimately relented, and in May of 1971, a new Marvin Gaye album was released, an introspective, jazz-laden, deeply political suite of music bearing the title *What's Going On* that produced three Top 10 singles and sold over two million copies.[101] *What's Going On* was the last major Motown work recorded in Detroit and the first Motown LP to credit studio musicians, including a special nod to "the incomparable James Jamerson," whose bass playing on the album (particularly its title track) is regarded as some of the finest of his career. *What's Going On* was a landmark moment, a Motown artist fighting Gordy on the creative end and winning, musically and commercially, striking a clean blow for individual vision and autonomy.

Gaye's victory did not go unnoticed. Eight days before the release of *What's Going On,* after the album's title track had raced up the Pop singles chart, Stevie Wonder turned twenty-one. In a shrewd show of chutzpah, Wonder had informed Gordy that, having become an adult, he intended to void the contract with Motown that he had signed as a minor. Gordy, well aware of the young Wonder's enormous musical gifts and still-boundless commercial and artistic potential, agreed to an unprecedented deal with the young singer, instrumentalist, songwriter, and producer, granting Wonder total artistic control over his future albums and half the publishing royalties to his songs.[102]

Wonder's ascent from child prodigy to the most powerful artist in the history of Motown spanned nearly the entire life of the company. Wonder had signed with the label in 1961, at the age of eleven, and had enjoyed his first number one hit the following year, a bizarre and thrilling live recording called "Fingertips, Part 2." Many at Motown initially saw Wonder as a gimmick, and Gordy privately worried that he would have to drop the singer once his voice changed.[103] His fears were dispelled in late 1965 with the success of "Uptight (Everything's Alright)," a song recorded and cowritten by the then-fifteen-year-old Wonder, whose transition into his adult voice had apparently only bolstered his confidence as a singer. Wonder followed this up with a stirring cover of Bob Dylan's "Blowin' in the Wind" that cracked the Top 10 in 1966, a gospel-infused rendition of the folk classic that hinted toward the young performer's versatility, his diversity of influences, and his own growing political awareness. A month after his seventeenth birthday the Beatles released *Sgt. Pepper's Lonely Hearts Club Band*, and Wonder later recalled being transfixed by the album.[104]

Wonder's appetite for non-Motown music did not stop him from becoming one of the label's most consistent hitmakers, with songs like "I Was Made to Love Her," "My Cherie Amour," and "For Once in My Life" all reaching the upper echelons of the *Billboard* Pop chart in the late 1960s. In June of 1970 Wonder released the single "Signed, Sealed, Delivered, I'm Yours," the first song on which he held sole producer credit, and an album called *Signed, Sealed & Delivered* was released two months later.[105] The album's second track was a cover of a 1965 Lennon-McCartney composition, "We Can Work It Out"; released as a single the following spring, Wonder's version reached number thirteen on the Pop chart.[106]

The Beatles' original recording of "We Can Work It Out" was released as a single in December of 1965, only days before the release of *Rubber Soul*.[107] The song was packaged as a "double A-side" with "Day Tripper" and went to number one in both the U.S. and the U.K. "We Can Work It Out" was a collaborative piece of songwriting on the part of McCartney and Lennon: McCartney wrote the song's verse sections, with its breezy, major-key melody, while Lennon contributed the bridge, a minor-key segment that includes a brief shift into a waltzing triple meter on the final bars of each phrase. At its core "We Can Work It Out" is a song about mending a relationship, although not without its turns of ambiguity. The song's bridge contains perhaps its most hopeful statement but seems contradicted by its minor, vaguely dirgelike quality, and lines like "do I have to keep on talking till I can't go on?" carry a frustrated exhaustion.

Wonder's version, recorded five years later, completely reimagines the song. Wonder's version is recorded only a half-step higher than the Beatles' original and at a nearly identical tempo, but the energy of his recording is startlingly different from the original. Wonder's version opens with a distorted clavinet playing three bars of introduction, then explodes into the song's verse as a cluster of voices shout an emphatic "hey!" The song's rhythm section is pure Motown dance pop: a four-on-the-floor kick drum; a percolating, elaborate bass line (played by Jamerson acolyte Bob Babbitt); a clean guitar playing staccato chord bursts on the backbeat.[108] Wonder's lead vocal possesses all the fiery urgency of "Uptight" but is more controlled and adult, a thrilling combination of commanding precision and flamboyant virtuosity.

Wonder's revision of "We Can Work It Out" differs from the Beatles' original in innumerable ways, but a few stand out. The first is the outsized and almost hyperactive role of backup vocal parts, which punctuate the song with exclamatory "heys." The effect achieved is a rollicking call-and-response, but with a notable twist: through studio multitracking Wonder provides all the backing vocals himself, which are then filtered through audio compression, giving the vocals a mechanized, techno-futuristic tinge. This is particularly notable in an interlude section that comes on the heels of Wonder's harmonica solo: as the clavinet riff from the song's beginning appears again, Wonder repeats the phrase "work it out with me, baby" as a swell of voices, intoning a wordless "ahhh," rises up around him, until a charging drum fill shoves the song into its final verse and out-chorus. As the gospel tradition of participatory musical community is wedded to modern recording technology, "We Can Work It Out" finds Wonder in communion with himself, giving the song an uncanny but riveting power.

A second difference is the song's bridge: as opposed to the Beatles' version, where a wheezing pump organ and brief shifts into waltz time lend a melancholic lament, Wonder's version increases in intensity. A tambourine arrives, jangling away on a driving eighth-note pattern, and the backup vocals soar into an upper-register head voice, performing the entire bridge in harmony with Wonder's lead. Wonder's bridge forgoes the Beatles' transition to triple meter, remaining in 4/4 time and employing a descending diatonic melodic hook to transition back into the verse, a flourish that sounds distinctly like a self-homage to the famous opening electric sitar riff of "Signed, Sealed, Delivered."

Wonder's vocal performance is also drastically different than McCartney's, particularly during the song's chorus. In the Beatles' version, McCartney swings the word "we" into the word "can," so that the emphasis unmistakably falls on the second word, while the first is more staccato: "we CAN work it out / we CAN work it out." In Wonder's version, both words are sung as straight eighth notes and the emphasis falls on the first word and third words: "WE can WORK it out / WE can WORK it out." Rhythmically, this creates a slight lag on the first word, leaning it against the rhythm section in a way that is, for lack of a better term, distinctly funkier than the original rhythm. Furthermore, the emphasis on "we" and "work" alters the meaning of the song's refrain, privileging the suggestion of togetherness over irresolvable differences.

Taken on the whole, this is the greatest accomplishment of Wonder's "We Can Work It Out": with its exuberant energy and revisions of form and phrasing, Wonder's version transforms the Beatles' song about the ambivalent reparation of a relationship into a statement about community and the unfulfilled possibility of reconciliation. By wedding the Beatles' song to his own unique blend of rock and roll and techno-gospel, Wonder explodes the song's text and stretches it into unimagined dimensions. At a time when Wonder's own music was expanding into new and increasingly political directions, he shifts the song's meaning, so that it's no longer about a quarreling couple but rather an affirmation of resilience and unity. If Gaye's version of "Yesterday" had brought a dark and piercing introspection to McCartney's composition, Wonder reimagines "We Can Work It Out" as a statement of extroverted generosity.

Much in the way that "Yesterday" was released as a turning point in the career of Marvin Gaye, at the end of his fealty to Gordy's system as he stood on the precipice of *What's Going On*, "We Can Work It Out" sounds a similar moment of transition in the career of Stevie Wonder. In 1972 Wonder would release *Music of My Mind*, an album that he wrote, produced, and performed almost entirely himself, a testament to both his own talent and to an expanding technological wizardry heard in inchoate form on "We Can Work It Out." "We Can Work It Out" contains many technologies that would become staples of Wonder's 1970s music, from the distorted clavinet of the introduction to the densely tracked backing vocals, whose compression and timbre carry hints of the vocoder or "talkbox" technology employed by Wonder throughout the 1970s.

By the time "We Can Work It Out" hit the Pop charts in 1971 Motown had all but left Detroit. The last act that Gordy personally shepherded to stardom in the manner that he had for so many Motown artists was a quintet of youngsters called the Jackson 5. The Jacksons themselves were not from Detroit but from Gary, Indiana, and their material was recorded almost exclusively in Los Angeles, with L.A. session musicians. The group's lead singer, a child prodigy named Michael who recalled no one so much as Little Stevie Wonder, would become one of the label's biggest stars before leaving for CBS Records in 1975. Wonder, for his part, has remained on Motown for his entire career.

As Wonder suggests in the epigraph to this chapter, it is impossible to imagine the history of 1960s popular music without the Beatles and Motown. The revolutions that they wrought on the music industry—commercially, artistically, sociologically—were the product of extraordinary vision and extraordinary circumstances: both took the loose and amorphous strands of rock and roll music into directions no one could have foreseen. The musical and commercial dominance of Motown and the Beatles pointed to something like a "sound of Young America" that exceeded the limits of America itself. The visions that enabled both were rooted in similar beliefs: that four young men from a British port city could play American rock and roll music and become more popular than even Elvis Presley; that white teenagers who'd long been accustomed to pale imitations of black music might give their ears and money to a black company directly, if given the chance.

By connecting "Money (That's What I Want)" from the beginnings of Motown to its appearance as the closing track on *With the Beatles* at the dawn of Beatlemania, by tracing the influence of James Jamerson through *Rubber Soul* and *Revolver,* by hearing the Motown transitions of Stevie Wonder and Marvin Gaye at the dawn of the 1970s through a pair of Lennon-McCartney hits from 1965, a web of musical commonality is revealed that exceeds the racially hermetic discourses surrounding these artists. In standard tellings, the Beatles helped invent white avant-garde rock while Motown was overly assimilationist, aesthetically compromised in its pursuit of white audiences. Both of these judgments are narrow and in crucial senses ahistorical. They position the Beatles and Motown into contexts and comparisons that are determined more by retrospective ideologies than musical realities.

In a 1970 interview, John Lennon remarked of the Beatles, "We were just a band that made it very, very, big, that's all. Our best work was never recorded."[109] It is a quote that has since become famous for its perceived irony, as if anyone could look back upon the 1960s and declare the Beatles to be "just a band." But it is also true, and while the "best work" refers to what a caustic Lennon had come to see as the band's idyllic, prefame years, it also gestures to the ineffability of truly grasping onto music of this magnitude. While Motown and the Beatles remain so familiar that to speak of their importance can often feel like a cliché, hearing them together suggests that they are perhaps differently important, and perhaps even more important, than we have previously allowed. Chapter 4 explores the new landscape of rock and roll music left in their wake, when a singer from Detroit and another from Texas further changed the way listeners thought about white and black music in the 1960s, while another singer from England sought a stateside invasion of her own.

"Being Good Isn't Always Easy"

Aretha Franklin, Janis Joplin,
Dusty Springfield, and the Color of Soul

What does Webster's *say about soul?*

—Gil Scott-Heron, "Comment No. 1," 1970

ON JUNE 6, 1965, the Rolling Stones released a single entitled "(I Can't Get No) Satisfaction." Clocking in at three minutes and forty-seven seconds, "Satisfaction" was a creative watershed that finally proved Mick Jagger and Keith Richards could produce songwriting of both quality and commercial viability to rival anything in popular music. The fuzzy guitar riff that opened the song became instantly iconic—Richards himself later recalled that he had imagined it as a horn line—and the band had never sounded better, with drummer Charlie Watts holding down a driving R&B backbeat, complemented by a relentless tambourine smacking out three eighth-notes on the back end of every measure, as Richards and Brian Jones snaked together lithe and sinewy guitar parts.[1] The lyrics, sung by twenty-two-year-old Jagger with swaggering confidence, were funny and edgy, worthy of the Stones' songwriting heroes such as Willie Dixon and Chuck Berry. The song also managed to further the air of controversy that had become the band's trademark, as its final verse, in which Jagger lamented that he "can't get no girlie action" and cryptically refers to a "losing streak," was initially deemed too risqué by many radio programmers.[2] Taken altogether, the song's sneering critique of celebrity and advertising culture fit snugly with the Stones' well-crafted scofflaw image.

"(I Can't Get No) Satisfaction" shot up the American charts. On July 10, 1965, it knocked the Four Tops' "I Can't Help Myself (Sugar Pie Honey Bunch)" from the top slot on the *Billboard* Pop charts and held the top position for four straight weeks, making it the Rolling Stones' first American number one single.[3] After nearly two years of toiling in the shadow of the Beatles, who by July of 1965 had already enjoyed eight U.S. number ones, "Satisfaction" gave the Rolling Stones a decisive stateside breakthrough. Over the next year the Stones would place five more songs in the *Billboard* Top 10, including two more number ones.[4]

So popular was "Satisfaction" that it even achieved a notable "reverse" crossover, reaching number nineteen on *Billboard*'s newly revamped R&B charts, meaning that the song was highly successful in record stores catering to African Americans and in solid rotation on black radio. "Satisfaction" also became the first original Rolling Stones composition to be widely covered by the American rhythm and blues artists whom the Stones idolized. Otis Redding had a hit with his own version of the song in 1965, a fitting exchange given that the Stones had covered a song popularized by Redding, "That's How Strong My

Love Is," on *Out of Our Heads*, the same album that contained "Satisfaction."[5] Redding's version moved Richards's famous guitar riff to the horn section and ratcheted up the tempo, and the singer's own vocal performance brought a frenetic exuberance to the material. Redding's version hit number thirty-one on the Pop charts and went to number four on the R&B charts.

By 1967, when a cover of "Satisfaction" appeared as the opening track on *Aretha Arrives*, the second album recorded by vocal sensation Aretha Franklin for Atlantic Records, "Satisfaction" had become one of the most famous rock and roll songs ever written.[6] Released in early August of 1967, at the height of what *Ebony* writer David Llorens would famously describe as the "summer of 'Retha, revolt and Rap," *Aretha Arrives* also included what would become Franklin's third consecutive Top 10 hit, "Baby, I Love You."[7] By the end of 1967 Franklin had released two more Top 10 singles, leaving the album's title less an alliterative boast than a vast understatement.

The version of "Satisfaction" that opens *Aretha Arrives* is exciting and new, boasting a driving four-on-the-floor kick-drum groove surrounded by swirling, churchy organ, pounding piano (played by Franklin herself), and piercing horn bursts. Franklin's vocal carries all of the commanding composure found on her more famous Atlantic sides, her performance a blend of the bluesy complaint of Jagger's original and the thrilling energy of Redding's cover. The musicians on Franklin's version hint around the song's iconic riff but never explicitly play it, and Franklin avoids the song's final verse entirely, choosing to riff extemporaneously on her inability to get "satisfaction" as opposed to Jagger's more specific griping over sexual frustration.

This is not a chapter about the Rolling Stones, but it is a chapter about Aretha Franklin and about the circulation of songs and the power of repertoire. More specifically, it is a chapter about how three female singers—Franklin, white American blues-rock singer Janis Joplin, and British pop star Dusty Springfield—used musical materials that were rarely of their own creation to navigate a historical moment during which conversations about race and musical authenticity reached new levels of intensity. This chapter roughly spans 1967 to 1970, a period that begins with the meteoric emergences of Franklin and Joplin and ends with Joplin's death from a heroin overdose in October 1970. During this time Dusty Springfield would travel to the United States and record the album *Dusty in Memphis* for Atlantic Records, a quirky and unique landmark in Southern rhythm and blues that found Springfield collaborating with many of the same musicians and producers who had worked with Aretha Franklin.[8]

During these years American critics, readers, and listeners were increasingly consumed with a peculiar subject of musical debate: "soul." For a word that conjures timelessness, the centrality of "soul" as a discursive subject in this period was in fact extremely timely, tied to burgeoning discourses of black cultural nationalism and often specifically to the rise of Franklin herself.[9] The far-flung metaphysicality embedded in the word's implications made it an ideal vehicle for a host of complicated discussions about cultural ownership versus cultural availability, racial essence versus racial transcendence, music as a utopian sphere of unraced democracy versus music as a delineation point of racial authenticity.

Who "had" soul and who didn't were questions that found their way into high-profile national publications, with figures such as Franklin and Janis Joplin serving as straw figures in discussions of the power of black music on the one hand and the proclivities of white performers trying their hand at said music on the other. Dusty Springfield, renowned for her facility within black musical styles in her native England, maintained only a side presence in the "soul" debates in the United States, her marginal position due mostly to a relative lack of commercial success and mainstream stardom in comparison to Franklin and Joplin.

This chapter examines the discourse of "soul," and the ways these artists functioned within and outside these conversations, both in a historically specific context and in relation to larger constellations of ideas about black and white music making. In the late 1960s ideas about soul gestured toward music while carrying claims that were distinctly extra-musical: "soul" was a way of using music to talk about race, and vice versa. In the years since this pattern has extended into historiography, and many histories of 1960s rhythm and blues music have focused on the social conditions of race and the essential relation of these conditions to musical performance. From a political standpoint such historiography has a long and important intellectual lineage, stretching back at least to LeRoi Jones's *Blues People* (1963), which drew a causal relationship between black musical activity and the legacies of slavery and emancipation.[10] Arguments for a defining, essential power in African American music have long been a powerful way of guarding said music against a white dominant culture that has repeatedly pillaged it, as well as a way of celebrating a cultural tradition whose legitimacy white America has long degraded, or simply denied.

All that said, one problem with such projects is their tendency to view musical practice as primarily determined by, or reducible to, race itself. In the historiography of 1960s R&B this tendency has often manifested itself in three distinct but occasionally overlapping ways. The first is histories that hold 1960s rhythm and blues music as a hermetically black undertaking, fundamentally resistant to and endangered by the influence of a white music industry; the second is histories that consider the music predominantly in terms of its relation to broader currents in African American political culture, specifically the civil rights movement; and the third is histories that focus on the interracial demographics of labels like Stax and locales like Muscle Shoals and that hold up the music as a metaphor for triumphalist integration narratives.[11] While there is surely some truth to all three of these threads, Charles Hughes has pointed out that narratives which hold R&B musicians as "vessels for authentic racial identity" tend to neglect that these musicians were "craftspeople, not conduits," and that soul music was both art and product made by people who labored at it.[12] Before it was anything else, soul music was mass culture, performed by professional musicians and marketed by record labels. The foremost goal of most soul music was to make black *and* white people buy it, and dance to it, in either order.

While both the material realities and imaginary capacities of race and its relation to musical performance will receive extensive attention in this chapter, I will also take up a subject that is too often neglected in discussions of popular music generally: namely, the question of repertoire, or the creation, selection, and performances of the songs themselves. Who was singing whose songs, for whom, and what does "whose songs" actually signify? How might Franklin's performance of "Satisfaction," a song originated by a band often categorized by the somatically disingenuous subgenre "blue-eyed soul," complicate or otherwise alter understandings of "soul," both its ontology and its aesthetic character? In a discursive landscape preoccupied with the relationship of racial category to authentic musicality, what happens when we examine specific musical material itself?

Race-based theories of musical practice almost always take root at the level of *performance,* while ignoring the variety of materials and motivations behind these performances. These are important topics, particularly within the context of commercial popular music. By focusing on repertoire I follow the work of Karl Hagstrom Miller, who has taken a similar approach in his study on race and its relation to the folk music industry in the early twentieth century. Miller writes of the benefits of looking at repertoire as a way "to identify interracial and transregional conversations" and to "avoid the potential dangers of overstating the differences between black and white performance styles."[13] Focusing on performance at the expense of repertoire naturalizes musical production, leaving the activity of music making susceptible to preconceived ideas about innate musical proclivities and tendencies.

Focusing on repertoire also allows us to recognize the performance *of songs* as a creative act in itself, one that is separate from but no less important than writing them. In so doing we might begin to undo a tendency in popular-music discourse—and rock music discourse specifically—to elevate the allegedly self-contained artist to the highest plane of artistic authenticity. Rock ideology fetishizes "originalism," and frequently trumpets the fact that nearly all of the genre's greatest heroes wrote the vast bulk of their own material.[14] This primacy of self-containment is, of course, conducive to the conviction that rock is above all a genre of authentic self-expression, and it helps tamp down anxieties about the music's relationship to mass culture and commerce's role in the artistic process. After all, going outside oneself for one's material implies a level of calculation a bit too cozy with naked commercialism.

This emphasis on originalism tends to misunderstand the complexities of songcraft and also discredits artists who do not often write the material they perform. This disavowal has been particularly damaging to female rock and roll and pop performers of the 1960s, who were often neither expected to nor usually encouraged to write their own material. Its persistence is just one reason that by the mid-1970s Ellen Willis could confidently and accurately accuse rock as "basically a male club,"[15] and Angela McRobbie and Simon Frith could state that "in terms of control and production, rock is a male form. . . . Female creative roles are limited and mediated through male notions of female availability."[16]

The conflation of authorship with authenticity means that artists who perform songs written by others—a standard practice for the vast bulk of American musical history—are implicitly denigrated. Franklin, Joplin, and Springfield did not write the majority of their own songs in this period, and for the most part they sang either songs written by professional songwriters or "cover" versions of songs originated by other artists. Of the nine singles that Franklin placed in the Top 10 on the *Billboard* Pop chart from 1967 to 1970, only two were credited as having been written by the singer ("[Sweet Sweet Baby] Since You've Been Gone" and "Think," both co-authored); similarly, the vast majority of Joplin's recorded output during her brief career originated from sources other than herself. Springfield rarely wrote her own material, and *Dusty in Memphis* is made up entirely of compositions by professional songwriters.

Paying attention to repertoire and its relation to performance, therefore, gives agency to performers who have been devalued by the cult of autonomous (male) creativity, and it also helps us to unravel certain race-based ideas of musical authenticity. As has been noted repeatedly in this book, these ways of thinking about music and performance are not unrelated, and both are fundamentally unequipped to confront the reality of a popular-music landscape in which no musician or musical community existed in hermetic isolation. Particularly in rhythm and blues during this period, many of the singers were black but many of the session musicians and songwriters were not. Triumphalist narratives aside, during a period in which rock music was becoming increasingly the province of white men, Southern rhythm and blues was, ironically, perhaps the most racially integrated corner of late 1960s popular music.

That word "ironically" gestures in a few directions. By insisting upon a view of musical performance and musical authenticity that was rooted in ideas of racial difference, the boundary policing of "soul" redrew lines of musical segregation, sometimes to the material detriment of musicians. In 1970 Wilson Pickett complained to an interviewer, "As I travel around the country I listen to what is being played and find that only on the soul stations is our music heard. A few years back it wasn't uncommon to find that on any radio station featuring the top pop artists we made up at least 40 per cent of the sounds they played."[17]

Even more troublingly, the fixation on soul as an object of conversation, controversy, and celebration also provided a way for the genre of "rock" to further consolidate itself as "white"; after all, if what Franklin was doing was a definitively "black" thing, why wouldn't the mirror image apply to the Beatles, Bob Dylan, or, for that matter, Janis Joplin? Much as Franklin was dubbed the "Queen of Soul," during her lifetime Joplin was hailed as the "undisputed 'Queen of Rock.'"[18] After her death Joplin would endure as the most vaunted female performer in the late 1960s rock pantheon, her exceptional femaleness confirming rock ideology's fundamental maleness, her death rendering her a perpetually malleable symbol, or token. And yet her own whiteness granted her access, furthering a notion that white performances of black-derived music were beginning to take on their own imagined musical ontology. A tragically unintended consequence of the discourse of "soul" was to further nudge African American performers from a rock and roll musical mainstream that they had disproportionately helped to create and sustain.

Writing the Sound of Soul

The cover of *Time* magazine's June 28, 1968, issue bore a painting of singer Aretha Franklin with the title "The Sound of Soul."[19] "Soul" was a concept that had long floated around African American culture but was experiencing a newly energized "crossover" into the white American mainstream, to sometimes embarrassing degrees: in February of 1968, Hubert Humphrey, the vice president and also a presidential candidate, was widely ridiculed in the media after referring to himself as a "soul brother" to an audience of black students.[20] The April 1968 issue of *Esquire* had featured its own report on "soul," complete with a chart seeking to answer the question "who's got soul?" (Lou Rawls, Muhammad Ali, and Jackie Kennedy were deemed to have it; Richard Nixon, Norman Mailer, and Humphrey himself were less fortunate).[21]

With regards to *Time,* the nation's most iconic newsmagazine, the image of Franklin combined with the story's title confirmed that Franklin was a figure of significance, that "soul" was significant, and that Franklin and "soul" were one and the same, a conflation that was borne out in the article: "In all its power, lyricism and ecstatic anguish, soul is a chunky, 5-ft. 5-in. girl of 26 named Aretha Franklin singing from the stage of a packed Philharmonic Hall in Manhattan."[22] Of course, the question of what soul exactly *was,* aside from simply Franklin herself, proved more complicated. *Time* defined it as follows:

> The force radiates from a sense of selfhood, a sense of knowing where you've been and what it means. Soul is a way of life—but it is always the hard way. . . . Where soul is really

at today is pop music. It emanates from the rumble of gospel chords and the plaintive cry of the blues. It is compounded of raw emotion, pulsing rhythm and spare, earthy lyrics—all suffused with the sensual, somewhat melancholy vibrations of the Negro idiom. Always the Negro idiom.[23]

In *Esquire,* writer Claude Brown seemed to agree, in less clinical tones:

> Soul is sass, man. Soul is arrogance. Soul is walkin' down the street in a way that says, "This is me, muh-fuh!" Soul is that nigger whore comin' along . . . ja . . . ja . . . ja, and walkin' like she's sayin', "Here it is, baby. Come an' git it." Soul is bein' true to yourself, to what is *you.* Now, hold on: soul is . . . that . . . uninhibited . . . no, *extremely* uninhibited self . . . expression that goes into practically every Negro endeavor. And there's swagger in it, man. It's exhibitionism, and it's effortless. Effortless.[24]

The March 29, 1968, issue of the Atlanta *Daily World,* an African American newspaper, included an article called "This Is 'Soul'" in which the author, Thaddeus T. Stokes, proclaimed that "soul is a poor-paying job where 'white' is the only color respected for upgrading and job-promotion. It is a smuty [sic] joke and loud laughter to destroy the black picture facing most of the unlearned."[25] Al Rutledge of the Baltimore *Afro-American,* in an article from July of 1968 entitled "The Root of All Soul," was quick to tie the concept of soul to black Christianity, although he noted that "young British musicians were the first whites to express enough musical genius and guts to venture into the blues idiom with any sense of real dedication" and praised the Rolling Stones and Beatles for their crediting of African American influences.[26] And in June the *Chicago Tribune* published an essay by Albert Murray entitled "Soul: 32 Meanings Not in Your Dictionary"; number seventeen read, pointedly, "Any Negro 'thing' imitated by white people."[27]

Nearly all commentators on the nature of "soul" agreed that it derived in a deeply significant and irreducible way from the African American experience. The particulars of that derivation varied in the telling—in her 1969 book *The Sound of Soul,* one of the first full-length treatises on the subject, the journalist Phyl Garland explicitly tied it back to slavery—but it was widely agreed that soul was most basically the province of African Americans.[28] But was it exclusively such? Could whites, with some proper combination of study, self-possession, enlightenment, and panache, attain soul, musically or otherwise?

The question of who had soul, who didn't, and how this correlated to racial identity, arose in almost every discussion of the subject. For every Al Rutledge who seemed to hold soul as a relatively democratic proposition, there were other commentators who saw it as an exclusive resource to be protected, lest it be corrupted or pillaged. The writer Clayton Riley, in an essay published in the *New York Times* entitled "If Aretha's Around, Who Needs Janis?," declared:

> In order to write of whites who sing and play Black, it is first necessary to call the imitators by their rightful names. Thieves. Bandits. That way. Just like this. Don't have to say the thing too loud, don't haveta lean on the truth. Crooks. Say it long but eeeeasy, so that *evvy*-body knows. Because you begin and end any description of white rock musicians by correctly categorizing them. They are good thieves or they are bad thieves.[29]

And there was LeRoi Jones, who, in his seminal 1967 essay "The Changing Same (R&B and New Black Music)" argued that "R&B

is straight on and from straight back out of traditional black spirit feeling. . . . Even so, as the arrangements get more complicated in a useless sense, or whitened, this spontaneity and mastery is reduced. The R&B presents expression and spontaneity, but can be taken off by the same subjection to whitening influences."[30] A few pages later Jones put the matter more bluntly: "the more intelligent the white, the more the realization he has to steal from niggers. They take from us all the way down the line."[31]

Perhaps unsurprisingly, white writers often felt differently. One of the most controversial defenses of whites' access to soul came from the critic and provocateur Albert Goldman. In late 1969, Goldman penned an article for the *New York Times* with the title "Why Do Whites Sing Black?" "There is," wrote Goldman,

> something providential about the occurrence of this musical miscegenation just at the moment when the races seem most dangerously sundered . . . black and white are attaining within the hot embrace of Soul music a harmony never dreamed of in earlier days. . . . They [whites] are *not* trying to pass. They are trying to save their souls. Adopting as a tentative identity the firmly set, powerfully expressive mask of the black man, the confused, conflicted and frequently self-doubting and self-loathing offspring of Mr. and Mrs. America are released in to an emotional and spiritual freedom denied them by their own inherited culture.[32]

For Goldman, white access to soul music had emancipatory potential, and the white practice of "singing black" held a moral—even spiritual—component. Black music, in this telling, was the path to white racial transcendence and redemption. Goldman's column was met with a flurry of letters, some supportive and others indignant. The most stinging response came from a group of female African American students at Smith College:

> We wish to inform you and Albert Goldman that no white can *ever* sing black. . . . The thing you white people always get mixed up over is that black music cannot be dissected into meters and patterns. For every black song there are a hundred ways a black person can sing and play it. The music is his soul expressed. . . . The white man is like a child. As soon as he sees a black man enjoying anything, despite all he (the white man) has done to destroy blacks, he decides he is going to take it away and keep it for himself.[33]

This letter in turn brought its own wave of responses from the *Times'* readership, with one particularly aggrieved correspondent comparing the Smith students to Nazis and declaring that "it is particularly depressing that a group of people who presumably have seen the worst side of racism should use racist arguments to deny the universality of musical expression."[34]

From a musical standpoint, discussions of the viability of white soul, or "blue-eyed soul"—a term believed to have been coined by black Philadelphia disc jockey Georgie Woods in 1964, to describe the Righteous Brothers—were almost absurdly over-determined, and at their core they boiled down to arguments over whether whites had the natural talent or even simply the ethical right to play black music.[35] Adding to the density of these questions was the historical backdrop of an American music industry that had long seen white artists disproportionately compensated in comparison to their black counterparts, even— indeed, especially—when the forms being performed were African American in origin. The discourse of "thievery" found in

Jones, Riley, and other black critics of white appropriation in this period is multivalent, the accusations of cultural theft nearly inseparable from legacies of economic inequity and exploitation. It was rightly understandable that many of the more proprietary definitions of "soul" derived from the fact that it was one of the rare things that white people heard, wanted, and were unable to take from black people for themselves.

Most striking about white writers', readers', and performers' envious relationship to soul is that the concept was almost always framed in terms both of blackness and also of oppression and hardship. To have "soul" was to have suffered at the hands of an unjust white society; if this was the case, how, then, could whites have soul, and wasn't there something deeply tormented about whites wanting it? Perhaps Goldman was right that an envious, aspirational white relationship to soul was in fact an initial step toward redressing racial guilt; or perhaps Jones was right that it was simply another iteration of white exploitation.

In its cover story on Franklin, *Time* went out of its way to tie soul to hardship, to degrees that would prove contentious when Franklin's husband, Ted White, filed a defamation suit against the magazine a few weeks after publication. "Her mother deserted the family when Aretha was six and died four years later, two shocks that deeply scarred the shy, withdrawn girl," wrote *Time*, a deeply personal revelation. The article went on to argue that "personally, she remains cloaked in a brooding sadness, all the more achingly impenetrable because she rarely talks about it—except when she sings," a strange assertion given that the piece was largely based around interviews with the singer. "Negroes," the author finally observed, "have been singing their sorrows in songs like this for centuries."[36]

Time insisted upon an intermingling of musical and racial imagination in which Franklin's blackness—signified by various imagined torments—and her enormous musical gifts are bundled together under this idea of "soul." In this framing Franklin's music becomes so magical that the source of its power is quite literally unknowable for *Time*'s white readership. The critic Michael Awkward has noted long-standing critical tendencies to characterize black female singers as dysfunctional or damaged, in which "the cultural significance of these female artists involves their capacity both to endure deeply troubled blues lives and to transform the resultant pain into great, highly emotional singing."[37] With regards to herself, in her 1999 autobiography Franklin traced the origins of this tendency to the *Time* article, and she complained of its persistence throughout her career.[38]

Time also glossed over the fact that Franklin had in fact grown up under rather extraordinary circumstances, just not in terms of the deprivations the article emphasized.[39] Franklin's father, the Reverend C. L. Franklin, was one of the most successful preachers in America, and Aretha Franklin had made her first commercial gospel recordings as a young teenager. In 1960, at the age of eighteen, she had been signed to Columbia Records by the legendary talent scout John Hammond, the same man who would sign Bob Dylan just a year later. While *Time* presented Franklin as a hardscrabble success story—and she had surely endured her share of professional disappointments in the eight years between her signing with Columbia and the publication of the *Time* article—at best this was an incomplete account. Franklin's musical exploits had received coverage in the national African American press since as early as 1957, and she'd first attracted the attention of the *New York Times* shortly after signing her Columbia deal.[40] In 1961, at the age of nineteen, she won "New Female Vocal Star of the Year" in the *Down Beat* magazine critics' poll, and "Best New Vocalist" in the *Playboy* jazz poll the same year.[41]

The six albums that Franklin released on Columbia between 1961 and 1966 did not sell commensurate to expectations, though, and when she and the label parted ways at the end of 1966, Atlantic Records Vice President Jerry Wexler was eagerly waiting in the wings. Wexler had long admired Franklin from afar, and he imagined her as a singer with crossover potential the likes of which Atlantic had never seen. For all of Atlantic's R&B success in the 1960s, it still lagged well behind Motown in terms of presence on the Pop charts. The details of Franklin's first (and only) recording session at Fame Studios in Muscle Shoals, Alabama, have been amply recounted elsewhere, but it was a day fraught with a distinctly Southern mix of musical ingenuity and racial antipathy.[42] All of the musicians on the session aside from Franklin herself were white, including a trumpet player who made a pass at Franklin after sharing copious amounts of alcohol with her husband, Ted White. The incident led to a conflict between White and the musician that transformed into a conflict between White and Fame's owner, Rick Hall. The session ended with Franklin having completed only one song; the singer would never record at Fame Studios again.

Luckily for Atlantic, that song was "I Never Loved a Man (the Way I Love You)," written by Ronnie Shannon and transformed by Franklin and the Muscle Shoals house band into a landmark of 1960s music. "I Never Loved a Man" established Franklin as a star, and the single's follow-up, a dramatic reworking of Otis Redding's "Respect" reached number one on the Pop charts and propelled her to superstar status. Between the release of "I Never Loved a Man" in January of 1967 and her *Time* magazine cover story roughly eighteen months later, Aretha Franklin released seven Top 10 Pop singles and three Top 10 albums, winning two Grammy awards. The same year that the Beatles released *Sgt. Pepper's Lonely Hearts Club Band* and a guitar virtuoso named Jimi Hendrix gained notoriety for setting fire to his instrument at the Monterey Pop Festival—a year that also saw the tragic death of Otis Redding, author of "Respect," in December— Franklin established herself, seemingly overnight, as the most successful female solo performer of the rock and roll era, and in the process she gained a nickname that remains with her to this day: the "Queen of Soul."

Franklin was not the only riveting vocalist to emerge in American music in 1967. The same Monterey Pop Festival that occasioned Hendrix's breakthrough included a band from San Francisco called Big Brother and the Holding Company that featured a lead singer named Janis Joplin. Joplin was born to middle-class parents in Port Arthur, Texas, on January 19, 1943.[43] Port Arthur was a conservative and fiercely segregated community, its 40 percent African American population kept at a legal if not always physical remove from its white population. In a 1969 interview with the *New York Times*, Joplin recalled Port Arthur thusly:

> Port Arthur people thought I was a beatnik, and they didn't like beatniks, though they'd never seen one and neither had I. I read, I painted, I thought, I didn't hate niggers. There was nobody like me in Port Arthur. It was lonely, those feelings welling up and nobody to talk to. I was just "silly crazy Janis." Man, those people hurt me.[44]

Although Joplin is most commonly associated with the late 1960s San Francisco music scene that produced such bands as Jefferson Airplane and the Grateful Dead, she was, like Bob Dylan before her, very much a product of the 1960s folk revival. Joplin came of age musically in an Austin, Texas, college folk scene not entirely dissimilar to that which Dylan frequented in Minneapolis. Like many young revivalists, the young Joplin and her friends in Texas were drawn to music seemingly untrammeled by modernity. By her own account Joplin's formative musical moment came from hearing the music of Huddie Ledbetter, or Lead Belly, the famed singer and songwriter who'd become an icon of the second stage of the folk revival before his death in 1949.[45] The only singer whose influence was more profound on Joplin as a young singer was Bessie Smith, the great female blues queen of the 1920s, whom Joplin frequently lauded in interviews and revered to the point of financing a new tombstone for Smith shortly before Joplin's own death in 1970.

The peculiar racial politics of the folk revival have been discussed in Chapter 1, but these peculiarities took on a more complex significance amidst the context of the rigidly enforced segregation found in Texas. For starters, unlike the Northern folk scenes of a Cambridge or Greenwich Village, many of the venues where Joplin performed in Texas were whites-only.[46] The image of young white people performing black music on stages where African Americans themselves were not allowed contains echoes of what Michael Rogin has called the "exclusionary" element of blackface minstrelsy, where, notes Rogin, the color line was always "only permeable in one direction."[47] Although Joplin herself never performed in blackface (a crucial distinction that cannot be overemphasized), for a singer who would come to be a flashpoint in debates over the viability of white soul as the 1960s progressed—as well as a frequent target of allegations of cultural theft—this strange aspect of Joplin's musical upbringing is at least worth acknowledging.

After several extended trips to California in the mid-1960s, Joplin moved to San Francisco in 1966 at the urging of her friend Chet Helms, the manager for a band called Big Brother and the Holding Company who were looking for a lead singer. Joplin's incendiary performances quickly brought Big Brother a strong local following in the Bay Area, and after their triumphant performance at Monterey Pop in June of 1967 Big Brother and the Holding Company began receiving national media attention. Their five-song set at Monterey, which culminated in an extended rendition of "Ball and Chain," garnered the group and its front woman widespread acclaim (although a prominently placed *Los Angeles Times* photo of Big Brother and the Holding Company referred to the band's lead singer as "Janice" Joplin).[48] In another parallel to Bob Dylan, the Monterey Pop performance garnered the interest of Albert Grossman (Dylan's manager), who quickly signed the band and secured them a recording contract from Columbia Records (Dylan's label).

As Joplin rapidly rose to stardom, her audacious, spectacular renditions of the blues made her a polarizing figure, and more than occasionally an unwilling foil to Aretha Franklin in debates over who did or did not have "soul." Much in the way that Franklin's musical abilities were often conflated with personal difficulties, profiles of Joplin frequently focused on her "outsider" status. In a 1968 interview Joplin told Nat Hentoff:

> I never seemed to be able to control my feelings, to keep them down. When I was young, my mother would try to get me to be like everybody else . . . before getting into this band, it tore my life apart. When you feel that much, you have superhorrible downs. . . . Now, though, I've made feeling work for me, through music, instead of destroying me. It's superfortunate. Man, if it hadn't been for the music, I probably would have done myself in.[49]

The language of exceptionalism was constant in coverage of Joplin, from both the singer herself and from fans and critics, at least those in the singer's corner. Robb Baker of the *Chicago Tri-*

bune, one of Joplin's most vocal admirers, declared that Joplin was "the first [woman] to have complete control of the blues since Bessie Smith and Billie Holiday" and he went on to compare her favorably against Aretha Franklin and Nina Simone.[50] Ralph Gleason, one of the most respected music critics in the country, gushed in the *San Francisco Chronicle* that "back over the decades of American pop music, from Sophie Tucker to Peggy Lee and Patti Page, many white women have sung black blues for their audiences in this country, but Janis Joplin is the first one to make you believe she really means it."[51] A profile in the *Los Angeles Times* described her as a "southern mean mama, bitch, suffering woman, little girl—and now not woman at all but energy incarnate," while across the Atlantic, *New Musical Express* mythologized her as a "beatnik rebel, the girl from the Deep South who mixed with Negroes."[52]

On account of her commercial success, spectacular performance style, and frequent outspokenness, from the moment of her emergence Joplin became a catalyst for controversies over what it meant for whites to sing in styles that were imagined to be black, and for every writer who sang her praises there were others who saw Joplin as a musical counterfeit and cultural thief. Reviewing *Cheap Thrills* in the *New York Times* in 1968, William Kloman called the album "a stereophonic minstrel show, and probably the most insulting album of the year" and called the group "the embodiment of the hippie fantasy: middle-class kids with long blond hair pretending to be black."[53] Columnist Hollie West of the *Washington Post* declared that "Miss Joplin is a poor excuse for a blues singer. She is probably well on her way toward ruining her voice under the strain of trying for the harsh, raucous sounds that black performers use naturally."[54] African American publications rarely covered Joplin, and when they did their valuations were often dismissive.[55] The *Los Angeles Sentinel*'s

Stanley G. Robertson, reviewing Big Brother and the Holding Company's performance at the Monterey Jazz Festival, wrote that "Miss Joplin, a very bad imitation of a Negro blues singer (She is Caucasian.) only made the band, which played much, much too loud, only seem more ridiculous than it was."[56]

The criticisms were not limited to writers either. Miles Davis told an interviewer in 1969 that the record industry "don't sell no black folks. . . . They sell nothing but white skin, blond hair and blues eyes. They sell that rock by Janis Joplin . . . sounds like a Xerox copy of Otis Redding."[57] Even Wexler, Franklin's producer, weighed in: "I don't really believe [Joplin]. When a person truly sings the blues, there's no strain, no trying to make it sound right. I can always hear Janis straining. I don't know. There are people who think she's almost an unwitting parodist." He then conceded "but I'd give anything to produce her."[58]

In the late 1960s Franklin's soul was deemed authentic and unimpeachable while Joplin's performances were often described as a parlor trick, even by the singer's champions.[59] *Rolling Stone,* a publication generally friendly to the singer, suggested in 1969 that Joplin's music belonged "more to the realm of carnival exhibition than musical performance."[60] A Columbia Records press bio for Big Brother and the Holding Company claimed that "Janis Joplin defies physiology, her voice clutched in a shuddering huskiness or shrieking as a witch exorcising demons."[61]

For her part, Joplin saw blues and soul music as a democratic proposition. "I ain't gonna sit here and defend my soul to anybody, man," she told the *San Francisco Chronicle.* "Anybody who feels things has paid dues; everybody with feeling, man, has paid dues whether you can sing or write or just iron. . . . Black people have the blues because they can't have this and they can't have that. Me, I was brought up in a white middle class family—I could have had anything, but you need something more in your gut, man."[62] Elsewhere, in response to accusations of stylistic theft, Joplin replied, "I don't sing black. I just sing. I don't think I copy at all. And anyway no one has a monopoly on soul."[63] And yet, in one of Joplin's most provocative answers to the question of why she worked "in vocal black face" (the phrasing of her interviewer, Albert Goldman), she stated her hope that "being black for a while will make me a better white."[64] This last response is perhaps the most interesting response to this question that Joplin ever gave, carrying traces of the intertwining of music and racial politics found in the earlier years of the folk revival, where, as discussed in Chapter 1, the performance of black music was thought to be a way into a more robust political consciousness and, by extension, a form of self-actualization.

While Joplin was an avowed antiracist, her outspokenness on race could also lead her to overlook her own whiteness in ways that could appear naïve, if not offensive. She was prone to broad statements on the nature of African American music: in 1970, she told an interviewer that "young white kids have taken the groove and the soul from black people and added intensity. Black music is understated. I like to fill it full of feeling."[65] She freely dropped the word "nigger" into her speech, and in another *Rolling Stone* profile Joplin boasted of her intention to add "a great big ugly spade cat" to her band.[66] While it is tempting to excuse remarks as relics of a different era, a year earlier Jerry Wexler had declared to the same magazine, "One of my pet peeves is this noxious hippy use of this word 'Spade.' It's just disgusting to me the way they cavalierly throw it around. . . . I don't think this word is sanctioned, accepted or condoned by any Negro people."[67]

While Joplin sold far more records than Big Mama Thornton, Bessie Smith, and most of her African American blues forebears, the suggestion that white performers of black music in the late

1960s were necessarily guaranteed success—that blue-eyed soul was invariably more lucrative than brown-eyed soul—wasn't always borne out. A prime example of this is the case of Dusty Springfield, a British pop star renowned in her home country for her abilities as a rhythm and blues singer who spent the latter part of the 1960s in a quixotic and ultimately unsuccessful attempt to gain a secure foothold in American pop music.

Springfield never achieved enough success in the United States to warrant consistent inclusion in debates over "soul" and "blue-eyed soul." In England, however, she had long been known as a singer of tremendous versatility and a tireless evangelist for African American music. Born Mary O'Brien on April 16, 1939, Springfield first rose to prominence as a member of the folk-pop group the Springfields, who were formed in 1960 and enjoyed a Top 20 hit in the United States in 1962 with "Silver Threads and Golden Needles," one of the rare pre-Beatles British groups to find American chart success.[68] She left the group in 1963 and embarked on a solo career that soon made her one of the most famous singers in England. By 1967 Springfield had enjoyed eight Top 10 hits in the United Kingdom, three of which crossed the Atlantic to reach the U.S. Top 20: "I Only Want to Be with You" (1963), "Wishin' and Hopin'" (1964), and "You Don't Have to Say You Love Me" (1967), which reached number four on the *Billboard* charts and gave Springfield the biggest American hit of her career.

By 1968 Springfield's success in the United States had mostly come through sugary pop songs and melodramatic ballads—what the musicologist and Springfield scholar Annie Randall has referred to as the "Sixties pop aria"—and American audiences would have likely been unaware of the degree to which Springfield was associated with American rhythm and blues within her native country.[69] British pop star Cliff Richard frequently referred to Springfield as the "White Negress," and Springfield's 1964 solo debut album, *A Girl Called Dusty*, contained seven covers of songs originally performed by African American artists.[70] Like Joplin, Springfield mixed a love of black music with a fierce personal antiracism, though Springfield was far more politically active. In late 1964 she was forced to leave South Africa after her refusal to play before segregated crowds; her expulsion was widely publicized in England, and even garnered coverage from African American newspapers in the United States.[71] In 1965 she was instrumental in spearheading the landmark *Ready, Steady, Go: Sound of Motown* television special, which brought artists such as the Supremes, the Miracles, the Vandellas, and the Temptations to prime-time British television. Springfield herself hosted the special and performed alongside the artists, dueting with Martha Reeves on "Wishin' and Hopin'."[72]

In 1964 Springfield told a *Melody Maker* interviewer "I have a real bond with the music of the coloured artists in the States. I feel more at ease with them than I do with many white people." She later remarked that "I wish I'd been born coloured. When it comes to singing and feeling, I just want to be one of them and not me. Then again, I see how some of them are treated and I thank God I'm white."[73] The frankness and honesty with which Springfield discussed her own racial identity and insecurities are striking. One biographer has claimed that "Dusty Springfield is likely to have her skin colour alluded to more than any other British white cultural figure," a perhaps hyperbolic statement that nonetheless indicates the extent to which race factored into discussions of the singer.[74] If Joplin sought to deny race's salience to singing ability and general musical authenticity, Springfield often rendered it paramount, with a peculiar mix of insecurity and apology.

In 1968 Springfield's contract with England's Philips Records expired; seeking greater stateside success, Springfield signed with Atlantic Records, one of America's most esteemed rhythm and blues labels and the home of Aretha Franklin. Jerry Wexler had long admired Springfield's talents, and he saw in her a way into tapping both the lucrative British import business and the burgeoning market of "blue-eyed soul." The year 1968 saw the release of Springfield's last album for Philips, *Dusty . . . Definitely* (a U.K.-only release), as well as the recording sessions that would beget the singer's most famous album for Atlantic Records, *Dusty in Memphis,* recorded in the fall of 1968 and released in January of 1969.

During this period Springfield crossed musical paths with both Joplin and Franklin while rarely managing to insinuate herself into the polarized discourse of "soul" that these performers tended to dominate. In the end most discussions of "soul" came down to vague ideals of musical performance that dovetailed with equally vague definitions of innate black and white character and expressive capacity. In short, they were discussions that obscured the role of craft and practice in the performance of popular music, abstracting these things into indecipherability through the fuzzy listening of race. The remainder of this chapter looks at the songs these three artists sang and how they sang them; in doing so, I show that the issue of "soul"—who may or may not have had it, what it may or may not have been—was a far vaster, more complicated, and ultimately much richer subject than many of its listeners may have realized.

"Piece of My Heart": (Erma) Franklin to Springfield to Joplin

In 1967, the same year Aretha Franklin burst into superstardom, her older sister Erma Franklin scored the first and only hit of her career with a song called "Piece of My Heart."[75] "Piece of My Heart" was written by Jerry Ragovoy and Bert Berns, white northerners who were established songwriters before Erma Franklin brought "Piece of My Heart" into the world. Berns had already written a classic, "Twist and Shout" (popularized by the Isley Brothers and later covered by the Beatles), as well as a number one Pop hit in "Hang on Sloopy" for the McCoys in 1965.[76] Ragovoy was perhaps best known for his composition "Time Is on My Side," an R&B standard made famous by Irma Thomas in 1964 that also became the Rolling Stones' first Top 10 U.S. hit later that same year.[77] After Erma Franklin enjoyed success with "Piece of My Heart" in 1967, the song would be recorded the following year by both Dusty Springfield and Janis Joplin.

Both the composition and these three performances of "Piece of My Heart" offer an object lesson in the capacious heterogeneity of rhythm and blues music· in the late 1960s. From a harmonic standpoint "Piece of My Heart" is exceedingly simple, based around a nearly unwavering I-IV-V chord progression.[78] Like most good pop songs its chorus is its most memorable part, the famous "come on, come on, come on, come on" building into the "take another little piece of my heart now, baby" refrain. Its lyrical text is strikingly masochistic, reveling in the pain of surrendering oneself to someone who may not have one's best interests at heart. "You know you've got it / if it makes you feel good" is the chorus's final line, and the declaration carries a potential double meaning: is the singer merely surrendering to a situation out of her control, or actually willingly offering herself up to her antagonist, out of a desire to "make [him] feel good?"[79] "Piece of My Heart" is a song about pain that is not necessarily about powerlessness, its major-key fervently suggesting that perhaps the singer's tormentor is not the only one who "feels good" about this couple's arrangement.

Erma Franklin's version of the song is relatively spare and re-strained; aside from the vocal, the dominant instrument heard over the verse is a piano, playing simple chords peppered with oc-casional flourishes while drums and bass play a mid-tempo 4/4 groove behind her. As Franklin hits the chorus, a horn section arrives, and her backup singers punctuate "take another piece of my heart" and "break another little piece of my heart" lines with staccato instances of "take it!" and "break it!," recalling the girl-group pop of the Shirelles or the Crystals earlier in the decade. The bass also assumes a more prominent role on the song's chorus, playing eighth-note and sixteenth-note runs that lift the song out of the ballad feel suggested by its opening verse. The song moves from its first verse to its chorus, then to the second verse into the second repetition of the chorus, then fades out on a final chorus.

Erma Franklin's recording of "Piece of My Heart" is an effec-tive if somewhat by-the-numbers piece of mid-1960s R&B. Franklin is a capable vocalist who suffers in comparison to her younger sister Aretha (as does almost everyone else), who was al-ready a star by the time Erma Franklin had her brief moment with "Piece of My Heart." Erma Franklin's recording of "Piece of My Heart" performed well on the R&B charts and even crossed over to the Pop charts, reaching number sixty-two. It was by far the biggest hit of her career.

"Piece of My Heart" would become an iconic piece of 1960s pop music, thanks to Janis Joplin, who performed the song in 1968 on Big Brother and the Holding Company's *Cheap Thrills* album, but the song also received a notable 1968 reworking at the hands of Dusty Springfield. Springfield's version of the song, re-titled "Take Another Little Piece of My Heart," appeared on her 1968 album *Dusty . . . Definitely,* her final album recorded for Philips Records in England.[80] For the most part the instrumentation and arrangement of Springfield's version mirror Erma Franklin's original, but its intensity exceeds the original by a number of degrees. Springfield's rendition opens with a similar piano figure to Franklin's but the piano is overdriven and drenched in reverb, reminiscent of Phil Spector's famed "Wall of Sound" productions of the early 1960s. The tempo is quicker and the bass is mixed extraordinarily high in the track, louder than both the drums and guitar, and the prominence of the instrument and the busyness of its player (likely frequent Springfield collaborator Doug Reece) gives the recording a driving effervescence from its opening moments that is missing from Franklin's original, lending a sunny breeziness to what had previously been imagined as a mid-tempo soul ballad.

Springfield performs the song a half-step lower than Franklin (her version is in D, whereas Franklin's is in E-flat), and she sings the first verse in a smoky, sultry voice, playing with phrasing and singing with relaxed nonchalance. Springfield's greatest gifts as a singer were her preternatural senses of time and phrasing, and in the case of "Piece of My Heart" this measured ease amplifies the paradox at the heart of the song: Springfield is singing a song about pain in a style that evokes nothing if not pleasure. Lines such as "didn't I give you everything a woman possibly can?" are sung with such casual certitude that they answer their own question, and there is a sense of empowerment at the heart of the performance, that the "piece" is being given as opposed to taken, and that if there is dysfunction or pathos in this relationship it is a mutually agreed-upon proposition.

Dusty . . . Definitely was not released in the United States, and most American listeners in 1968 would not have heard the singer's inspired take on Ragovoy and Berns's composition. It is also highly unlikely that, when recording *Dusty . . . Definitely* in August of 1968, Springfield would have yet encountered Big Brother and the Holding Company's version of the song, which featured an explosive vocal performance by Joplin and reached number twelve on the *Billboard* Pop charts in late 1968, making it the most successful single from *Cheap Thrills* and one of the biggest hits of Joplin's career.[81]

Big Brother and the Holding Company's rendition of "Piece of My Heart" is drastically different than either Franklin's or Springfield's. The track opens with loud, distorted electric guitar, and the vocal begins on the "come on, come on, come on" repetition that normally precedes the song's chorus, only here it leads into the first verse. Big Brother and the Holding Company were a famously haphazard musical outfit, and according to Joplin's biographer Alice Echols it was partly frustrations over this that caused the singer to leave the band shortly after the release of *Cheap Thrills*.[82] John Simon, the producer of *Cheap Thrills,* refused to even put his name on the album, and as *Rolling Stone* reported at the time, Simon "feels that this album is as good as the band and that's about it."[83]

"Piece of My Heart" reflects this. The guitars are only moderately in tune, the rhythm section is chaotic, and changes in dynamic often sound like the result of studio punch-ins rather than organic crescendos and decrescendos.[84] For all of the technical troubles of the production, however, Joplin's vocal performance is arresting and thrilling. She throws herself into the song, and there is a desperate ferocity that is absent from Springfield's and Franklin's versions. While Springfield's easy restraint subverts the lyric's themes of heartbreak and agony, Joplin's version attacks the text at its most literal, eschewing the potential pleasure that might lurk behind the pain in favor of exploring pain on its own terms.

Joplin's voice is ravaged and pushed to its limits, giving the sense that the singer is in fact inflicting physical pain on herself, a common sensation while listening to the singer's music that would later cause a *Rolling Stone* writer to remark that "Janis doesn't so much sing a song as to strangle it to death right in front of you. It's an exciting, albeit grisly, event to behold."[85] Or, as Joplin herself once noted to an interviewer, "maybe they can enjoy my music more if they think I'm destroying myself."[86]

In Joplin's rendition of "Piece of My Heart" we can hear almost every aspect of the controversy swirling around the singer. Her performance is stunning, but its reliance on spectacle raises the question of whether Joplin's performance is genuine catharsis for the singer and her audience, or an exaggerated parody of what said audience might expect from musical emotion. In a sense Big Brother and the Holding Company's recording of "Piece of My Heart" can be heard as a strange apotheosis of the naturalist overtones of the "soul" concept, the idea that musical proficiency was most directly linked not to practice or craft but simply to one's proximity to "feeling."

Negative reviews of *Cheap Thrills* often seemed to recognize this, deriding the album for its amateurism. "Among other problems, the musicians in the group have some very peculiar ideas about rhythm," wrote the *New York Times*, which complained of the band's "screeches and arbitrary twangs geared to listeners who can't distinguish between sexual yearning and prickly heat."[87] *Rolling Stone* described the album as "a real disappointment" and sarcastically noted that *Cheap Thrills* was "a good representation of Big Brother and the Holding Company, as good a one as could have been expected and as good a one as there ever will be."[88] Still, *Cheap Thrills* shot to the top of the *Billboard* album charts in the summer of 1968. Joplin's performance of "Piece of My Heart" quickly became the most iconic rendition of the song, vastly exceeding Erma Franklin's original in sales and exposure, and most of the American audience so enthusiastic for Joplin's "Piece of My Heart" would never even hear Springfield's version.

"Son of a Preacher Man":
Franklin to Springfield to Franklin

Only a few months after Big Brother and the Holding Company brought "Piece of My Heart" to its greatest chart success, Springfield enjoyed her final brush with stateside success in the 1960s, when her recording of a song called "Son of a Preacher Man" cracked the *Billboard* Top 10. "Son of a Preacher Man" was a song that had originally been written for Aretha Franklin; upon first encountering the song Franklin rejected it, then finally recorded it herself in 1970, after Springfield's success convinced her to revisit it. "Son of a Preacher Man" is an extraordinary song, one whose cultural career defies expectation at all turns. Written by two white Southern men (John Hurley and Ronnie Wilkins) for a black woman from the North (Aretha Franklin), only to be made a hit by a white Englishwoman (Springfield), "Son of a Preacher Man" attests to soul music's immense variations during this period, as well as music's own resistance to stories we tell about it. Finally, the song's journey reveals some of the ways that convoluted beliefs about genre and authenticity worked to drown out the very music they were attempting to describe and delineate.

"Son of a Preacher Man" is a song so direct that its strangeness can elude detection on first listen. Most pop songs are sung *to* someone—there is usually an object of address, sometimes a named person but often simply "you," and most are directed to someone who is inspiring either affection or heartbreak. "Son of a Preacher Man" is a song about "Billy Ray," a preacher's son, and sung by a woman, although exactly when and to whom is unclear.

It's a story song, but its indeterminacies of temporality and address lend a hazy ambiguity: it's really a song about memory. The first verse establishes that Billy Ray would accompany his preacher father to the narrator's house, and "when they gathered round and started talking / that's when Billy would take me walking," the song's heroine at first too demure to offer details of what happens next, even if the chorus's revelation that Billy Ray was "the only boy who could ever reach" her fills in some of the blanks.

The second verse heightens the level of suggestion. "Being good isn't always easy / no matter how hard I try" is the opening line, an eloquent statement on the struggle between propriety and desire that doubles as a beautifully halfhearted protestation. The rest of the verse establishes Billy Ray as sexual initiator, and when we reach the second iteration of the chorus this knowledge has infused the once-simple statements of "the only one who could ever teach me" and "the only one who can ever reach me" with carnal overtones. As we approach the bridge, "Son of a Preacher Man" is now a song about a sexual awakening.

And then the bridge arrives and changes everything again. "How well I remember / the look that was in his eyes," is the first line, and the entire narrative frame is shifted. This is a song that is being told much later, about something that presumably once was but is no longer. Suddenly a song about memory is also a song about loss, and the couplet "taking time to make time / telling me that he's all mine" reveals the betrayal of a false promise. This was a love rooted in the physical that disappeared long ago, and on the final repetition of the chorus the suggestion that this was the "only one" takes on a melancholic defiance, and the very act of recounting the tale an assertion of selfhood.

"Son of a Preacher Man" belongs to the genre of the forbidden love song, and such songs were not uncommon to Southern rhythm and blues at the time: James Carr's "The Dark End of the Street," Clarence Carter's "Slip Away," and Wilson Pickett's "In the Midnight Hour" all stand as classic explorations of the illicit or unattainable. And yet "Son of a Preacher Man" departs from these in its invocation of religion, and it is here that it strays into its most peculiar territory of all. In one sense this can be seen as an indictment of Southern social mores, a suggestion that underneath genteel morality all is not as it seems, or, perhaps, it celebrated the more sensual and erotic aspects of Southern religiosity, evident to anyone who'd ever heard a particularly impassioned Holiness sermon or gospel performance.

Whatever it was, it was too much for the woman for whom it was written. When Atlantic brought Hurley and Wilkins's composition to Aretha Franklin, she rejected it. For all of the erotic undertones of Franklin's Atlantic work—with songs such as "Dr. Feelgood" and "You Make Me Feel Like a Natural Woman" often heard as anthems of sexual empowerment—the open combination of religion and sex in "Son of a Preacher Man" was apparently too much for Franklin, a preacher's daughter herself, at least initially.[89]

Franklin's loss was Springfield's gain. Along with American Studios' formidable stable of session musicians, Springfield turned "Son of a Preacher Man" into one of the more unique moments in Southern soul music.[90] Perhaps the most remarkable aspect of Springfield's "Son of a Preacher Man" is its use of quiet. The song's opening guitar riff is spacey and surreal, so cleanly played that it almost chimes, while a Wurlitzer electric piano hums underneath it. Gene Chrisman's drum performance is delicately understated, his high hat and cymbals played almost at a whisper, his fills sparse and laconic. Tommy Cogbill's bass is the most melodically active instrument on the record, bubbling delicately underneath Chrisman's drumming.

This quiet has several effects. From a thematic standpoint it heightens the song's undercurrents of illicit suggestion while evoking a setting of thick, slow Southern evenings. Musically, the quiet directs our attention to even the slightest moments of dynamic emphasis, such as Chrisman hitting a snare-drum backbeat just slightly harder than he did in the previous measure, or Cogbill's bass line providing a particularly nimble flourish. Even Springfield's vocal begins with careful breathiness, as though confessing a secret, the British pop chanteuse as parody of a Southern belle.

The arrival of the bridge following on the heels of the second chorus transforms the recording. Horns play sustained pads, while the electric guitar plays chopping rhythm chords for the first time in the song. Even more significantly, the song's bridge modulates up an entire fourth, an unusually wide interval that forces Springfield into the upper registers of her vocal range, where she remains for the song's final chorus. We hear ad libbing from Springfield, as "Son of a Preacher Man" becomes "sweet-talking son of a preacher man," then "sweet-lovin' son of a preacher man," as her backup singers take on their fullest role yet, essentially filling out the entirety of the chorus. Chrisman's drum part moves to polyrhythms on the cymbals, and as the song soars toward its fade the listener is swept away in the mixture of exuberance and lament that haunts the song's text.

The success of "Son of a Preacher Man," both commercially and artistically, in large part resulted from the tremendous influence of the composition's inspiration, Aretha Franklin. Not only does the recording feature numerous musicians who were veterans of Franklin's sessions—including Cogbill on bass, and the horn section of Andrew Love and Wayne Jackson—it also features Franklin's backup singers, the Sweet Inspirations. "Son of a Preacher Man" is basically an Aretha Franklin track without

Aretha Franklin; it is almost impossible to imagine the song being recorded in this way prior to Franklin's emergence. Of course, Springfield's vocal range and capacity were nowhere near the equal of Franklin's, and the production and arrangement are tailored around this. By placing the white British Springfield in a recording studio with a song written for Aretha Franklin and musicians who backed up Aretha Franklin, what emerged was one of the great R&B records of the 1960s, a recording whose peculiar, atmospheric power is truly unique.

Franklin herself returned to "Son of a Preacher Man," after the success of Springfield's version changed her mind about the song's worth. Recorded in Miami during the sessions for Franklin's 1970 album *This Girl's in Love with You*, from a stylistic standpoint her recording is a stark departure from Springfield's, abandoning the latter's ambient sparseness for a full-on, gospel-rock aesthetic.[91] An electric guitar plays fills behind Aretha's vocal as her piano churns, and Barry Beckett's organ playing more directly evokes the song's religious underpinnings. Jerry Jemott's bass playing is more insistently rhythmic and less melodic than Tommy Cogbill's, and drummer Roger Hawkins brings a funky, driving backbeat to the proceedings. Perhaps the most striking difference between the two recordings is the role of the backup singers—again, the same voices heard on Springfield's recording—who intone the chorus in syncopated, staccato bursts, then move to a "hallelujah" in response to "oh, yes, he was" rejoinder.

The "hallelujah" is a clear indication of the foregrounding of religion in Franklin's version, but Franklin's own vocal is powerfully church-infused as well. Franklin improvises around the song's melody far more than Springfield, and the most striking example of this is heard in the song's bridge, which is a stark departure from Springfield's. In opposition to Springfield's bridge, where the intensity of the track is dramatically heightened in terms of both dynamics and arrangement, in Franklin's version the entirety of the backup track drops out behind her, save for her own piano playing and, later, an organ. The entire bridge is out of time, with Franklin guiding the chord changes along with her vocal in an almost theatrical variation on the gospel tradition of testifying. The band crashes back in behind her as the final chorus arrives, and, like in Springfield's version, the song fades.

Franklin's version is louder and more bombastic than Springfield's. The religious undertones of the song are heightened, and by calling more explicit attention to the song's intimations of sex, the production loses the haunting hesitation of Springfield's, its sense of dilemma and awakening. By explicitly foregrounding the connection between religion and sex that is only hinted by its predecessor, the version on *This Girl's in Love with You* skirts over the complexities of both sex and religion in favor of an exaggerated performance of both. While Franklin's own influence looms over *Dusty in Memphis,* Springfield's rendition of "Preacher Man" leaves Franklin's own version in something of a stunted state. Franklin and her producers may have felt the same way, as her version of "Son of a Preacher Man" was never released as a single.

It is hard to know what accounts for this discrepancy. It is possible that Franklin was still uncomfortable with the song, as many of the other performances on *This Girl's in Love with You* are brilliant. It is also quite possible that Franklin was not used to performing a rendition of a song previously performed by another female singer, so recently and with such success. As others have noted, beginning with her hit version of Otis Redding's "Respect" in 1967, Franklin overwhelmingly gravitated toward songs first performed by male artists when it came to choosing covers in this period.[92] *This Girl's in Love with You* alone features five such songs.[93]

A more intriguing possibility lies in the messy thicket of genre. As Jerry Wexler later acknowledged, Atlantic was looking for inroads into the burgeoning white "rock" market and saw Aretha's talent as so monumental that she might be capable of bridging the rapidly solidifying boundaries between black and white music. The first single released from *This Girl's in Love with You* was a cover of the Band's "The Weight," featuring a young session guitarist named Duane Allman on slide guitar, which Wexler later expressed regret over.[94] Although Franklin's cover of "The Weight" is original and inspired, it failed to find the success Atlantic had come to expect from her.

The arrangement choices on Franklin's version of "Son of a Preacher Man" may reflect this concern with cross-genre appeal: the song has a louder, more aggressive feel than Springfield's original version, and Franklin's version exaggerates the gospel elements of the song to stereotypical extremes. Wexler's visions of Springfield as the blue-eyed soulstress who would bring Atlantic that crossover demographic never materialized, much in the way that Aretha never quite became the "rock" star the label hoped she would become in the early 1970s. Ironically, the British band that would finally give Atlantic the "rock" success it craved was recommended to the label by Springfield herself, when she pointed executives in the direction of a newly-formed quartet called Led Zeppelin.[95]

For her part, Springfield was never able to hear "Son of a Preacher Man" the same way after Franklin's version, and she was perpetually convinced that Franklin had "done it better."[96] A self-conscious performer perpetually aware of her own whiteness and mistrustful of her own "soul"-ful authenticity, Springfield was mortified at the thought of being compared to

Franklin, even if their moment of overlap had produced arguably the most brilliant performance of her career.

"Eleanor Rigby": Lennon/McCartney to Franklin

Franklin's own career was in a state of flux at the time of *This
Girl's in Love with You*. She had recently ended her marriage to
Ted White and had opted to record *This Girl's in Love with You*
in Miami instead of New York, where she had made her earlier
Atlantic recordings. Franklin had not had a Top 10 hit since late
1968, and *This Girl's in Love with You* is an unusual album, one
that found the singer working with a wide array of material,
among which were a pair of songs by British artists who were far
more well known to American audiences than Dusty Springfield:
John Lennon and Paul McCartney. The fourth and fifth tracks
on *This Girl's in Love with You* are Franklin's renditions of "Let
It Be" and "Eleanor Rigby," the first of which was in fact released
before the Beatles' version—McCartney sent Franklin a demo of
the song, in hopes that she would record it—and the second of
which reimagined one of the most famous tracks from the Beatles' 1966 album *Revolver*.

Franklin's recording of "Eleanor Rigby," recorded at the dawn
of the 1970s, is a compelling study in the vestigial interracialism
of 1960s music, a reclamation of rhythm and blues from a Beatles song that originated at a moment when the band were widely
heard as moving away from black musical influences, as discussed in Chapter 3. Franklin's "Eleanor Rigby" finds one of the
most famous singers of the 1960s tackling one of the most famous
songs of the 1960s and making it unmistakably her own, and in
doing so the recording offers a powerful counter to gathering
ideologies of originalism, high-minded masculinism, and racial
hermeticism in rock music.

The version of "Eleanor Rigby" on *Revolver* features Paul Mc-Cartney on lead vocal, backed by a double string quartet arrangement in E minor; the song moves between E minor and C major chords on the verses, then proceeds to a chromatically descending Em7/D–Em6/C#–C–Em pattern on the song's chorus ("all the lonely people / where do they all come from?").[97] "Eleanor Rigby" is unusual among Beatles songs of this era in that it is told entirely in the third person, McCartney's narrator delivering a story of "lonely people," such as the titular heroine and "Father McKenzie." The Beatles' version was notable both for its chamber-music backdrop—although both John Lennon and George Harrison sing backup vocals on the track, none of the four Beatles play instruments—and for its themes of loneliness and isolation, more somber than anything the Beatles had previously released.[98]

Franklin's version of "Eleanor Rigby" transforms the song. Franklin's recording features a full band with a driving rhythm section that performs the track as an up-tempo dance number. The recording opens with a rumbling minor-pentatonic piano introduction before going into the first verse. Franklin's version completely does away with the Beatles' harmonic structure as well, instead sticking to a two-chord vamp throughout the entire song, moving from two bars of D7 to two bars of G7 (I to IV), then repeating this progression through the entirety of the song.

Most notably, Franklin's version discards the third-person narrative structure entirely. "*I'm* Eleanor Rigby," Franklin declares in the song's opening line, and she sings the entire song in the person of McCartney's main character. Suddenly the text is turned from a storylike elegy into a bluesy, personalized complaint. On the song's chorus Franklin's backup singers come in behind her, singing in tightly syncopated staccato bursts, and a warm electric piano plays fills around Franklin's vocal. After the song's second chorus much of the band drops out for an eight-bar "breakdown" section that essentially serves the purpose of a bridge, capped by a short drum solo by Bernard Purdie. As the song moves toward its fade Franklin goes into a shout chorus, with the singer improvising around the song's lyrics—recalling the end of the version of "Satisfaction" that opens this chapter— as her backup singers intone variations of "Eleanor Rigby" and "all the lonely people," and the electric piano solos behind them.

Franklin's "Eleanor Rigby" remakes McCartney's quasi-classical rumination into a rollicking R&B song. More than that, by moving the lyrics from the third person into the first person, Franklin conceptually reimagines the song as a blues, and she invests the character of Eleanor Rigby with a distinctly feminist defiance. It is an audacious revision of what was already by 1970 a canonical popular-musical text, and in many senses Franklin's rendition of "Eleanor Rigby" is as bold a genre-bending exercise as the Beatles' original version.

As I argued in Chapter 3, large swaths of the Beatles' *Revolver* can be heard as an avant-garde R&B album. The string octet version of "Eleanor Rigby" on *Revolver* would seem to be an exception to this, but Franklin's rendition suggests that even this needn't be the case, and that the musical commonalities between the Beatles and Ray Charles—indeed, there's no performer whom Franklin's version of "Eleanor Rigby" more distinctly recalls, down to the rolling Wurlitzer piano—are still far thicker and more meaningful than the musical commonalities between the Beatles and Johann Sebastian Bach. Franklin's "Eleanor Rigby" stands as a tribute to soul music's potential resistance to the rigidities of racialized genre discourses, a potent statement that ideas about what white and black musicians can and cannot do rarely hold up under the scrutiny of actual musical practice. Most potently, it stands as proof that when a song the quality of

"Eleanor Rigby" and a singer the quality of Aretha Franklin find one another, the possibilities are boundless.

The discourse of "soul" that percolated so feverishly during the late 1960s was a strange and deeply ideological conversation. While often celebratory in nature, its terms drew on long-standing beliefs about innate black musical ability that were deeply rooted in the history of American racism. By using music to make arguments about race and race to make arguments about music, "soul" became a way to artificially stabilize the instabilities wrought by the conflation of racial and musical ideology, and in doing so the actual music that it sought to describe was often obscured.

There were, of course, numerous ironies to this. First, the policing of "soul" as a musical boundary sometimes created real problems for many of the artists it was ostensibly celebrating. Through suggestions that white and black music, white and black musicians, and white and black audiences were inherently *different* from one another, the popular-music industry redrew the very lines of market segmentation and segregation that musicians themselves had challenged. More distressingly, the discourse of "soul" provided a backdoor opening for white "rock" music to further stake itself as inextricably different than black music. Although it was almost certainly not her intent, this is clearly embodied in the figure of Janis Joplin. Recall Joplin's statement that "young white kids have taken the groove and the soul from black people and added intensity." The extremity of emotion and pathos of Joplin's "Piece of My Heart" marks many of Joplin's most iconic performances, and Joplin's ideal of blues and soul performance was theatrical in almost every sense of the word, an exaggerated rendering of what she, and presumably large segments of her audience, believed to be black musical expression. As Gayle Wald has written, "In Joplin's rock performance we can detect an emulation of black female blues artists that borders on a reactionary romanticization of their artistic achievement and a reification of racial difference."[99] Perhaps the strongest trace of Joplin's folk-revival roots in her move to rock music was this very romanticization, which exalted black music to an impossible position populated by figures such as Leadbelly and Bessie Smith, irrevocably lost to the past but whose imagined tormented authenticity was carried forward by musicians like Joplin.

But most fundamentally, these conversations often missed musical connections where connections were plentiful, and they invented differences when differences were minimal. The story of Dusty Springfield, Aretha Franklin, and "Son of a Preacher Man" is a potent example of this: a song written by two white men for a black woman, performed by a white Englishwoman in the black woman's stead with musicians from the black woman's band, many of whom themselves were white; then re-recorded by the black woman for an album for which she was explicitly courting a white audience, an album featuring a mixed-race band that included one member—Allman—who would become a rock icon in his own right. Through their shared encounter around "Son of a Preacher Man" and also through their shared status as talented artists performing R&B music and attempting to find success among white *and* black audiences, Springfield and Franklin may have had more in common with one another than many were ready to concede.

In her 1969 book *The Sound of Soul,* Phyl Garland conceded that upon a visit to Stax Studios in Memphis, "I found it difficult if not impossible to distinguish a white sound from what was supposedly a black sound." Al Jackson, the African American drummer for the interracial Stax house band Booker T. and the

MGs, told Garland that, "in today's white market, the general market that uses the term soul, they think of Negroes only. . . . I'd say that soul has no *color.* It's a matter of exposure."[100] "Soul" was not so much a way for Americans to talk about the music they were making and consuming as it was a way for them to talk about themselves. The problem with "soul" was that it abstracted musical practice to a magical realm: instead of music being something people did, music became something people *were.* As Chapters 5 and 6 will now show, similar beliefs in unbridgeable difference and ideologies of musical boundary-policing were finding a home in rock music as well.

CHAPTER 5

House Burning Down

Race, Writing, and Jimi Hendrix's War

People should see more violence on the stage, maybe they'd get it out of their system—wouldn't have to fight wars.

—Jimi Hendrix, 1969

IN SEPTEMBER OF 1969, a few weeks after his already-legendary performance at the Woodstock Music and Art festival, guitarist Jimi Hendrix was asked by an interviewer to categorize his music and explain himself to a world that often seemed bewildered by his presence. Frustrated by a question he'd confronted countless times previously, Hendrix spun a metaphor: "What I don't like is this business of trying to classify people," he responded. "It's like shooting at a flying saucer as it tries to land without giving the occupants a chance to identify themselves."[1]

The remark is as perfectly Hendrix as anything that emerged from the guitarist's Fender Stratocaster: its resistance to definition, its witty extraterrestrial imagery, and its invocation of violence, a topic that, as the epigraph to this chapter indicates, fascinated him. Like many musicians in the late 1960s, Hendrix felt compelled to transpose the violence around him—assassinations, the Vietnam War, urban rebellions in the United States and abroad—into his art, to express his dismay and dissatisfaction with the world he lived in through his groundbreaking music. But more than that, between 1967 and his death in 1970 the guitarist also waged audible war against musical possibility and racial confinement, raging against a cultural and discursive landscape that was rapidly circumscribing, if not outright denying, the possibility of his own existence. Hendrix was an African American musician playing a musical form that was quickly and assiduously being reimagined as a whites-only enterprise: as mentioned in the Introduction, by the time Hendrix died in September of 1970 one prominent obituary described him as "a black man in the alien world of rock."[2] In his pioneering and hugely impactful explorations into the aesthetics of musical violence, it was in part this "alien world," and the logics that created it, that Hendrix was seeking to destroy and remake.

Chapters 5 and 6 are about the conjunction of music and violence in the work of two of the 1960s' most influential artists: Jimi Hendrix and the Rolling Stones. The music made by both these artists in this period has come to uniquely symbolize violence in popular-cultural settings, with songs like "All along the Watchtower," "Voodoo Child (Slight Return)," "Jumpin' Jack Flash," "Gimme Shelter," and others serving as instantly recognizable audible markers of violence in movies, television shows, and other media.[3] I want to argue that both of these artists' preoccupations with violence can be heard as responses to hardening racial ideologies in popular music that left each in an embattled and precarious position in the late 1960s. Hendrix and the Rolling Stones were perhaps the most racially complex and controversial musicians of their era: Hendrix, a black man playing a music that was fast coming to be imagined as a whites-only enterprise; the Rolling Stones, a white band obsessed with black music to a degree that left them in a minority of rock acts still directly engaging with black music as a living form.

For Hendrix, explorations of violence in his music were ways of audibly remaking the tumult of the world in which he lived. If the Rolling Stones were rock and roll's greatest hedonists, Hendrix was the music's greatest utopian, a man prone to describing his music in terms like a "sky church sort of thing," "Western sky music," or "sweet opium music."[4] "I want to write mythology stories set to music, based on a planetary thing and my imagination in general," he told an interviewer in 1967.[5] Paul Gilroy has since argued that "the substantive issue is not that Hendrix was ahead, but rather that he was able to pronounce another time—sculpting temporality itself so that his listeners could, in effect, be transported from one time to another."[6] In the wake of all the cultural mythology that surrounds him it's tempting to treat Hendrix's utopian dreams as clichéd hippie hallucination, but such a reading overlooks the many ways that Hendrix's musical utopias were so frequently—indeed, almost compulsively—wrought from conditions of dystopia.

One of these conditions was a discursive landscape increasingly invested in policing the stakes and possibilities of black musical creativity. To return to a recurring theme in this book, these boundaries most often arose around ideas of authenticity. As Chapter 4 showed, certain discussions of "soul" during the late 1960s served as bulwarks against white appropriations of black culture, musical and otherwise. While these conversations were frequently driven by African American commentators, white writers were drawing their own racial-cum-musical dividing lines during this period, most prominently through the increasingly influential medium of rock writing. Hendrix's rise to stardom almost directly coincided with the emergence of rock criticism as a mainstream, marketable form: only five months after the guitarist's international breakthrough at the Monterey Pop Festival in June of 1967, *Rolling Stone* magazine was founded in San Francisco. Hendrix was thus one of the first rock and roll superstars understood in accordance and negotiation with what newly vocational "rock critics" were saying about him.

This chapter begins with an overview of the rise of rock writing during this period, focusing on the role that race played in the form's emergent self-definition. I'll then turn to a discussion of Hendrix and the guitarist's position within this context, before moving to extended examinations of three of the guitarist's most famous performances in "Voodoo Child (Slight Return)," "All along the Watchtower," and "Machine Gun." I will focus on themes of violence in these compositions, both Hendrix's deployment of violent imagery through lyrical and musical devices—mostly notably in his deployment of "scratching" guitar techniques—and also the ways that this violence was received and rearticulated by his listeners. If Hendrix's musical experimentations were a critique of the musical and social conditions surrounding him, after the guitarist's death these critiques were absorbed and incorporated into subgenres like heavy metal and "cock rock," which transformed Hendrix into a foundational figure for a new sort of hegemonic white masculinism. Finally, I will briefly explore the discursive swarm occasioned by the rise of one of rock's earliest and greatest post-Hendrix guitar heroes, the Mexican-born San Franciscan Carlos Santana, whose Latino identity and musical eclecticism prompted a descriptive crisis wrought with exoticism and nostalgia in the "alien world" Hendrix had recently left behind.

The Rise of Rock Writing

There are any number of possible reasons why rock criticism exploded in the mid- to late 1960s: a generation of intellectuals raised on Elvis and Little Richard, and later the Beatles and Bob Dylan, came of age and gained access to media venues; the political and discursive energies of the New Left counterculture found an artistic form that it could claim as its own, to theorize, debate, and celebrate; an older and more established generation of critics, including Albert Goldman in New York, Kenneth Tynan in London, and Ralph Gleason in San Francisco began taking the music more seriously and using their various podia to trumpet its virtues. But perhaps the most compelling reason is also the simplest: in the wake of all the music that's been discussed previously in these pages, there was really quite a lot to write about.

Simon Frith has characterized popular music criticism as "not just producing a version of the music for the reader but also a version of the listener for the music"; in other words, music criticism doesn't simply describe or evaluate music, it instructs us on how to hear it, how to think about it, how to categorize it.[7] The rise of rock criticism in the late 1960s helped consolidate ideologies about what rock music was, wasn't, and ought to be, and in doing so it produced ideas about what rock fandom should be, what it should value, and the sorts of conversations it should conduct. Rock writing, and of course rock reading, offered new ways of fashioning musical consumption into expressions of one's identity. Crucially attendant to this, of course, were discussions about race, and the position of black music and musicians within new modes of musical thinking being formulated by writers who were, by and large, overwhelmingly white.

In June of 1966, just shy of his twenty-second birthday, Richard Goldstein's first "Pop Eye" column appeared in the *Village Voice*, a landmark moment in American music criticism.[8] Goldstein was not the first rock writer, nor was the *Voice* the first venue to publish serious rock criticism: as a seventeen-year-old Swarthmore College student, Paul Williams had founded *Crawdaddy!* magazine, widely considered the first rock magazine in America, four months before Goldstein's column debuted. But in June of 1966 *Crawdaddy!* remained a typed, mimeographed affair with minimal circulation; Goldstein, on the other hand, had a column in the most celebrated weekly newspaper in the most influential city in America.

Goldstein was a deeply intellectual and prodigiously gifted prose stylist, passionate, funny, and opinionated, as well as a fierce advocate that rock and roll be taken seriously as a cultural form. In an article on Bob Dylan from 1966, he attacked the singer's "parochial critics," who, he declared "face a practically insurmountable obstacle in their unwillingness to accept the fact that a poet can work in a medium such as rock 'n' roll. . . . Just as reprehensible as the widespread ignorance of the classics among the youth is the widespread ignorance of the current among adults."[9] Such statements made Goldstein among the premier rock-critical voices of the late 1960s and arguably the most influential. So respected was Goldstein that he maintained his critical credibility even after panning the Beatles' *Sgt. Pepper's Lonely Hearts Club Band* ("fraudulent") in the *New York Times* in 1967.[10] Goldstein departed the *Voice* in 1968, and by 1970 his legacy was such that *Rolling Stone*'s Jon Landau credited him with bringing "literacy, the first sign of civilization," to rock discourse.[11]

Goldstein was not shy about addressing race in his writing, and like many other white critics of his era, he felt strongly that white performers had access to "soul." "Soul is intimately tied to sorrow, and sorrow is not a racially exclusive enterprise," he noted in an early "Pop Eye" column; later he would explicitly attack "the myth that soul and gospel wailing has to be all black to be good."[12] As the decade progressed, Goldstein and other critical voices grew increasingly interested in the intersection of rock music and the concept of "revolution," particularly after the tumultuous spring and summer of 1968. In November of 1968, Goldstein wrote a column in the *New York Times* discussing the revolutionary language sweeping through rock and roll and argued that "rock contains in its live performance an implicit statement of rebellion against restraint." He then connected this to rock's roots in black music:

> To do away with revolution in rock, one would have to ban the music itself, since revolt is inherent in its nature as a charged version of blues. . . . [R]hythm and blues was an agent of liberation in a climate of crippling repression. It grew in the ghettos with the zeal of a political movement, and it was as certain a sign of impending revolt as the first sit-in.

He went on to write that "the contact between folk and rock musicians on both sides of the Atlantic has produced a hybrid music which is as vital to the restive youth of the sixties, as R. and B. [*sic*] was a generation before."[13]

The critic and historian Bryan Wagner has argued that cultural imaginings of the itinerant blues singer, so frequently held as a paradigm of authenticity in African American music, are rooted in fantasies of violence and racial threat—the bluesman as a social and existential "outlaw."[14] We can see strong traces of this formulation in Goldstein's passage above, in which he ties rock's emerging aggression and rebellion to the blues and "impending revolt." And yet Goldstein also suggests that this connection is essentially *past*: note the telling phrase "a generation before." In fact, nearly every artist discussed in Goldstein's article—from the Beatles to the Rolling Stones to the MC5—was white. In this telling black music provided the imaginative basis of rock's rebellion, but belonged to an earlier generation: it is not of a piece with rock, but rather something that preceded and enabled it.

Shortly after Goldstein's column, the *Los Angeles Times* ran an article by Mike Gershman entitled "The Blues, Once Black, Now a Shade Whiter" that echoed Goldstein's thesis that white musicians had expropriated successfully aggression and danger from black musical traditions. Gershman added a twist, though, excoriating contemporary black music for not living up to the author's own ideas of blues tradition. Gershman complained of "denatured Negroes" who "have learned only too well . . . the value of getting Top 40 airplay" and ended his article with the following statement:

> The thrust of writing message songs has passed from Negroes to whites. We are getting a kind of musical integration, but at the expense of Negro blues, the most honest and meaningful contribution of black people. Blues fans can be thankful that young musicians like John Kay and Stevie Winwood are keeping the faith. Even though they are white.[15]

Gershman claimed that by chasing commercial success black artists were losing authenticity, which was in turn being snatched up by white artists. By picking up an imagined political and philosophical torch of black music, white men had taken the blues tradition and made it their own, while black musicians had lost it while attempting to "integrate." Here was a vision of music in which appropriations of black music only added to white authenticity, while courting white audiences left black musicians spiritually degraded and politically suspect.

Why would a white writer take to the pages of a national newspaper and confidently level such claims? In fact, Gershman was neither the first nor the most prominent voice to do so. In the autumn of 1967, *The American Scholar* published a lengthy essay by the *San Francisco Chronicle*'s renowned music critic Ralph J. Gleason, who later that year would become a founding editor of *Rolling Stone* magazine. The article, entitled "Like a Rolling Stone," extolled the musical contributions of the 1960s counterculture. "I daresay that with the inspiration of the Beatles and Dylan we have more poetry being produced and more poets being made than ever before in the history of the world," Gleason declared.[16] He then launched into a lengthy rumination on the relationship between white and black music in contemporary times. He lamented the "Ed Sullivan TV-trip to middle class America" that he saw James Brown, the Supremes, the Four Tops, and other African American performers pursuing, and he then declared that "the only true American Negro music is that which abandons the concepts of European musical thought, abandons the systems of scales and keys and notes, for a music whose roots are in the culture of the colored peoples of the world."[17]

Leaving aside that one would need to go back several hundreds of years to find an "American Negro music" that was entirely separate from "the concepts of European musical thought," Gleason's endorsement of musical segregation is strikingly brazen, and he even goes so far as to claim inspiration from Stokely Carmichael. Gleason then proceeded to praise recent white rock music for its purported banishment of African American influences. "Today's new youth, beginning with the rock band musician . . . is not ashamed of being white," wrote Gleason.

> He is remarkably free from prejudice, but he is not attempting to join the Negro culture or to become part of it. . . . For the very first time in decades, as far as I know, something important and new is happening artistically and musically in this society that is distinct from the Negro and to which the Negro will have to come, if he is interested in it at all.[18]

He went on to cite the Beatles' 1967 single "Strawberry Fields Forever" as "one of the more easily observed manifestations" of music that "exists somewhere else from and independent of the Negro."[19] Such statements reveal the ease with which racial essentialisms slip into tautology. In one breath Gleason assails Motown for aspiring to middle-class respectability; in the next he praises the Beatles for partaking in the bourgeois trappings of classical music. Gleason's "new music" is thus defined in terms of its *distance* from black culture, even as he acknowledges that it was born from that culture.

Such appraisals were not limited to the American side of the Atlantic. In 1968 a twenty-two-year-old British writer named Nik Cohn wrote an influential volume called *Awopbopaloobop Alopbamboom,* subtitled *The Golden Age of Rock.*[20] *Awopbopaloobop,* one of the earliest attempts at writing the history of rock and roll, was argumentative, romantic, and deeply nostalgic—Cohn later recalled writing the book as a series of "farewells," feeling that commercialism and artistic pretention was destroying the music he'd loved as a youth.[21] The heroes of *Awopbopaloobop* are figures such as Eddie Cochrane ("pure rock") and Little Richard ("the most exciting live performer I ever saw in my life"); even the Beatles and Bob Dylan are treated ambivalently ("with their followers, there was nothing beyond pretension").[22]

Awopbopaloobop is a lively mix of hagiography and declension narrative, a construction of tradition that simultaneously laments said tradition's passing. Its cast of characters is remarkably white—while early African American rock and roll artists receive generous treatment in the book's early chapters, no black artist is the subject of a stand-alone chapter, as Elvis, the Beatles, the Rolling Stones, Dylan, and other white artists are afforded. Contemporary African American music is considered extensively only once in the book, in a chapter entitled "Soul." Here, like Gleason, Cohn found the current state of black music lacking: "Most soul singers come on like windup dolls, they almost sleep-walk and they smirk, leer and grimace like so many nigger minstrels. They don't act like people and they don't treat their audience like people either. It's all depressingly Tom."[23] Also like Gleason, Cohn saw Motown as a primary problem in all this, complaining of Berry Gordy's tendency to put his acts into white markets, which "is fine for the acts themselves, because they make more money, but a bit rough on their long-time followers, because the music turns lousy."[24]

Again, such critiques contain a near-incoherent double standard. Black artists are derided as "Toms" for aspiring to make money, then castigated for conforming to expectations of musical blackness on the part of white listeners—of which Cohn is one. In each of these examples we see white critics relegating black music and musicians to an impossible position. To court mainstream success and white audiences is to sacrifice authentic blackness, particularly if one does so by conforming to inauthentic white expectations of blackness—expectations that themselves are being articulated by white writers. The only "real" black music becomes that which has no contact with white styles and white listeners, even though the entire history of American music is made of such encounters, including rock and roll itself. Here was musical segregation that disproportionately punished black artists, a separate-but-unequal vision of popular music's landscape: white musicians were celebrated for pursuing musical styles that were both associated with their race (such as the Beatles' experimentations with European art music) and outside of it (such as white blues musicians playing the blues), while black musicians were decried as fraudulent for not adhering to standards imagined as properly "black."

The Jimi Hendrix Problem

It was into this climate that James Marshall Hendrix emerged as the most controversial American rock and roll star since Elvis Presley.[25] The Seattle-born Hendrix was twenty-four when his performance at the Monterey Pop Festival in June of 1967 made him a global superstar, but he had been toiling as a professional musician since being discharged from a one-year army stint in 1962, performing and recording as a sideman and session musician for a variety of R&B acts. In 1964 he moved to Harlem, and by 1966 had secured a residency at the Café Wha? in Greenwich Village. While in New York he attracted the attention of Chas Chandler, ex-bassist of the Animals, who convinced the guitarist to move to London. Upon arriving, Hendrix formed a band, the Jimi Hendrix Experience, with drummer Mitch Mitchell and bassist Noel Redding (both white Englishmen). By the end of 1966 Hendrix's was the hottest name in British music. The *New Musical Express* called him "a one-man guitar explosion," and *Melody Maker* put him on its cover in February of 1967, noting that the guitarist had "broken box office records up and down the country."[26]

During his London days Hendrix's race was a topic of endless fascination. *Melody Maker*'s first major profile of Hendrix contained the following description: "He possesses the aura of a man who has seen and been through a lot of life. His own started in Seattle, Washington, in 1945, and took off from there. Tenements, rats and cockroaches, poverty, colour prejudice, hitching around the South, the occasional gig. Eventually he joined a blues tour but was soon penniless again."[27] While this description contains numerous inaccuracies (including the year of Hendrix's birth, which was 1942), it clearly seeks to position Hendrix within the lineage of the premodern, itinerant bluesman and its attendant fantasies of outlaw authenticity. Hendrix had surely paid his dues as a musician, but he'd grown up in the north, attended an integrated high school, and served as a paratrooper in the military. Jimi Hendrix was many things, but Robert Johnson was not one of them.

Still, many British music fans held their own fantasies of black musical authenticity, and Hendrix represented the physical embodiment of these. In a 1968 interview with *Rolling Stone,* Hendrix's friend Eric Clapton remarked:

> When he first came to England, you know English people have a very big thing towards a spade. They really love that magic thing, the sexual thing. They all fall for that sort of thing. Everybody and his brother in England still sort of think that spades have big dicks. And Jimi came over and exploited that to the limit, the fucking tee. Everybody fell for it.[28]

While Clapton's quote has lived in infamy, its sentiment speaks bluntly to an entwinement of musical and racial imagination with which Clapton himself was surely familiar. The 1960s had already seen an explosion of young British musicians onto the international musical scene, and while the backgrounds

and styles of these musicians varied widely, almost all were profoundly indebted to African American musical traditions. Years
after Hendrix's death, the Who's Pete Townshend told writer
Charles Shaar Murray that

> there was a tremendous sense of him choosing to play in the
> white arena, that he was coming along and saying, "You've
> taken this, Eric Clapton, and Mr. Townshend, you think
> you're a showman. This is how *we* do it. This is how we can do
> it when we take back what you've borrowed, if not stolen . . ."
> There was a real vengeance there.[29]

While it's likely that Townshend was projecting some of his
own confessed discomfort with Hendrix onto his interactions
with the guitarist, his words indicate the complex economy
of exchange that these musicians found themselves operating
within, and the precarious racial dynamics of such transactions.
In England Hendrix's blackness was a potent if combustible
commodity, a marker of authenticity, desire, envy, and always
difference.

Hendrix's race would become the topic of even greater fixation upon his breakthrough into international stardom. The
Jimi Hendrix Experience's set at the Monterey Pop Festival—
immortalized in D. A. Pennebaker's film of the concert, *Monterey
Pop*—remains one of the most iconic performances in popular
music. The set included an assortment of the guitarist's U.K.
hits as well as a litany of covers, including Howlin' Wolf's "Killing
Floor" and Bob Dylan's "Like a Rolling Stone." The most widely
discussed number was the Experience's rendition of the Troggs'
"Wild Thing," which closed the set and culminated in Hendrix
setting fire to his guitar onstage.[30]

Hendrix's music was virtuosic and titillating. His performance style played into myths of black male sexual potency

and produced a complex and occasionally tense relationship between the guitarist and his overwhelmingly white concert audiences. Steve Waksman has described Hendrix's guitar as a
"technophallus," "an electronic appendage that allowed Hendrix
to display his instrumental and, more symbolically, his sexual
prowess."[31] Feminist critic Germaine Greer articulated this dynamic more directly in a 1970 obituary for the guitarist, in which
she described Hendrix's audience at the Isle of Wight Festival
shortly before he passed away:

> They wanted him to give head to the guitar and rub it over his
> cock. They didn't want to hear him play, but Jimi wanted, as
> he always wanted, to play it sweet and high. So he did it, and
> he fucked with his guitar, and they moaned and swayed
> about, and he looked at them heavily and knew that they
> couldn't hear what he was trying to do and they never
> would.[32]

Hendrix's race produced a crisis in popular-music discourse.
He presented a mix of stereotype and subversion, seemingly
playing to racist clichés of black menace and sexuality while performing music that contradicted contemporary expectations of
black sound. One of the most common accusations lobbed at
Hendrix in this period was that of racial inauthenticity, or even
race treachery. After Monterey a young Robert Christgau wrote
a scathing appraisal of Hendrix's performance in the pages of
Esquire, describing Hendrix as "terrible" and accusing him of
being "just an Uncle Tom" who "had tailored a caricature to [the
audience's] mythic standards and apparently didn't even overdo
it a shade."[33]

The "Uncle Tom" remark is startling, and because of Christgau's later fame as music critic for the *Village Voice* it has had a
long and frankly undeserved afterlife. In context the epithet is

clearly meant as much as a commentary on the audience's reaction to Hendrix as it is on Hendrix himself, and Christgau, more so than many of his peers, was often highly critical of racial attitudes in the white rock counterculture—in fact, he spent a significant portion of the same article decrying the "paucity of Negro acts" at Monterey.[34] And Christgau was by no means the only critic to make similar claims about Hendrix during this period. In early 1968 the *Washington Post* wrote that "Jimi Hendrix is the P. T. Barnum of rock. He assesses, and fills, the needs of his crowd. His blackness is an Uncle Tom blackness."[35] The article also noted that "it is entirely necessary, in fact, that Hendrix is a Negro. His music is Chuck Berry filtered through the Beatles and the West Coast electronic freak-out, back through a black man to a 99 per cent white audience," a sentiment conveyed more caustically by Richard Goldstein, who remarked in his own review of Hendrix's Monterey performance: "his major asset seems to be his hue."[36] *Rolling Stone* magazine eschewed the Uncle Tom epithet but wondered if Hendrix was simply a "psychedelic superspade."[37] Never one to be outdone, in a *New York* magazine article entitled "SuperSpade Raises Atlantis," Albert Goldman mused on what he saw as Hendrix's preference of "playing to almost exclusively white audiences" and "consorting with white women" and concluded that "Hendrix's blackness is only skin deep."[38]

Such commentary casts multiple layers of aspersions on Hendrix's person and music. By playing to white audiences in a "rock" style, Hendrix was accused of being an inauthentic black man; by calculatedly pandering to his audience's fantasies, he was an inauthentic performer; by virtue of his race, he was an inauthentic rock star, simply a curiosity. After all, one cannot conceive of an equivalent slur to "psychedelic superspade" being directed at, say, John Lennon or Jim Morrison during this period—its entire function is to mark Hendrix as an outsider, as Other.

African American writers were also ambivalent toward Hendrix, similarly preoccupied over his credibility as a black artist. One of the earliest mentions of Hendrix in the African American media came in an article in the *Chicago Defender* that compared Hendrix to the Young Rascals (a white soul group) in arguing that traditional race-based distinctions between white and black music no longer applied; while the article was generally positive, the clear implication was that the white Rascals were making "black" music while Hendrix was not.[39] Others were far less charitable; writing in the *Washington Post*, African American columnist Hollie West complained of Hendrix's "watered down black sexual imagery" and "absurd mélange of electronic sound and guitar burnings."[40]

Throughout his career Hendrix deflected attempts at categorization from all sides, characterizing his own music in extraterrestrial, supernatural terms. The Jimi Hendrix Experience's first album, *Are You Experienced?*, released in August of 1967, was a watershed in psychedelia: tracks such as "Purple Haze," "May This Be Love," and "The Wind Cries Mary" linked the opaque lyrical style of Bob Dylan to a musical experimentalism that chased after noisy futurism, cutting-edge studio trickery, and breathtaking guitar virtuosity. His second album, *Axis: Bold as Love,* found the guitarist embracing quieter and more lyrical styles on tracks such as "Little Wing," "Wait Until Tomorrow," and "Castles Made of Sand," each of which bore the strong influence of R&B star Curtis Mayfield.

By the time of the Experience's third album, a double LP entitled *Electric Ladyland* and released in October of 1968, Hendrix was moving in still new directions.[41] While officially credited to the Jimi Hendrix Experience, large portions of *Electric Ladyland* featured guest artists, or simply Hendrix overdubbing parts himself. The album opened with a one-minute-and-twenty-second introduction, cryptically titled ". . . And the Gods Made

Love," then burst into its sumptuous title track, the Mayfield-infused "Have You Ever Been (to Electric Ladyland)." The album boasted crisp rhythm and blues ("Crosstown Traffic," "Long Hot Summer Night"), dreamy pop ("Burning of the Midnight Lamp"), and a cover of Earl King's New Orleans standard "Come On (Let the Good Times Roll)."

Electric Ladyland also contained an air of violence and ominousness that was stronger and starker than on his first two albums. Since Hendrix's meteoric rise to stardom, violence had been a recurring fixation in discussions of his music. Goldstein had characterized his Monterey performance in the *Voice* as "a strange moment for the love generation, aroused by all that violent sexuality into a mesmerized ovation."[42] The *Los Angeles Times* wrote that "his appearance, with wildly backcombed hair and a fantastically colored wardrobe of embroidered satin gear, is violent and his guitar-smashing, musically-crashing act is even more violent."[43] The *Washington Post* described Hendrix as "more evil than Elvis ever dreamed of being," and the *Chicago Tribune* wrote that Hendrix's music "lets you know there is a war in Viet Nam and there will be more big city riots next summer . . . there are things like sex and drugs and violence which people are afraid to talk about but maybe should."[44]

On *Electric Ladyland* the two most striking tracks in this regard came at the LP's end, a cover of Bob Dylan's "All along the Watchtower," which became a hit in the fall of 1968, and "Voodoo Child (Slight Return)," a ravaging sprawl of blues-infused mayhem that remains one of Hendrix's best-known performances.

Described by critic John Morthland as "galactic Muddy Waters," the verse structure of "Voodoo Child (Slight Return)" is twelve bars long and employs a strophic, A-A-B lyrical scheme, in the fashion of a classic blues.[45] "Voodoo Child" is a tour de force of guitar playing, and Hendrix's instrument dominates the track. The album's stereo mix makes the sound of Hendrix's guitar swoop between channels, savage and snarling, saturating sonic space. The instrument itself becomes an intricate tapestry of sound: we can hear the bending of strings, the attack of his pick, the pop and hiss of the pickups. The lyrical content of the song is distinctly tumultuous, even apocalyptic, from its opening lines—"Well I stand up next to a mountain / chop it down with the edge of my hand"—to its final couplet: "I don't need you no more in this world / I'll meet you on the next one, so don't be late."

"Voodoo Child (Slight Return)" took Hendrix's preoccupation with violence to new heights, both lyrically and musically: the world-destroying imagery, the pounding drums, the overdriven distortion, the swaying, thrashing Fender Stratocaster. In fact, the mood of violence is established before the song even begins, during its famous introduction. The track opens with Hendrix employing a pick-scratching technique to his guitar strings— rhythmically running his pick across the strings with his left hand while using his right to mute the fretboard (Hendrix was left-handed) so that conventional tones are not produced, almost like one would play a washboard—then playing a two-bar, minor-pentatonic riff on a guitar run through a wah-wah pedal.

While it's impossible to know who the first guitar player was to rhythmically scratch a pick across muted strings, for Hendrix's purposes it's likely that his most immediate influence for the technique was Jimmy Nolen, a guitarist in James Brown's band, who employed the maneuver—often referred to as the "chicken scratch"—on many of Brown's mid-to-late 1960s recordings.[46] Nolen used the "chicken scratch" primarily as a rhythm-guitar technique; when Hendrix brought the device to his music, it was more often a sort of flourish or trope, one that often served as a musical signifier of violence. The most direct example of this is "Machine Gun," in which the scratching is actually used to aurally imitate the sound of a weapon, but the effect can also be heard in Hendrix's cover of Bob Dylan's "All along the Watchtower," the track that precedes "Voodoo Child (Slight Return)" on *Electric Ladyland* and that reached the Top 20 on the *Billboard* Pop charts in the fall of 1968, the biggest U.S. hit of Hendrix's career.[47]

In musical style and recording technique "All along the Watchtower" shares little in common with "Voodoo Child (Slight Return)." "Watchtower" is centered around a two-bar, three-chord vamp that repeats throughout the song and boasts a driving performance on drums by Mitch Mitchell.[48] The recording is lush and airy, with layers upon layers of guitar, acoustic and electric, and a active, highly melodic bass line played by Hendrix himself. As opposed to the electrified tumult of "Voodoo Child," Hendrix's guitar here is careful and lyrical, full of fills and flourishes, the song's solo sections a dazzling array of textures and techniques, from reverb-drenched slidework to trembling wah-wah to blindingly fast melodic runs.

The lyrical content of "Watchtower" is all ominous portent, its text a litany of cryptic Dylanisms: " 'There must be some kind of way out of here,' / said the joker to the thief," is the song's opening couplet, its language evoking both general paranoia and the Animals' 1965 hit "We Gotta Get Out of This Place."[49] While Dylan's original version of "Watchtower" is spare, haunting, and ambiguous, Hendrix takes the text's latent dread and explodes it.[50] As the musicologist Albin Zak has written, "Dylan's arrangement imparts an air of detachment, while Hendrix, in deepening the musical problem both sonically and syntactically, situates himself firmly at the center of the song."[51]

A crucial device in accomplishing this effect is the same scratching technique heard in the beginning of "Voodoo Child," which is here performed on an overdriven twelve-string acoustic guitar: the sound is first heard in between the lines "there's too much confusion / I can't get no relief" during the first verse, then throughout the song, always in short, staccato bursts; Hendrix also employs the technique on the electric guitar, in the fourth chorus of his extended guitar solo in between the song's second and third verses. Again we hear the scratching technique employed as a marker of violence and turmoil. Such moments abound in "Watchtower," perhaps most notably following the song's final line—"two riders were approaching / and the wind began to howl"—when Hendrix plays an ascending, tremolo guitar line that resembles nothing so much as howling wind itself.

Electric Ladyland was the final studio album released in Hendrix's lifetime. For all of Hendrix's renown as a live performer, "Voodoo Child (Slight Return)" and "All along the Watchtower" are extraordinary displays of recording technique and studio invention. As Waksman writes, the recording studio was "a sonic sanctuary where Hendrix could escape the burdens of performing according to a set of expectations that he had helped to foster and yet had no ability to manage, expectations that came with the position of being a black hipster artist playing amidst the predominantly white counterculture of the late 1960s."[52] The utopian space of the recording studio was the only location where Hendrix's race was effectively rendered invisible, and he was free to explore sound entirely on its own terms. "Voodoo Child" and "Watchtower" exemplify these explorations and also demonstrate that Hendrix's sonic epiphanies were growing increasingly violent.

Nineteen sixty-nine was a transitional year for Hendrix; early on he replaced bassist Noel Redding with Billy Cox, an African American rhythm and blues player who was a friend of the guitarist's from his army days. Hendrix became more reclusive, spending extensive amounts of time with blues and jazz musicians at a mansion in upstate New York and clearly searching for new directions. Attendant to these shifting musical and professional ambitions was an increased interest in reaching out to the African American community. "It bothers me that some black people now can't get into our music right away because they are so hung up about other things," he told a British interviewer in early 1969, a provocative if typically cryptic statement.[53] Hendrix's popularity among black listeners—or lack thereof—has long been a subject of controversy, and Hendrix received far more coverage in the mainstream white press and more airplay on white radio stations than he did in the African American press or on black radio stations.[54] Hendrix never appeared on the *Billboard* R&B charts, although this may have had more to do with *Billboard*'s charting practices than actual sales.[55]

As the year wore on, Hendrix was exploring new and more explicit racial politics in both his musical practice and his personal dealings. He was increasingly drawn to the Black Power movement and had even begun introducing "Voodoo Child (Slight Return)" as the "Black Panthers' national anthem" during live performances.[56] In September of 1969 Hendrix played a benefit for the United Block Association (UBA) in Harlem; reporting on the event, the *New York Amsterdam News* pointedly noted that "many people in the black community are unaware of Hendrix as being an entertainer," although the two thousand audience members that the newspaper reported in attendance suggest otherwise.[57] He was particularly attuned to racial violence, and its relation to power, telling an interviewer:

"They make black and white fight against each other so they can take over at each end. If they can get the Black Panthers fighting the hippies—who are really the young whites—then we will all be right back where we started off 20 years ago. This, it seems to me, is what they are trying to do."[58]

And yet Hendrix remained steadfastly resistant to racial confines on his creative output. At the Harlem UBA benefit he told an interviewer, "Sometimes when I come here people say, 'he plays white rock for white people. What's he doing up here?' Well, I want to show them that music is universal—that there is no white rock or black rock."[59] Asked the following year about rumors that he was starting an "all-black recording enterprise," Hendrix dismissed the idea, describing it as "like being Catholic or something," a remark that hints at a belief that race was imaginary and ideological, to be accepted or rejected, believed or disbelieved.[60] He extended this to other musicians as well: asked by an interviewer from *Jazz & Pop* about white blues guitarist Mike Bloomfield's band, Hendrix replied, "The Bloomfield band is ridiculously out of sight and you can feel what they're doing no matter what color the eyes or armpits might be. . . . [L]ike I said before, it all depends on how your ears are together and how your mind is and where your ears are."[61]

On December 31, 1969, and January 1, 1970, Hendrix, Cox, and drummer Buddy Miles united to play four shows over two nights at New York City's Fillmore East, under the name Band of Gypsys. The shows were recorded, and March of 1970 the album *Band of Gypsys* was released on Capitol Records.[62] Band of Gypsys was the only band Hendrix ever fronted that featured an all-black lineup; the group ended up playing together for less than a month, their final show a disastrous appearance at a Madison Square Garden benefit concert in which Hendrix, allegedly under the influence of bad acid, got in a verbal altercation with an audience member and left the stage.[63] Miles was fired shortly thereafter, and Hendrix rehired Mitch Mitchell, with whom he would play, alongside Billy Cox, until the end of his life.

Band of Gypsys is the only authorized live recording of Hendrix released during his lifetime, and it is probably best known for its second track, a twelve-minute opus entitled "Machine Gun." "Machine Gun" is a searing meditation on violence and war, a sprawling piece of music that features some of the most inventive guitar work of Hendrix's recorded catalogue. The track opens with the following spoken introduction by Hendrix, in which he dedicates the song to "all the soldiers that are fighting in Chicago, and Milwaukee, and New York. Oh yes, and all the soldiers fighting in Vietnam." Hendrix then begins playing his guitar, alone, four bars of wah-wah blues guitar. At the beginning of the fifth bar he returns to the pick-scratching technique heard at the beginning of "Voodoo Child (Slight Return)" and throughout "All along the Watchtower," and the rapid-fire sixteenth notes are clearly imitative of a machine gun itself. After four more bars the drums come in, playing the same rhythmic device, and the effect is unmistakable, Hendrix using his instrument and band to create a direct invocation of war through music.

Unlike "Voodoo Child" and "Watchtower," "Machine Gun" is a modal piece of music: the song is in D Dorian and contains no chord changes to speak of. Its lyrical text is sparse and impressionistic—"Machine gun, tearing my body all apart" is the song's opening line, repeated twice. Hendrix doubles his vocal melody on the guitar, obscuring the lyrics, which are pointedly vague, occasional references to "farmers" and "bombs" suggesting Vietnam while the "only families apart" sentiment implies something domestic.

At the time of *Band of Gypsys* much had already been written of Hendrix's rendition of "The Star-Spangled Banner" in the early morning hours of the Woodstock Music and Art Festival in August of 1969, a performance that found the guitarist re-imagining his country's most famous song at one of the most iconic events of the decade.[64] The real meaning of Hendrix's "Banner" is difficult to pin down, though: for all of the speculation that the invocation "Taps" near its end suggests a statement on Vietnam, biographer Charles Cross points out that Hendrix himself never declared it as such, and a few weeks later Hendrix suggested that the performance may have been given in the spirit of patriotism: "We're all Americans . . . it was like, 'Go America!' "[65] Hendrix's "Star-Spangled Banner" is a pointedly ambiguous statement, clear in its sonic adventurousness but less so in its politics.

"Machine Gun" is a far more explicit and darker meditation on violence, war, and betrayals of humanity. One of the most interesting facets of the song's lyrics is its preoccupation with technology: "I pick up my axe and fight like a farmer," sings Hendrix, a metaphor that, juxtaposed against the weapon of the song's title, suggests a world upended by misbegotten progress, and that carries a knowing nod to the militarized potential of Hendrix's own instrument ("axe" being a common slang word for guitar). This conceit is all the more striking in light of the degree to which Hendrix himself was preoccupied with technology, with regards to the studio techniques discussed previously and also simply to his own instrument: the very pick-scratching technique, crackling through Hendrix's Marshall amplifier in imitation of the song's title, is a product of modern technology, yet another way in which Hendrix's guitar and the gun become one and the same.

By the dawn of 1970 Hendrix seemed to be unraveling: firing his band, then firing his new band, creatively striving but frustrated by confinements forced upon him. The musician who had long spoken of music in the terms of limitless potential seemed increasingly torn in different directions. Before the Band of Gypsys shows Hendrix confessed a desire "to get back to the blues, because that's what I am," an uncharacteristic statement from a musician who tended to speak solely in terms of progress, and who was normally loath to present his own music as being a "return" to anything.[66] "Machine Gun" can be heard as a sort of undoing, its seriousness and gravity tinged with ambivalence, performed by a man who imagined music as a transformative force but was surveying a world that seemed inured to correction.

Less than ten months after the New Year's shows at the Fillmore East, Hendrix was dead, a victim of an overdose of sleeping pills at the London flat of his German girlfriend, Monika Danneman. As in life, coverage of Hendrix's death fixated upon his race. In a story detailing Danneman's insistence at the inquest that Hendrix had not seemed depressed on the eve of his overdose, the *Philadelphia Tribune* ran the salacious headline "Black Rock Singer Died Happy Man, Blond Moans."[67] The *Los Angeles Times* called him "the first black sex symbol in rock music for white America," while the *Philadelphia Tribune* described him as "a kind of black sex symbol to thousands of female fans."[68] Hendrix had embodied the interracial possibilities of 1960s music as much as any other musician: a black man who'd trained on the rhythm and blues circuit, then moved to England to pioneer psychedelic rock alongside white musicians, then returned to America where he played with racially mixed bands. And yet in death he was still an outsider, an "alien."

More than forty years after his death Hendrix remains the lone black hero in the "classic rock" pantheon, his image endlessly memorialized on t-shirts, posters, tattoos, and other accoutrements of fandom, the single exception that confirms the essential whiteness of the genre's self-understanding.[69] Ironically, for a man whose authenticity was so widely debated in his life, he has become for rock ideology the embodiment of a vanished musical blackness that was lamented by writers even during his own career. Even more ironically, the primary way Hendrix has been incorporated into rock's construction of white male authenticity is the very tool he often used to resist it: his explorations of violence.

The topic of violence in rock music could fill a small library, and after the 1960s violent imagery in hard rock and heavy metal became ubiquitous as to be almost constitutive. The cover of Led Zeppelin's landmark first LP, released in January 1969, featured a photo of the *Hindenburg* disaster; one of Metallica's most beloved albums is titled *Kill 'Em All*; the names Black Sabbath, Megadeth, and Slayer speak for themselves. This obsession has often been understood in terms of a hyperaggressive masculinism that came to proliferate certain corners of rock music in the 1970s and beyond. In 1978 Simon Frith and Angela McRobbie wrote of a genre they called "cock rock," which they described as "music making in which performance is an explicit, crude, and often aggressive expression of male sexuality."[70] Jimi Hendrix's performance style, his "technophallus," was seen as hugely influential to the development of this musical ethos, so much so that Greg Tate calls cock rock "largely, and inadvertently, a Hendrix invention."[71] In his study of 1980s heavy metal, Robert Walser argued that while some of the violence and aggression in that form were misogynistic, much of it trafficked in what Walser deems "exscription," the use of an exaggerated masculinity to create a world in which women simply do not exist.[72] Walser describes Hendrix as one of heavy metal's most revered figures, and Steve Waksman also notes that Hendrix's music is often held up either as a direct predecessor to heavy metal or as an early example of the genre.[73]

And yet to hear Hendrix's flirtations with musical violence as simply promulgating an aggressively sexual, hegemonic masculinism would be to define his music in terms of that which came after it. Moreover, it reinscribes the very stereotypes of black male hypersexuality that haunted Hendrix in his own lifetime; unlike his later progeny Hendrix rarely sang about sex with any degree of explicitness.[74] One of the many tragedies of Hendrix's passing is that it allowed his own radicalism to be co-opted by scenes and genres that were often loudly and proudly reactionary, and which would have been even less hospitable to the guitarist than the musical world in which he lived. And Hendrix's own insistence that he and his music existed beyond category, his own denial of race's salience to musical activity, would be adopted by white rock music as a sort of strategic colorblindness, Hendrix's silent presence in rock iconography a bulwark against confronting its own whiteness. As Maureen Mahon writes, in rock circles Hendrix has become "not black, not white, just Jimi."[75] It is a deep irony that one of Jimi Hendrix's most enduring contributions to rock's racial imagination was the fact that he himself had so little use for it.

Coda: Carlos Santana and the New Beginning

If Hendrix had disrupted rock ideology's emergent racial definitions, he had not disrupted its starkly dichotomous conviction that music existed as either black or white, a dyad that, as the Introduction notes, continues to hold far too much sway in conversations about American popular music. In rock music this vocabulary received its first prominent challenge in the year before Hendrix's death, by a distinctly post-Hendrix figure, the electric-guitar virtuoso Carlos Santana.

Born in 1947 in Autlán de Navarro in the Mexican state of Jalisco, Carlos Santana's family moved to San Francisco when he was an adolescent. He first caught the attention of famed Bay Area promoter Bill Graham in 1966, when Santana was tabbed as a last-minute substitution for a gig at Graham's Fillmore West auditorium. When Santana put together his own band, first calling it the Carlos Santana Blues Band before shortening the name to Santana, the powerful and influential Graham was one of the group's most avid promoters. "What impressed me is that it was an attempt at fusing rock and Afro and Latino and getting a rhythmic sensuous sound into rock, which I've always thought it lacked in many cases," Graham told an interviewer in 1972.[76]

Partly through Graham's influence, Santana secured a slot at the Woodstock festival before the group had even released an album, where they wowed spectators. Their self-titled debut was released on Columbia shortly after the festival and reached number four on the *Billboard* charts, buoyed by the buzz generated from the band's Woodstock performance as well as the band's popular cover of Clarence Henry's "Evil Ways," which became a Top 10 hit. In 1970 the group returned with *Abraxas*, which hit number one in the United States and produced two more hit singles, "Black Magic Woman" and "Oye Como Va." *Abraxas* would ultimately sell over five million copies, and it solidified Santana's status as rock and roll's first Latino superstar since the death of Ritchie Valens in 1959.

Santana's music was a unique and sprawling mélange of influences, one of the most prominent of which was Hendrix himself, although Santana generally tended to eschew feedback experimentation and other sonic pyrotechnics for a cleaner and more studiously melodic sound. He and his band were a product of the communitarian San Francisco scene that had spawned Big Brother and the Holding Company, the Grateful Dead, Sly and the Family Stone, and many others. Like the Family Stone, Santana's lineup was remarkably diverse, featuring (among others) a white drummer and second guitar player, an African American bass player, and a Nicaraguan percussionist.

Santana himself was unusual in that he was the front man for a rock band without being its lead singer, and he wasn't a particularly avid songwriter. The band's first three hits—"Evil Ways," "Black Magic Woman," and "Oye Como Va"—were all covers. Of course, Santana was also unusual in that he disrupted the black-and-white racial imagination of 1960s popular music discourse. All of this contributed to the profound confusion with which Santana was met upon his breakthrough, and early coverage of the group betrays something like a crisis of description. Their music was characterized variously as "Afro-flavored jazz," "Mexicano blues," "Mariachi rock," "Afro-Cuban rock," "supercharged Latin," "Rock 'n' Roll's answer to Xavier Cugat," a "fusing of Latin-jazz and rock," and "Chicano blues" that was "raw and basic, primitive in its percussive beat and demanding urgency."[77] This far-flung and somewhat incoherent collection of descriptions speaks to the originality of Santana's music and also the way he confounded rock music's racial imagination: there were surely some predictable, clumsy attempts at stereotyping, but for the most part there was simply bafflement. With a few exceptions the band was nearly universally praised but remained inscrutable.[78] The *Baltimore Sun* suggested that the band might have "a strong appeal for Third-World people," while the *Baltimore Afro-American* fell back on the topic of "soul," writing that the group was "proof that soul is not exclusively a black commodity . . . the Latin and African drums and rhythms fused beautifully with the electric guitars of group leader Carlos Santana and Neal Schon."[79]

In the wake of Santana's success there was also a run on trend pieces. The *New York Times* remarked that "rock with Latin influences has grown in vogue recently," while the *Hartford Courant* asked "Will La Lupe and Tito Puente be the next cultural heroes? Will the 'guido' take its place with the tambourine as a classic rhythm instrument?"[80] A *Rolling Stone* critic described the group as "a popularized Mongo Santamaria" and suggested that "they might do for Latin music what Chuck Berry did for the blues."[81]

This didn't really come to pass—while rock certainly maintained an occasional, if touristic, interest in Latin music through the 1970s and beyond, nearly a half century after his emergence Carlos Santana remains the most famous Latino rock star by a wide margin. Moreover, the suggestion that Santana was the first to bring "Latin" musical influences to the music was remarkably shortsighted: most contemporary coverage of Santana failed to mention Ritchie Valens, a strong indicator of the extent to which rock music had already whitewashed its early history, nor is there mention of mid-1960s Chicano-led groups like Sam the Sham and the Pharaohs, and the Mysterians, and Thee Midniters. Going back even further, Cuban music had long exerted considerable influence on American rhythm and blues, as both the "Bo Diddley beat" and Ned Sublette's scholarship on the subject attest.[82]

But the invocation of Chuck Berry is suggestive in that it speaks to an interesting sense of possibility that runs through much early writing on Santana—namely, the guitarist's potential as a figure of renewal. By the early 1970s some of the same critics who had championed rock's emancipatory potential in the

1960s were newly disillusioned with the state of the music. Massively successful bands like Grand Funk Railroad and Led Zeppelin prompted widespread critical opprobrium, not least of all for their purportedly perfidious relationship to African American blues and R&B.[83]

Santana offered a renewed contact with Otherness for the white genre of rock, a gateway to an untapped vein of exotic authenticity. Interestingly, the writer who gave perhaps the most full-throated voice to this conviction was Ralph Gleason himself, who just a few years earlier had praised rock music for moving away from black forms. Writing for *Rolling Stone* in 1972, Gleason effused:

> Santana is more deeply committed to the music defined and still played by Tito Puente, Machito, Mongo Santamaria, and all the glorious combinations of brass and rhythm that made the old Sunday afternoon dances such a delight, than to the Rolling Stones. . . . Sometime I would like to see an analysis of the rhythms and patterns used by Santana done by some ethno-musicologist who could relate them to traditional Cuban, African and Haitian music and styles. I suspect it would be quite revealing. I am convinced that this band . . . is solidly linked to the hill country, the savannahs and the inland plains music of Africa and Cuba and the other sources of that magic rhythmic power of which they are such compelling examples.[84]

This passage now reads as exoticizing to the point of near-absurdity. The "magic rhythmic power" that Gleason extolled was provided by drummer Michael Shrieve and bass player Douglas Rauch, both of the savannahs and inland plains of San Francisco. Santana's music was surely innovative, but the suggestion that one might require an ethnomusicologist to unlock its secrets is simply fanciful. For all of Gleason's effusiveness, his insistence that Santana's music lay so far outside of rock-and-roll tradition that the band had more in common with Tito Puente— born in Harlem to Puerto Rican parents in 1923—than they did with the Rolling Stones was simply another racial sorting mechanism dressed up as a musical one. In fact, Santana's biggest hit, "Black Magic Woman," was written by British blues guitar virtuoso Peter Green, cofounder of Fleetwood Mac and another of Santana's most prominent musical influences.

Santana's emergence reaffirmed the notion that anyone non-white coming to rock music would be doing so as an outsider, a fount of mystical, premodern source material to be mined for white fantasy. By turning Santana into an exotic cudgel with which to flail at contemporary music, by placing him outside of rock and roll tradition in order to elevate him to a pedestal of authenticity, writers and listeners missed just how much he fit into that tradition. Furthermore, they missed the possibility that perhaps there was an alternative tradition to be found all along, one in which Chuck Berry, Ritchie Valens, the Beatles, Bob Dylan, Jimi Hendrix, and Carlos Santana shared far more commonality than rock ideology was prepared to allow. Ironically, the white rock band who may have been most committed to this alternative tradition were also on their way to becoming perhaps the most racially troublesome in all of rock music: namely, the Rolling Stones. Their extraordinary adventures at the intersection of music, violence, and racial imagination are the subject of Chapter 6.

Just around Midnight

The Rolling Stones and the End of the Sixties

> There is at the heart of this music a deep strain of mysterious insurrection, and the music dies without it.
>
> —Stanley Booth, *The True Adventures of the Rolling Stones*

> Paint it black, you devil!
>
> —Female Rolling Stones fan, November 1969

ONE OF THE MOST IMPORTANT rock and roll records of the late 1960s came out of nowhere, even though it was recorded by the second-most famous band in the world. "Jumpin' Jack Flash," released by the Rolling Stones in May of 1968, opened with an overdriven and distorted acoustic guitar, pummeled by guitarist Keith Richards into a riff that sounded a little like "(I Can't Get No) Satisfaction" in reverse but that seemed to come from somewhere harsher and more desolate.[1] After eight bars of instrumental introduction, singer Mick Jagger grunted "watch it!" as the track exploded into a quagmire of guitars, bass, and drums. "I was born in a crossfire hurricane / and I howled at my ma in the drivin' rain" was the entirety of the first verse, as though the song itself could barely wait for its own chorus: "Jumpin' jack flash / it's a gas, gas, gas." The nonsensical playfulness of the phrase belied a lyrical text that was stalked by violent chaos. "I fell down to my feet and I saw they bled," sang Jagger; "I was crowned with a spike right through my head." The musical backdrop only added to the song's atmosphere, a propulsive machine of driving rhythm and angry distortion, all clinging to Richards's churning guitars.

The lyrics to "Jumpin' Jack Flash" were grim and opaque, and when Jagger slurred "I was drowned / I was washed up and left for dead" at the beginning of the song's final verse, the sentiment was fitting, as only a few months earlier the Rolling Stones had been in a state of crisis that appeared to threaten their very existence. While 1967 had been an extraordinary year in popular music generally—one that saw, among other things, the release of the Beatles' *Sgt. Pepper's Lonely Hearts Club Band*, and the rise of Aretha Franklin, Jimi Hendrix, Janis Joplin, the Doors, and Sly and the Family Stone—for the Rolling Stones it had been calamitous. In February Jagger and Richards had been arrested in a widely publicized drug bust at Redlands, Richards's estate in Sussex, and the attendant trial drew international attention for much of the year. During the same period Richards began an affair with Anita Pallenberg, the girlfriend of the Stones' other guitarist, Brian Jones, exacerbating already-strained relations between Jones and his bandmates. By the end of 1967 the group would part ways with its longtime manager and producer, Andrew Loog Oldham, who had overseen the Stones' rise from London club act to international stardom.

The pressures wrought by the Redlands trial and personal and professional tensions caused the band's creative pace to slow, but finally in December a new album arrived. Adorned with an ornate hologram cover and the bizarre title *Their Satanic Majesties Request,* the LP found the Stones venturing curiously far down the newly paved pathways of psychedelia.[2] *Satanic Majesties* was clearly influenced by the Beatles' *Sgt. Pepper,* and it suggested that for all their successes the Stones remained preoccupied by the enormous shadow of their countrymen. Musically, *Satanic Majesties* presented a bold departure from the ramshackle R&B that had gained the group its biggest successes; it was undoubtedly the Rolling Stones' most musically adventurous project to date.

It was also a disaster. *Their Satanic Majesties Request* was the band's first album that failed to yield a Top 10 hit in either the United Kingdom or the United States. "This could be art for art's sake," speculated *Melody Maker.* "But what emerges is merely studio teamwork, dedicated at being obscure, at hinting, at nudging and playing children's games with instruments, musical and otherwise."[3] Stateside, *Rolling Stone* magazine called it "insecure" and "embarrassing," while the *Los Angeles Times* lamented its "excesses of gimmickry."[4] The Rolling Stones had capped a year of turmoil and upheaval—one in which the artistic landscape of popular music had profoundly and definitively shifted—with an album that was widely viewed as the worst they'd ever made.

When "Jumpin' Jack Flash" reached number three on the American charts and number one in the United Kingdom in the early summer of 1968, it revived and transformed the Rolling Stones.[5] After the disaster of *Their Satanic Majesties Request,* the Stones had made a musical rebuttal to the entire ethos that spawned it, the first great "answer record" to psychedelia. It was, in some senses, a return to the band's roots—upon the single's release the *Chicago Tribune* described the song as "back in the old blues-hard rock vein of 'Satisfaction' and 'Get Off of My Cloud' "— but it was also a single that took a sidelong glance at the receding Summer of Love and loudly announced it wanted nothing to do with it.[6] "Jumpin' Jack Flash" did all this through an aesthetic that embraced a thundering and explosive vision of musical violence, one that would carry the Rolling Stones through the end of the 1960s and beyond.

This chapter explores the music of the Rolling Stones at the close of the 1960s, a period of creative triumph for the band that also saw them become arguably the most iconic rock band of all time. While the Beatles' musical and commercial impacts surely outstripped those of the Stones, the stance that the Rolling Stones staked out in the late 1960s has likely exceeded the Fab Four in terms of its hold on the rock imaginary. The hedonism, the sexual transgressions, the intimations of Satanism, the air of violence and evil that were cultivated by the band, then lavishly embellished by fans and commentators: all of these were pioneered by the Rolling Stones during this period. In the 1970s the group's influence could be seen across far-flung corners of the genre, from the antic freneticism of Iggy Pop to the sullen swagger of the Ramones to the leering arena blues of Led Zeppelin and Aerosmith.[7] It is a great truism of popular music that there has never been another Beatles: while there has never been another Rolling Stones either, I would argue the history of rock music has seen considerably more attempts toward the latter.

Crucial to the fomentation of the Rolling Stones' mythology was the band's purported connection to blackness and racial transgression, both in a musical sense and a more vague, imaginative one. As this chapter shows, from their earliest coverage in both the British and American presses the Stones were characterized as harboring a preternatural fluency within black music and a prodigious knowledge of blues and rhythm and blues traditions. One of the band's earliest Decca Records press releases wrote of their "fanatic interest in R&B" and stated that the band learned their "uninhibited blues" from obsessive practice and "a record player on which they constantly played discs by artists like Chuck Berry, Bo Diddley, Little Walter and Jimmy Reed."[8] The Rolling Stones were also described as a public menace, scourges to society, the embodiment of all the fears of generational overthrow and cultural disruption that the cuter and cuddlier Beatles had so effectively managed to sublimate. Opining on the band in the *New York Post* in 1965, columnist Pete Hamill warned his readers: "We are the enemy, of course, you and I, because these are children and only children can sustain hatred of such pure fury. The Stones are the rococo to the Beatles baroque, and what had once seemed fresh and effortless with the Beatles has now turned nasty and predictable with the Stones . . . their moving passion is contempt."[9]

I will argue that these two narratives were not separate, but rather inextricably conjoined—hysteria around the band, particularly in their early, formative years, was keyed in the language and imagery of race and racial threat. As the 1960s progressed, the Rolling Stones' ongoing proximity to black music and musicians increasingly left them as outliers in a rock-music landscape rapidly distancing itself from black people, their musical-cum-racial mixings further validating the air of general transgression that the band and its handlers had long cultivated. "Paint it black, you devil!" a female fan shouts at Jagger before the Stones launch into "Sympathy for the Devil" on *Get Yer Ya Ya's Out,* a live album recorded in late 1969 at Madison Square Garden, just days before the band's disastrous appearance at Altamont Speedway: this chapter will show just how deeply her sentiment resounded.

The Rolling Stones' relationship to black music, and race it-self, is among the most complex and controversial of any white artists in the history of rock and roll. Over the long course of their stardom the band has weathered charges of minstrelsy from Black Arts Movement poets and white academics alike.[10] Yet for all of the long-standing and ongoing controversies over the ethics and particulars of the Rolling Stones' relationship to black music, the band was fiercely committed to a future for rock and roll in which black music and musicians continued to matter, deeply. During a moment in which rock-and-roll music was exploding in any number of directions, the Rolling Stones, a white British rhythm and blues band, presented a vision of the music obsessively rooted in tradition, and a black musical tradition specifically. While Jimi Hendrix's music had gestured toward supernatural utopia, the Rolling Stones embraced a pe-culiar role of conservators of a musical past that they had bor-rowed by their own admission and doggedly tried to make their own.

Like Hendrix, the Rolling Stones' experimentations with the musical future were rooted in a fascination with violence, ex-emplified in songs such as "Sympathy for the Devil," "Street Fighting Man," "Gimme Shelter," "Brown Sugar," and, of course, "Jumpin' Jack Flash." The Stones' flirtations with musical vio-lence during this period were creatively invigorating but ulti-mately brushed up against reality in catastrophic fashion. The murder of Meredith Hunter at their free concert at Altamont in December 1969 remains one of the more legendary night-mares of the 1960s, and it irrevocably altered the band's position within the public imagination.

In the aftermath of the 1960s the Stones would become the ar-chetypal rock band for all time, Jagger's and Richards's perfor-mance styles so naturalized that it would soon be notable when a rock star didn't sneer, slur, and strut. The Stones' obsession with black music and black musicians simply became part of the Rolling Stones, the band who'd wanted to be Muddy Waters now surrounded by a world of rock musicians that wanted to be them. This transition—the shift from the Rolling Stones being heard as the authenticated, to the Rolling Stones being heard as the authentic—is among the most significant turns in the racial imagination of rock.

Play with Fire: The Rolling Stones and Race

One of the many ironies of the Rolling Stones is that a band that has, at the time of this writing, existed for more than fifty years and has been touring under the mantel of "the world's greatest rock and roll band" for more than forty of them, never set out to be a rock and roll band at all. As described in Chapter 2, the Rolling Stones were born from the subcultural cauldron of British blues, an ersatz folk revival in which young British men developed obsessive relationships with African American music and the doorway to mystical authenticity and escape from postwar British whiteness that it provided. Early press coverage of the band went out of its way to emphasize that the group was strictly a blues or rhythm and blues band: "They are, they claim, first and foremost a rhythm-and-blues group. If you refer to them as a beat outfit, they frown. If you venture to suggest that they play rock 'n' roll, they positively glower."[11]

British blues had a relationship with black music that was deeply reverent but also fetishistic, the music's content often inseparable from its perceived danger and subversive liminality. As Adam Gussow has argued, the Southern blues tradition that the Rolling Stones and other British musicians so studiously absorbed is itself plagued by violence, both in its content and its broader relation to structures of racial terror in the American

South.[12] Fantasies of the blues' "threatening" capacity for social rebellion, as identified by Bryan Wagner and discussed in Chapter 5, took on uniquely powerful imaginative dimensions in England, where black American bodies were generally absent. From the beginning of their careers in England the Stones were linked to African American music, through both the imaginative work of journalists and the band's own self-presentation. The group unfailingly went out of its way to name-drop its influences: Mick Jagger told *Melody Maker* in early 1964, "We have always favoured the music of what we consider the R&B greats—Muddy Waters, Jimmy Reed, and so on—and we would like to think that we are helping to give the fans of these artists what they want," and in an accompanying profile the band listed its favorite artists as Reed, Waters, Chuck Berry, Bo Diddley, Ray Charles, and John Lee Hooker.[13]

The Rolling Stones did not take their own success as evidence of "colorblindness" or racial neutrality, and they often expressed frustration that their own performances of rhythm and blues were more popular among their countrymen than the original versions they so revered.[14] Some of the most pointed of these remarks came in an article written "by" the Stones for *Melody Maker* in 1964, when Jagger acknowledged that "it's the system that's sometimes wrong. Girl fans, particularly, would rather have a copy by a British group than the original American version—mainly, I suppose, because they like the British blokes' faces."[15] The sexism of this passage aside, Jagger's suggestion that the fans "like the British blokes' faces" implies that the singer recognized that the Stones' skin color had given them an undue advantage among audiences.

The Rolling Stones, particularly early on, were many things—controversial, musically erratic, image-obsessed—but they did not avoid the topic of race, or its salience to their own commercial success. This may explain an underexplored and perhaps unexpected aspect of the early career of the Rolling Stones: namely, the unusual enthusiasm with which the band was received by the African American press. In 1964 the *Los Angeles Sentinel* called the group "wonderful" and wrote that "each [member] has enough talent to take him well beyond the capabilities of the group."[16] A column in the *Chicago Defender* wrote that "the Stones are worth everyone's attention. Many of us are ardent R&B followers and believe me, the Stones are no less ardent. They love and feel this music and if the money was taken away, you would still find them playing and singing R&B. . . . [T]he Stones are R&B men in the truest sense."[17] In October 1965, the *Defender* printed an interview with Muddy Waters in which Waters said, "The Rolling Stones, sure I dig them, they're a part of me. . . . Those boys jam." The paper then quipped, "The man has spoken. Take a bow Stones."[18]

Such notices are more remarkable in light of the fact that a large portion of white press attention directed at the band was scathing, although much of this was orchestrated by the group's manager, Andrew Loog Oldham. In February of 1964 the Rolling Stones released their third single, a cover of Buddy Holly's "Not Fade Away"; it reached number three on the U.K. singles charts and turned the group into full-fledged stars.[19] That month also marked the first time that a writer named Ray Coleman profiled the band for *Melody Maker*, and over the coming months no journalist would wield more influence in shaping media coverage of the band.

Coleman's stories went to great lengths to chronicle public revulsion at the Rolling Stones. In his first profile, published in the February 8, 1964, issue, Coleman wrote of an anonymous taxi driver who "loathed the Rolling Stones. Like certain others he considers them downright scruffy, hairy horrors." In the interview portion of the story the band actually protested their own image, but Coleman disregards this, writing that "although they deny it, the truth is that they are angry young rebels who scorn conformity." The article closed with a description of the Stones leaving the restaurant where the interview had taken place: "People eating lunch looked up, aghast at such a sight."[20]

Coleman's coverage of the band in this period was consistently pitched in such tones: superficially sympathetic toward the band while insisting that polite British society loathed them. As a promotional strategy it was brilliant, positioning the Stones on one hand as deviant scofflaws, on the other as underdogs besieged by conservative moralism. In March of 1964 *Melody Maker* announced the band's forthcoming American tour with a screaming front-page headline: "Stones for States! Group Parents Hate Makes Big Hit." The same issue featured an article by Coleman that opened thusly: "What is your conception of the five far-out figures who make up the Rolling Stones? Nice boys—or ugly cave men? Do you wake in the middle of the night screaming with horror at the faces that stared at you from the TV screen a few hours earlier?"[21]

The most notorious piece of *Melody Maker* Stones coverage came in the March 14, 1964, issue, another piece by Coleman that was adorned with the headline "Would You Let Your Sister Go Out with a Rolling Stone?" The piece itself was fairly tame and by this point formulaic, each attempt at generating controversy vague and suspiciously undersourced. There was a claim that "elders groan with horror at the Rolling Stones" to go along with the rumored existence of a letter from an unnamed fan whose parents had barred her from attending a Stones concert.[22] The "Would You Let Your . . ." question would become iconic, though, appearing in various iterations in both the American and British presses, "sister" and "daughter" often substituted interchangeably.[23]

The scandal-driven discourse followed the band to the United States. When the Stones arrived in the United States in June of 1964 for their first American tour, the *Chicago Tribune* declared: "Thank you, Rolling Stones. You have been able to convince the world that no one, not even the Beatles, could be more repulsive than you."[24] Huge swaths of American coverage focused on their physical appearance, particularly their hair. The *Tribune* ran a story about a barber attempting to forcibly give the band a haircut: "The visit of the Rolling Stones, who say they are singers, ended abruptly yesterday on North Michigan avenue. A barber came along. . . . All wear tight trousers and haggard looks. All of them slouch. Each look unkempt."[25] The *New York Times* ran two lengthy articles on "androgynous" hairstyles and reported that the city of Cleveland would soon prohibit rock and roll performances at that city's Public Hall: "The ban goes into effect after tonight's Public Hall appearance of the Rolling Stones, another group of shaggy-haired English singers."[26] The *Los Angeles Times* compared the Rolling Stones to cavemen, chimpanzees, and "very ugly Radcliffe girls."[27]

A common aspect of nearly all the negative attention paid to the Rolling Stones by the American and British mainstream presses is the degree to which it traffics in the language and imagery of racial threat. The obsessions with physical appearance, the dehumanizing comparisons to Neanderthals and animals, the vague moral phobia (the Cleveland ban cited destructive effects on "the community's culture"), the miscegenation implications distinctly embedded in the headline about sisters and daughters: all of these were ways of marking the Stones' appearance and foreignness as indices of moral degeneracy and social danger. This is certainly not to suggest that the Rolling Stones were rendered as black, but rather that they were rendered something other than properly white, which to some readerships, particularly in more conservative corners of the United States, may have been even more threatening.

In England this had taken root in the band's identification with a British blues subculture, but when it traveled over to America it came incompletely and piecemeal: the Stones were seen as curiously obsessed with black American music and culture to degrees most American youths were not, and this in turn was met by moral conservatism and xenophobia. The Beatles had encountered wary hostility in some corners but the Stones were seen as far more dangerous. "Rolling Stones Lacking in Beatle-Like Finesse," declared the *Washington Post* in 1965, then went on to describe the band as "morbid and pathetic," even rendering Mick Jagger's speech in dialect.[28]

As the Rolling Stones became more successful this opprobrium continued to cling to them, but increased exposure and their own creative development caused certain aspects to change. As the band shifted away from playing covers to playing mostly original material, their transgressive image and the content of their music grew more and more intertwined. "(I Can't Get No) Satisfaction" and "Let's Spend the Night Together" were censored or banned from radio and television; songs like "Get Off of My Cloud," "Nineteenth Nervous Breakdown," and "Paint It Black" were anthems of nonconformity; "Mother's Little Helper" was one of the earliest rock and roll hits about drug abuse. The group was constantly on the defensive against charges of moral corruption, and even when they protested such treatment, coverage was often slanted against them. In early 1967 Jagger told the *Chicago Tribune* "I'm not leading the revolt. If the family unit is breaking down, if there is more illegitimacy around, parents might consider where they went wrong instead of blaming their children—or the lyrics of pop songs." In sensationalizing fashion, the headline of the story read simply "Singer Puts Blame on Parents."[29]

The Redlands drug bust of February 1967 only exacerbated the band's deviant image. When both Jagger and Richards were convicted in June of 1967—the former receiving three months in prison, the latter a year—there was public outcry on both sides of the Atlantic, including a famous editorial from William Rees-Mogg, editor of the London *Times*, entitled "Who Breaks a Butterfly on a Wheel?"[30] By the end of July, Richards's sentence had been overturned on appeal and Jagger's changed to a conditional discharge.

The Redlands affair further linked the Rolling Stones to hedonism and degeneracy. This lingering turmoil, coupled with the psychedelic disaster of *Their Satanic Majesties Request,* made the band's reemergence with "Jumpin' Jack Flash" in the spring of 1968 even more surprising. "Jumpin' Jack Flash" not only righted the band commercially, but also pointed toward a new musical direction, driven in large part by Keith Richards's increased reliance on open guitar tunings. Open tunings—most commonly open G—allowed Richards more facility in the creation of chord-based riffs that were often constructed out of harmonic movements in fourths, which in open G can be accomplished simply by repositioning two fingers against a barred chord.[31] The transition effectively allowed Richards to repurpose the rhythm guitar as a lead instrument, with loud, clattering chords such as those heard at the beginning of "Jumpin' Jack Flash" becoming the instrumental centerpiece for entire songs. In many senses it was a throwback to earlier rock and roll, particularly the guitar work of Richards's primary influence, Chuck Berry, but in terms of songwriting Richards drifted away from the conventional blues chords of I, IV, and V into more Aeolian textures facilitated by the open tuning, with bVI, bVII, and bIII chords appearing with increasing frequency.[32] "Jumpin' Jack Flash" was also the first Stones single produced by Jimmy Miller, an American who'd previously worked with the Spencer Davis Group and would go on to produce all of the Stones' major recordings through 1973. The recording had no extended solo sections or ornate instrumentation, and its most notable arrangement touch was the addition of maracas coming out of its second chorus, a small flourish that subtly transformed the shape of the song.

"Jumpin' Jack Flash" proved to be the most important Rolling Stones single since "Satisfaction," and if 1967 had been stunted by discord and dysfunction for the band, 1968 would be extraordinarily reinvigorating. By the end of the year the band released its first LP since *Their Satanic Majesties Request,* entitled *Beggars Banquet.*[33] *Rolling Stone* magazine called it "the best record they have yet done," adding that it "marks the comeback of the Stones from the disastrous *Their Satanic Majesties Request,* a recording episode as unfortunate as any for any group in the world."[34] The *Washington Post* called *Beggars Banquet* "their rawest, lewdest, most arrogant, most savage record yet. And it's beautiful."[35]

Beggars Banquet was ten songs long and presented the Stones in a state of renewed energy and versatility. There was the usual leering rhythm and blues—"Stray Cat Blues," "Parachute Woman"—but also moments of quiet introspection, such as "No Expectations" and "Factory Girl." Perhaps the album's most notorious track was its opener, a six-minute-plus opus entitled "Sympathy for the Devil." "Sympathy" was essentially a tour through history guided by Lucifer, one that began with the Crucifixion, wound through the Russian Revolution, and continued all the way up to the recent assassination of Robert Kennedy. It was an up-tempo and infectious song, with a slithering bass line and an instantly memorable refrain—"pleased to meet you / hope you guess my name."

"Sympathy for the Devil" furthered the notion of the Stones as diabolic and evil: when the *Chicago Tribune* ran an article on the rise of satanic imagery in rock music in September of 1968, the paper cited the band as central progenitors.[36] The *Washington Post* described the group as "satanic" and "demonic," while the *New York Times* soon wrote that Mick Jagger "combines bitterness, much hate, frustration, and defiance. . . . He adores his evil."[37] The Stones' embrace of satanic imagery was itself, of course, partly inspired by the blues tradition itself, where songs about the devil constitute a robust subgenre, although this lineage was often left out of mainstream press coverage that sought to portray the band as uniquely sinister.[38] While the Stones had flirted with occult imagery before—"Paint It Black" had similar overtones, and the title of *Their Satanic Majesties Request* speaks for itself—"Sympathy for the Devil" raised this theme to new heights.

Concurrent to this fixation on the band's evilness was a growing association with the Rolling Stones and violence, fueled by the lead single from *Beggars Banquet*, a raucous piece of music entitled "Street Fighting Man."[39] "Street Fighting Man" was released as a single in late August of 1968 and would reach number forty-eight on the American charts, an impressively high showing given that, once again, many American radio stations refused to play it out of fears that it would be an incitement to violence.[40] Released within a week of the 1968 Democratic National Convention into a summer already thick with unrest on both sides of the Atlantic, its "picture sleeve" boasted a graphic image of police brutality taken from Los Angeles' Sunset Strip curfew riots of 1966. The image was quickly withdrawn and the sleeve became a valuable collector's item.[41]

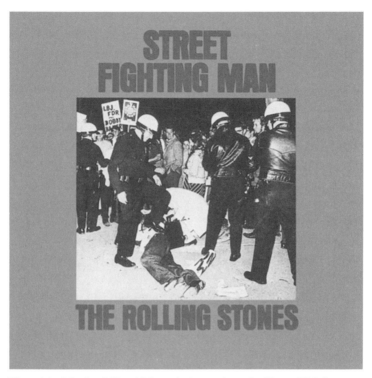

The original (and quickly withdrawn) picture sleeve for "Street Fighting Man" (1968). © ABKCO Records. Used by permission.

"Street Fighting Man" was the follow-up single to "Jumpin' Jack Flash" and was similar to its predecessor in energy and arrangement. Like "Jumpin' Jack Flash," "Street Fighting Man" opens with an overdriven acoustic guitar, playing a riff based in a I-IV chord progression. After two bars a pounding kick drum comes in, and after two more the full band: more acoustic guitars, bass, shakers, and percussion. Its first verse is brief but memorable: "Everywhere I hear the sound of marching charging feet, boy / But summer's here, and the time is right for fighting in the street, boy." The song's chorus—"But what can a poor boy do / Except to sing for a rock-and-roll band / Cause in sleepy London town there's just no place for a street fighting man" explicitly linked rock and roll to violence. The phrase "poor boy" contains both a class statement and its own hints of blues tradition: "A poor boy took his father's bread / and started down the road" is the opening line of Robert Wilkins's "Prodigal Son," which the Stones in fact covered on *Beggars Banquet*.

"Street Fighting Man" is an angry and relentless piece of music, a call to rebellion, and an excoriation of conformity. "I think the time is right for a palace revolution / but where I live the game to play is compromise solution," shouts Jagger in the song's second verse. Like "Jumpin' Jack Flash," its lyrical content is pointedly vague, and there are no references to any specific political concerns; it's an exploration of rebellion on its own terms, with rapt attention to the traditions that preceded it. Most notably, the phrase "summer's here, and the time is right" is a direct homage to Martha and the Vandellas' 1964 Motown hit "Dancing in the Street," a song that had itself already been speculated as being indirectly about urban unrest.[42] "Street Fighting Man" takes "Dancing in the Street" and made its allegorical uprising far more explicit, forcibly resituating the Vandellas and Motown into London, four years later, a thoughtful and serious homage that imaginatively repurposes its object for a vastly different political context.

The significance of the interracial exchange here should also not be overlooked, and it speaks intriguingly to Richard Goldstein's claim, quoted in Chapter 5, about the inherent "revolt" in black music, its historical power as an "agent of liberation."[43] But whereas Goldstein had located this power in the past, the Stones chose contemporary R&B music to infuse their "palace revolution," not some long-lost blues lineage. Here and elsewhere the Rolling Stones remained devoted to surrounding themselves with present-day black music and black musicians in ways that were becoming increasingly uncommon in late 1960s rock. On the Rolling Stones' 1969 tour Ike and Tina Turner and B. B. King were opening acts, and the band also frequently played alongside African American performers onstage and in the studio, most notably singer Merry Clayton, who will be discussed more shortly.

This ongoing affinity with black American music and culture often manifested itself in strange ways outside of the band. In 1968, French New Wave filmmaker Jean-Luc Godard made a feature-length film called *One Plus One* that would later be retitled *Sympathy for the Devil*. The film was a mix of long sequences of the Rolling Stones in the studio recording the title track, intercut with extended vignettes featuring black French "revolutionaries" reading aloud from the works of Eldridge Cleaver, Amiri Baraka, and other African American writers. In one of the more memorable sequences, revolutionaries kidnap and murder a group of white women, all wearing white dresses. Jagger himself provided the following description of the film to an interviewer: "Well it's [Godard's] wife who plays the lead chick. She comes to London and gets totally destroyed with some spade cat. Gets involved with drugs or something. Anyway, while she is getting destroyed we find the Rolling Stones freaking out at the recording studio making these sounds."[44]

Godard's film made visible what "Street Fighting Man" had made audible: an imaginative connection between the Rolling Stones, racial boundary crossing, and violence. In his 1968 review of *Beggars Banquet,* the critic Jon Landau had written: "The Rolling Stones are violence. Their music penetrates the raw nerve endings of their listeners and finds its way into the groove marked 'release of frustration.' Their violence has always been a surrogate for the larger violence their audience is so obviously capable of." This only increased in July of 1969, when former guitarist Brian Jones drowned in his swimming pool and only two days later the band played a free concert in London's Hyde Park to introduce his replacement, Mick Taylor. If the timing seemed in poor taste, as the *New York Times* noted in its coverage of the concert, "the Rolling Stones have always expressed the most savage urges and frustration of their followers."[45]

It was against this backdrop that the Stones would release their follow-up to *Beggars Banquet,* the evocatively titled LP *Let It Bleed,* in late 1969.[46] *Let It Bleed* sandwiched a diverse array of material between its opening track, "Gimme Shelter," and its conclusion, the seven-and-a-half-minute, whimsically elegiac "You Can't Always Get What You Want." Amidst the band's typical moments of bawdy rock and roll ("Live with Me," "Let It Bleed") was an understated Robert Johnson blues ("Love in Vain"), a folk ballad ("You Got the Silver") and a shambling ho-down ("Country Honk"). Furthering the band's obsession with depravity was "Midnight Rambler," a blues told through the eyes of a serial rapist and murderer. The album was well received by critics: "*Let It Bleed* presents the Stones in their strongest suit—heavy, black-tinged, passionately erotic hard rock/blues."[47]

For all of its eclecticism, *Let It Bleed*'s most striking moment was "Gimme Shelter," which found the Stones venturing even deeper into the dark recesses they'd explored in "Jumpin' Jack Flash," "Sympathy for the Devil," and "Street Fighting Man." Reviewing the album for *Rolling Stone* in late 1969, Greil Marcus wrote, " 'Gimmie Shelter' [*sic*] is a song about fear; it probably serves better than anything written this year as a passageway straight into the next few years. . . . It's a full-faced meeting with all the terror the mind can summon, moving fast and never breaking so that men and women have to beat that terror at the game's own pace."[48]

"Gimme Shelter" is an explicitly violent piece of music. The song begins with a quiet, tremolo-laden guitar intro, playing a straight-eighth-note figure that's little more than a decelerated version of the propulsive guitar introductions made famous by Chuck Berry in the 1950s on hits such as "Roll over Beethoven" and "Johnny B. Goode."[49] After the opening four bars of guitar introduction, more instruments layer on. Light percussion begins to creep through and a second guitar enters, playing sparse melodic fills. In the background we hear vocals, the falsetto voices of Jagger and Richards singing wordless "oooohs" in a sort of occult rendering of street-corner doo-wop. After eight more bars an electric bass enters, lightly plucking the root, and four bars later a piano crashes on the downbeat, striking an ominous octave in the low register. Charlie Watts cracks his snare twice and the full band enters like an explosion into a quagmire.

The text of "Gimme Shelter" is an apocalyptic flood blues. The song reads like a hybrid of Delta bluesman Charley Patton's 1929 classic "High Water Everywhere" and William Butler Yeats's "The Second Coming," the lyrics' description of a "mad bull, lost its way" bearing distinct echoes of Yeats's "rough beast" that "slouches towards Bethlehem to be born."[50] The song's opening verse is sung by Jagger in a slurred, melismatic bravado:

> *Oooh, storm is threatenin'*
> *My very life today*
> *If I don't get some shelter*
> *Oh yeah, I'm gonna fade away*

This opening stanza is representative of the lyrical imagery of "Gimme Shelter": the threat of the "storm" is vague, suggesting only a general atmosphere of dread, while the plea for "shelter" suggests that the impending destruction is inevitable and out of the speaker's control. Perhaps the most pointed phrase in the opening verse, one that is revisited later in the song, is the suggestion of "fading away," a reference to Buddy Holly's 1957 classic "Not Fade Away"—a cover version of which, again, served as the Rolling Stones' first major hit. Here we have another moment of the Stones gesturing to rock and roll history, and the reference to Holly, who in 1969 still represented the most famous death in the music's history, enhances the themes of death and destruction.

After the opening verse, "Gimme Shelter" enters its chorus. Here a second voice arrives, that of African American female backup singer Merry Clayton, who belts the song's refrain in harmony with Jagger: "War, children / it's just a shot away / it's just a shot away." The chorus's utilization of "children" carries a double edge, invoking both the gospel tradition of referring to one's audience as "children" and late-1960s images of Vietnamese children slaughtered in villages and fleeing napalm strikes: children as victims of war, children as ourselves.

Perhaps the most indelible moment of "Gimme Shelter" comes after its second verse and on the heels of a Richards guitar solo, when Clayton wails through four repetitions of the chorus, this time without the accompaniment of Jagger. The text shifts from "War, children / It's just a shot away" to "Rape, murder / It's just a shot away," and Clayton's voice teeters between a song and a shout, producing the unsettling experience of hearing a woman repeatedly cry the word "rape" on a rock and roll record. The song then enters its last verse, with Jagger and Clayton singing the final verse almost entirely in tandem:

> *Ooh, those floods is threatenin'*
> *My very life today*

Gimme, gimme shelter

Oh, I'm gonna fade away

The final verse is in many senses a restatement of the first, with several small but notable changes. The "storm" of the first verse has been replaced by "floods," carrying the implication of the storm's aftermath as well as that of blood running in the street. "If I don't get some shelter" has changed to "gimme shelter," and we have the repetition of "fade away," a line that now sounds more like fated resignation than impending threat. Like Hendrix's "Machine Gun," "Gimme Shelter" makes its violence explicit, though the Rolling Stones seem more interested in vicariously representing war than explicating or critiquing it. What's more, the song finds the Rolling Stones straying even deeper into musical history: the Chuck Berry intro, the Buddy Holly allusions, the knowing nods to entire various traditions such as flood blues, gospel, and doo-wop. Clayton's presence on the track also heightens the notion of racialized violence surrounding the band, five white men and a black woman in the recording studio, performing a song about rape and murder. As Farah Jasmine Griffin has written, "the black woman's singing voice can signal a crisis of national unity . . . Representations of the voice suggest that it is like a hinge, a place where things can both come together and break apart." [51] In the Vietnam-era context of *Let It Bleed,* I would suggest that in Clayton's voice can be heard the sound of things breaking apart.

"Gimme Shelter" remains one of the most iconic musical markers of violence in popular culture, appearing repeatedly in films, television shows, and other media. [52] Its cultural power has long since exceeded the specifics of its composition and original recording, however, due to its associations with a specific historical incident and the film that came out of it. On December 6, 1969, the Rolling Stones arrived at the Altamont Speedway, located a little more than fifty miles east of San Francisco between the towns of Tracy and Livermore, to perform a free concert before a crowd estimated at three hundred thousand people. The California air was already thick with portent, as newspapers were abuzz with reports of the recent apprehension of several members of the Manson Family, suspected in the brutal Benedict Canyon murders of the actress Sharon Tate and four houseguests the previous August. As details leaked out about the Manson cult, a story emerged that connected drugs, the occult, rock and roll, and Manson's own designs for igniting a "race war." "Bizarre Tale of 'Black Magic'" blared a *Los Angeles Times* headline in a front-page feature on the murders that ran just a day before the Stones' free concert.[53]

The disastrous run-up to the concert at Altamont has been recounted in a number of contexts, most notably in Albert Maysles, David Maysles, and Charlotte Zwerin's documentary *Gimme Shelter*.[54] The infamous decision to hire the Hell's Angels motorcycle gang as security was mostly a reflection of the poor planning for the concert, though there had been a precedent of the Angels maintaining a peaceful presence at rock concerts in the San Francisco area, and a London chapter of the Hell's Angels had presided over the Stones' earlier Hyde Park concert. Violence began erupting early in the day, with the Angels accusing audience members of vandalizing their motorcycles. The Stones were the final act on the bill and made their way through a disjointed and frequently interrupted set. It was during their performance of "Under My Thumb" that an African American teenager, Meredith Hunter, was stabbed to death by a Hell's Angel, his murder captured on film by the crew of *Gimme Shelter*.

National reaction to Hunter's death was initially subdued: perhaps ironically, it was *Rolling Stone* magazine itself that would play a leading role in transforming Altamont from circumstantial tragedy into an apocalyptic death rattle of the 1960s. The magazine devoted fifteen pages of coverage to Altamont in its January 21, 1970, issue, under the pointed headline "Let It Bleed." *Rolling Stone* compared Altamont to Hiroshima, and it quoted Ralph Gleason wondering aloud if Mick Jagger was guilty of murder.[55] In its next issue, *Rolling Stone* ran a second feature on Altamont; in both stories, the magazine erroneously reported that the Stones had been playing "Sympathy for the Devil" when Hunter was stabbed.[56]

The mythology of Altamont quickly grew. In a March 1970 article in the radical journal *Scanlan's Monthly*, writer Sol Stern dubbed Altamont "Pearl Harbor to the Woodstock Nation," and as the year rolled on more and more critics laid blame for the carnage at Altamont squarely on the Rolling Stones.[57] By the time the Maysles's and Zwerin's *Gimme Shelter* was released in theaters in December of 1970, Altamont had been elevated to the level of a cultural catastrophe. Famed film critic Pauline Kael despaired in the *New Yorker*, "But how does one review this picture? It's like reviewing the footage of President Kennedy's assassination or of Lee Harvey Oswald's murder."[58] The film redoubled hostility toward both the filmmakers and the Rolling Stones, who were often conflated as one and the same. In a column entitled "Making Murder Pay?," the *New York Times'* venerable film critic Vincent Canby essentially accused the Maysles of making a snuff film, decrying the movie's "exuberant enthusiasm with which it exploits the events" and wondering if "someone thought 'Wow, what luck!' when it was found that Meredith Hunter's death had been filmed."[59] Writing in the same paper a few weeks later, the excitable Albert Goldman raised the level of scorn even higher:

> Bravo, you measly brothers! You've captured on film the epic of a self-destructive generation. "Gimme Shelter" gives us the

thrills that so many porno-oriented Danish flicks have
failed to deliver. Who cares about the truth when we can
revel in the fantasies of *cinema verité*? Up with Mick Jagger!
Up with Angel Sonny Barger! Up with the fat, the naked, the
pathetically flapping victims of the camera as carnal
scourge![60]

The Altamont tragedy and its aftermaths seemed to actualize
and prophetically fulfill an already-existent imaginative connection between the Rolling Stones, racial transgression, and
violence. Hunter's race—and his involvement in an interracial
relationship—was mentioned incessantly in media accounts.
Rolling Stone compared his killing to "that [which] we've all seen
in photographs of redneck brutality against black people in the
South," and it quoted Hunter's sister's suspicion that "their being
a mixed couple . . . may have had quite a lot to do with it. The
Hell's Angels are just white men with badges on their backs."[61]
It has never been confirmed that Hunter's race played a role in
his death, but this element of the Altamont story captivated its
various tellers, from William F. Buckley's inflammatory characterization of Hunter as a "hopped-up Negro" to David Maysles's
own description of Hunter as wearing "a nigger zoot suit . . . you
wouldn't believe him if you saw him in a fiction film."[62]

In a 1972 article for *Creem,* Simon Frith took aim at what he
perceived as America's obsession with Altamont, and its self-
serving demonization of the Rolling Stones: "Altamont was an
American answer only. I used to believe all those stories in the
American press about how it was all Mick Jagger's fault but I've
now seen *Gimmie Shelter* [*sic*] and bullshit. Altamont was a
strictly family affair. The Stones went as tourists, clutching their
bunches of flowers, sticky fingered."[63] And yet the symbolic irony
of Altamont was hard to ignore: a young black man, framed as an

outsider, murdered at a rock concert at the end of the 1960s, a concert headlined by a white band who had mined black musical traditions with unprecedented creative energy. As historian Brian Ward notes, "Whereas blacks had once greeted the interracialism of early rock and roll dances and concerts as portents of a new era of race relations, the concert at Altamont had simply provided the occasion for another lynching."[64] The Rolling Stones' racial transgressions became absorbed into the figure of Hunter and the Altamont narrative, and Hunter's murder legitimized the idea that the violence found in the music of the Rolling Stones was in fact simply a "surrogate" for a wider violence lingering about the culture that embraced the band.

The Rolling Stones' insistence on the continued relevance of black music to rock and roll was never fully heard; like Hendrix, they became exceptional figures, their curious obsessions with blues and rhythm and blues simply becoming another way of being white rock stars. The clattering R&B of "Jumpin' Jack Flash," the reworked Motown of "Street Fighting Man," the tumultuous blues of "Gimme Shelter": songs like these could be heard as whole musical histories, works whose lives depended on a continual and conscious interaction with the music that came before them, much of which was black in origin. The problem was that the music the Stones were hearing as both a living past and something still present—"Summer's here, and the time is right"—was increasingly heard by its listeners solely as a past. The Rolling Stones' challenges to racially prescriptive ideas of music making, imperfect and muddled as they often were, were absorbed by rock discourses that denied the possibility of black participation while relegating black music to "source material," to be heroically mined by white men who would soon come to selectively mishear the Rolling Stones as the very originators they'd never claimed to be.

Coda: Cold English Blood Runs Hot

The Rolling Stones continued to record and perform after the events at Altamont, though in 1973 the band would part ways with producer Jimmy Miller, ending what would come to be widely regarded as their most fertile creative period. Before that separation the Rolling Stones did muster one more remarkable rendezvous at the intersection of rock and roll, race, and violence, however. In the spring of 1971 the band released its first album since Altamont. Entitled *Sticky Fingers,* the LP's cover was designed by Andy Warhol and showed the front of a pair of jeans, replete with a suggestively operative zipper.[65] The lead single to *Sticky Fingers,* entitled "Brown Sugar," was released in the United States in May and promptly went to number one on the *Billboard* charts, the band's sixth single to do so.[66]

Although it was released in 1971, "Brown Sugar" had in fact been recorded in early December of 1969, at the Muscle Shoals Sound Studios in Muscle Shoals, Alabama, an outfit started by some of the same musicians who'd performed on Aretha Franklin's most famous Atlantic recordings.[67] The Stones would debut the song live two days after wrapping in Alabama—in front of the fans at the free concert at the Altamont Speedway, in fact—but the studio recording sat on the shelf for over a year. By the time it was released, Hendrix and Joplin were dead, the Beatles were broken up, and the 1960s were over, the Stones—in the telling of some—having ended them.

"Brown Sugar" is an up-tempo and rollicking bit of rhythm and blues, its musical backdrop drawing from what were now hallmarks of Rolling Stones productions, from the slashing opening guitar riff to the trademark maracas on the final verse. From a purely formal standpoint it's a great performance, precisely the sort of lean, driving rock and roll that by the late 1960s

the Stones could churn out with inimitable, ramshackle precision. Jagger's vocal performance is emphatic and controlled, full
of grunts, shouts, and interjections.

As in many of his other performances the words are slurred
nearly beyond comprehension, but it's possible that here it's particularly deliberate, as "Brown Sugar" boasts some of the most
appalling lyrics ever written for a rock and roll song, a catalogue
of racial and sexual violence so gratuitous it seems to simultaneously critique and congratulate itself. "Brown Sugar" is a song
about the transatlantic slave trade that is startlingly explicit in
its imagery, starting with its opening verse:

> *Gold coast slave ship bound for cotton fields*
> *Sold in the market down in New Orleans*
> *Scarred old slaver, know he's doin' alright*
> *Hear him whip the women just around midnight*

"Brown Sugar" is an extended rumination on white-on-black
rape and the racial and sexual violence of the slaveholding South.
The song traffics in repugnant stereotypes of black female sexuality, and it mines the historical atrocity of slavery for white
male fantasy, while its rollicking and ebullient backing track implies galling flippancy toward its own subject matter. On this
level one can hear "Brown Sugar" as the most racially offensive
composition in the catalogue of one of the most racially troublesome bands in rock and roll, and it is certainly that.

But on another level one can hear "Brown Sugar" as the most
unflinching exploration of racial and musical imagination ever
put on record by a white rock and roll band, and it is quite possibly that, too. In a moment when conversations about musical
and racial authenticity had become dominated by claims about
innate white and black expressive capacity that could be traced

back to the most primordial origins of American racial thought, the Rolling Stones wrote a song about those origins. What's more, they implicated themselves, and their own country, in the process: "drums beating, cold English blood runs hot" is the opening line of the second verse, a chilling reminder of England's own role in the Atlantic history of racial terror. "Brown Sugar" is a song about many things: it's a song about desire, lust, and the horrific underside of history; it is a song about exploitation and relentlessly iterative violence; it is a song about musical power, carnal power, and the entwinement of the two; it is about the most grotesque and unseemly cultural politics of economies of pleasure; and it is about the ways race figures so centrally in all of the above. Heard this way, "Brown Sugar" is a song about rock and roll music itself, and all the histories that inform it. It is morally outrageous, and yet I am not sure it is more so than the many, many songs since that have sought to replicate its fantasies of white male sexual hedonism while assiduously obscuring the horrors that have fed those fantasies. "Brown Sugar" is a song that only the Rolling Stones could have written, a deeply troubling yet inescapable reckoning with both the world that made them and the world that they in turn made.

The Rolling Stones and Jimi Hendrix commanded the imagery of musical violence in the late 1960s to degrees previously unheard in rock and roll music. Their fascination with violence emerged in reaction to a musical landscape that was subtly but increasingly denying each artist the possibility of their own existence. For Hendrix these critiques took place in the future tense, in the form of a categorical denial of the legitimacy of race itself and its connection to genre and musical authenticity, and a notion of musical creativity that was profoundly individualist and anti-essentialist. The Stones' critiques took nearly the opposite shape: an obsessive and dogged insistence on the centrality of tradition to rock and roll, which the band saw as directly contiguous to a long and rich history of African American music.

In a sense the Rolling Stones' position was fundamentally conservative and Hendrix's fundamentally progressive, but both viewed rock and roll music as a space where race itself might be radically undone. Ultimately neither critique was successful, partly derailed by the intensity that enabled them and the self-destruction that it wrought. But they were also derailed by an ideology of white rock music that simply accepted them: Hendrix is the lone black star in the "pantheon" of rock heroes, the accusations of "Uncle Tom" long vanished, forgotten almost willfully. As for the Rolling Stones, they have continued to perform with African American musicians and still make a point of selecting black artists as touring partners: their 2006 North American tour found them sharing a bill with hip-hop star Kanye West. Still, this has now simply become part of the Rolling Stones' mythology, the band's obsession with black music merely seen as some essence of the Rolling Stones.

The Rolling Stones were never entirely able to separate their relationship to black music from a fantastical fetishization of that music, a fetishization present from the band's beginnings. The roots of the band's dangerous, outsider image sprang from the belief that for a white band to play black music was a transgressive and titillating act. The Rolling Stones themselves were by no means innocent in the construction of this image, and to no small degree it has lurked beneath the surface of nearly all of their work. If Hendrix held race as something that might be disbelieved as readily as believed, the Rolling Stones' ongoing flirtations with racial fantasy suggest that they were never fully able, or willing, to embrace this disbelief.

But most crucially, the flirtations with violence that marked the music of the Rolling Stones in this period were simply absorbed into rock ideology as affirmations of the music's own white authenticity, rather than as attempts to destabilize it. Part of this was due to the many issues described above, but a larger part was due to a discursive landscape that would silence the band's subversions by rendering musical iconoclasm into musical archetype. The complex case of "Brown Sugar" can be heard as a sort of fulcrum of this: for all its twisting and tortuous layers it is, at its most basic, a song about white male sexual conquest, and it is at this level that a white rock landscape would subsume the song into its consolidating canon. As rock continued into the 1970s an endless litany of bands made musical violence just another marker of white male hegemony; this violence often served no political purpose, and little imaginative purpose either. It simply became another way of being white, which was one thing that, for better and worse, the Rolling Stones were never interested in being.

Notes

Introduction

1 Margo Jefferson, "Ripping Off Black Music," *Harpers,* Jan. 1973, 45.

2 Maureen Mahon, *Right to Rock: The Black Rock Coalition and the Cultural Politics of Race* (Durham, NC: Duke University Press, 2004), 14.

3 Craig Werner writes that "attacks on disco gave respectable voice to the ugliest kinds of unacknowledged racism, sexism, and homophobia," while Dave Marsh called it "your most paranoid fantasy about where the ethnic cleansing of the rock radio could ultimately lead." Craig Werner, *A Change Is Gonna Come* (New York: Plume, 1998), 211 ; Tony Sclafani, "When 'Disco Sucks!' Echoed around the World," *MSNBC,* 10 Jul. 2009, http://www.today .com/id/31832616/ns/today-entertainment/t/when-disco-sucks-echoed -around-world/#.UVyAD6s0hk8.

4 *Back to the Future,* DVD, directed by Robert Zemeckis (1985; Los Angeles: Universal Studios, 2011).

5 Q104.3 New York, "Top 1,043 Songs (2011 Edition)," http://www.q1043 .com/common/top_songs/2011.html (accessed July 30, 2015).

6 Ernie Santosuosso, "Epitaph for Jimi Hendrix," *Boston Globe*, 19 Sept. 1970, 10.

7 See Linda Martin and Kerry Segrave, *Anti-Rock: The Opposition to Rock 'n' Roll* (New York: Da Capo, 1988), esp. 41–43, as well as Sacha Jenkins, Elliott Wilson, Chairman Jefferson Mao, Gabriel Alvarez, and Brent Rollins, *Ego Trip's Big Book of Racism!* (New York: HarperCollins, 2002), 91.

8 Guthrie P. Ramsey, *Race Music: Black Cultures from Bebop to Hip-Hop* (Berkeley: University of California Press, 2004), 121.

9 Josh Kun, *Audiotopia: Music, Race, and America* (Berkeley: University of California Press, 2005), 23.

10 "Rock 'n' Roll: Everybody's Turned On," *Time*, 21 May 1969; "Rule Sam Cooke's Death 'Justifiable' Homicide," *Chicago Defender*, 17 Dec. 1964, 1. Cooke was similarly described as such in mainstream white newspapers such as the *New York Times* ("a rock 'n' roll singer") and the *Los Angeles Times* (a "rock 'n' roll singer"), while the African American *Los Angeles Sentinel* referred to him as a "rock 'n' roll singing idol." "Shooting of Sam Cooke Held 'Justifiable,'" *New York Times*, 17 Dec. 1964, 82; "Mourners Jam Streets to See Sam Cooke Body," *Los Angeles Times*, 14 Dec. 1964, 25; Paul C. McGee, "New Shocking Evidence Looms; Push Sam Cooke Investigation," *Los Angeles Sentinel*, 24 Dec. 1964, A1.

11 Frith here in fact draws on the theoretical work of musicologist Franco Fabbri: see Franco Fabbri, "A Theory of Musical Genres: Two Applications," in *Popular Music Perspectives*, ed. David Horn and Philip Tagg (Exeter, UK: International Association for the Study of Popular Music, 1981), 52–81. As Frith himself writes, "It is through its generic organization that music offers people, even so-called passive at-home listeners, access to a social world, a part in some sort of social narrative . . . genre analysis must be, by aesthetic necessity, narrative analysis." Simon Frith, *Performing Rites: On the Value of Popular Music* (Cambridge: Harvard University Press, 1998), 90.

12 Ingrid Monson, *Freedom Sounds: Civil Rights Call Out to Jazz and Africa* (New York: Oxford University Press, 2007), 24.

13 See Michael Omi and Howard Winant, *Racial Formation in the United States, 3rd Ed.* (New York: Routledge, 2014).

14 Ronald Radano and Philip Bohlman, eds., *Music and the Racial Imagination* (Chicago: University of Chicago Press, 2001), 5.

15 Kun, *Audiotopia*, 26.

16 Lee Marshall, "Bob Dylan and the Academy," in *The Cambridge Companion to Bob Dylan*, ed. Kevin J. H. Dettmar (New York: Cambridge University Press, 2009), 105.

17 Two of the most influential early histories of rock and roll music, Nik Cohn's *Awopbopaloobop Alopbamboom: The Golden Age of Rock* (1969; New York: Grove, 2001) and Charlie Gillett's *The Sound of the City: The Rise of Rock and Roll* (1970; Boston: Da Capo, 1996), already gesture toward this division, Gillett explicitly and Cohn more implicitly (although more polemically).

18 For a history and analysis of this dichotomy, see John McMillian's *Beatles vs. Stones* (New York: Simon and Schuster, 2013). Also see Jim DeRogatis and Greg Kot, *The Beatles vs. the Rolling Stones: Sound Opinions on the Great Rock 'n' Roll Rivalry* (Minneapolis, MN: Voyageur, 2010).

19 Chris Roberts, "John Lennon," *Melody Maker,* 4 Apr. 1964, 3.

20 Probably the most well-known purveyor of this hardline view is Amiri Baraka, whose landmark 1963 history of African American music, *Blues People*, put forth a purity/dilution dialectic in its view of black music's proximity to white "influence," broadly defined. In his famous essay "The Changing Same (R&B and New Black Music)," Baraka accused the Beatles and Rolling Stones of minstrelsy. Amiri Baraka (as LeRoi Jones), *Blues People: Negro Music in White America* (1963; New York: Perennial, 2002); *Black Music* (1968; New York: Akashic, 2010), 234–235. Nelson George embraced a somewhat similar stance in his widely read polemic, *The Death of Rhythm & Blues* (New York: Pantheon, 1988).

21 Karl Hagstrom Miller, *Segregating Sound: Inventing Folk and Pop Music in the Age of Jim Crow* (Durham, NC: Duke University Press, 2010), 15. Emphasis added.

22 Eric Lott, *Love and Theft: Blackface Minstrelsy and the American Working Class* (New York: Oxford University Press, 1993). John Szwed likened Mick Jagger to a blackface minstrel as early as 1973, as Lott himself discusses (qtd. in ibid., 7). More recently, W. T. Lhamon's *Raising Cain: Blackface Performance from Jim Crow to Hip Hop* (Cambridge: Harvard University Press, 1998) is a long-ranging history of what Lhamon identifies as minstrel performances that enfolds white rock and roll musicians into its survey, and the frequency of minstrel discourse surrounding Bob Dylan is discussed extensively in Chapter 1.

23 Alexander Saxton, "Blackface Minstrelsy and Jacksonian Ideology," *American Quarterly* 27, no. 1 (Mar. 1975): 3–28.

24 Elijah Wald, *How the Beatles Destroyed Rock 'n' Roll: An Alternative History of American Popular Music* (New York: Oxford University Press, 2009), 235.

25 Chief among these is Brian Ward's outstanding *Just My Soul Responding: Rhythm and Blues, Black Consciousness, and Race Relations* (Berkeley: University of California Press, 1998). To name just two more that are also stellar: Craig

Werner's *A Change Is Gonna Come: Music, Race and the Soul of America* (New York: Plume, 1998) and Mark Anthony Neal's *What the Music Said: Black Popular Music and Black Public Culture* (New York: Routledge, 1997).

26 Emily J. Lordi, *Black Resonance: Iconic Women Singers and African American Literature* (New Brunswick, NJ: Rutgers University Press, 2013), 8.

27 Lester Bangs, "The White Noise Supremacists," in *Psychotic Reactions and Carburetor Dung,* ed. Greil Marcus (New York: Vintage, 1988), 272–282. For information on the article's reception and Bangs's apostasy from the punk scene, see Jim DeRogatis's *Let It Blurt: The Life and Times of Lester Bangs, America's Greatest Rock Critic* (New York: Broadway, 2000), esp. 172–173; Sasha Frere-Jones, "A Paler Shade of White," *New Yorker,* 22 Oct. 2007, 176–181. Shortly after Frere-Jones' piece was published, *New York* magazine's *Vulture* blog rounded up the backlash to Frere-Jones's piece in a post entitled "Finally, Some Outrage Over Sasha Frere-Jones' Latest Column!" *Vulture,* 18 Oct. 2007, available at http://www.vulture.com/2007/10/finally_some_outrage_over_sasha.html. "A Paler Shade of White" received a particularly thoughtful response by Carl Wilson in *Slate* (Carl Wilson, "The Trouble with Indie Rock," *Slate,* 18 Oct. 2007, available at http://www.slate.com/articles/arts/culturebox/2007/10/the_trouble_with_indie_rock.html), and in 2008 the Experience Music Project's annual Pop Conference held a roundtable devoted to discussion of Frere-Jones's essay.

28 The number of biographies and academic and nonacademic studies of Dylan and the Beatles are far too numerous to list, and the copious literature on these artists will be discussed more extensively in later chapters. It is worth noting, however, that recent years have seen Cambridge University Press release a *Cambridge Companion to Bob Dylan* and a *Cambridge Companion to the Beatles,* while, by the time of this writing, no African American musician from the period had received the same treatment. Dettmar, *Cambridge Companion to Bob Dylan*; Kenneth Womack, ed., *The Cambridge Companion to the Beatles* (New York: Cambridge University Press, 2009).

29 Fred Moten, *In the Break: The Aesthetics of the Black Radical Tradition* (Minneapolis: University of Minnesota Press), 149.

30 The most important work in the rock-and-roll-as-folk-expression canon is Greil Marcus's *Mystery Train,* which is likely also the most influential book on rock and roll music, period. Marcus's book is a brilliant collection of essays in the classical "myth and symbol" American Studies tradition that enfolds rock and roll into an exceptionalist American narrative that generally treats race as secondary to nation. Greil Marcus, *Mystery Train: Images of America in Rock 'n' Roll Music* (New York: E. P. Dutton, 1975). For other class-

based analyses of rock music, see George Lipsitz, *Time Passages: Collective Memory and American Popular Culture* (Minneapolis: University of Minnesota Press, 1990), and Lawrence Grossberg, *Dancing in Spite of Myself: Essays on Popular Culture* (Durham, NC: Duke University Press, 1997). Lipsitz, of course, has written perceptively about race and popular music elsewhere, particularly *The Possessive Investment in Whiteness: How White People Profit from Identity Politics* (Philadelphia: Temple University Press, 1998). For a discussion of class anxieties in the New Left, see Doug Rossinow's *The Politics of Authenticity* (New York: Columbia University Press, 1998), esp. 193–207.

31 Probably the most influential voice in Springsteen discourse is the rock critic and biographer Dave Marsh, who published his first biography of Springsteen, *Born to Run: The Bruce Springsteen Story* (New York: Dolphin, 1979) in 1979, then published a nearly seven-hundred-page "definitive" biography of the singer in 2004. Marsh, *Bruce Springsteen: Two Hearts: The Definitive Biography* (New York: Routledge, 2004).

32 David Remnick, "Bloodbrother: Clarence Clemons, 1942–2011," *New Yorker* (online), 19 Jun. 2011, available at http://www.newyorker.com/online/blogs/newsdesk/2011/06/bloodbrother-clarence-clemons-1942-2011.html.

33 Philip Auslander has written extensively of this with regards to the Milli Vanilli lip-synching controversy of the late 1980s, which led MTV to create its *Unplugged* series, the suggestion being that the stripped-down environs would preclude trickery and artifice (never mind that, obviously, the show was still thoroughly edited and produced). Auslander, *Liveness: Performance in a Mediatized Culture* (New York: Routledge, 1999), esp. 63–109. For an interesting collection of authenticity debates across popular-music genres, see Hugh Barker and Yuval Taylor's *Faking It: The Quest for Authenticity in Popular Music* (New York: W. W. Norton, 2007).

34 Keir Keightley, "Reconsidering Rock," in *The Cambridge Companion to Pop and Rock*, ed. Simon Frith, Will Straw, and John Street (New York: Cambridge University Press, 2001), 125.

35 Auslander, *Liveness*, 70.

36 Patricia J. Williams, *Seeing a Color-Blind Future: The Paradox of Race* (New York: Farrar, Straus and Giroux, 1999), 9.

37 Alexandra T. Vazquez, *Listening in Detail: Performances of Cuban Music* (Durham, NC: Duke University Press, 2013), 8.

38 Theodore Gracyk, *Rhythm and Noise: An Aesthetics of Rock* (Durham, NC: Duke University Press, 1996), 13. See Auslander, *Liveness*, esp. 63–109.

39 Eric Weisbard, *Top 40 Democracy: The Rival Mainstreams of American Music* (Chicago: University of Chicago Press, 2014), 196–197.

40 Kelefa Sanneh, "The Rap against Rockism," *New York Times,* 31 Oct. 2004, AR32.

41 Keightley, "Reconsidering Rock," 126.

42 Ronald Radano, *Lying Up a Nation: Race and Black Music* (Chicago: University of Chicago Press, 2003), 4.

43 Michael J. Kramer, *The Republic of Rock: Music and Citizenship in the Sixties Counterculture* (New York: Oxford University Press, 2013), 128.

44 Kun, *Audiotopia,* 187.

45 See Gayle Wald, *It's Been Beautiful: Soul! and Black Power Television* (Durham, NC: Duke University Press, 2015), and Matthew F. Delmont, *The Nicest Kids in Town: American Bandstand, Rock 'n' Roll, and the Struggle for Civil Rights in 1950s Philadelphia* (Berkeley: University of California Press, 2012).

46 Rob Bowman, *Soulsville, U.S.A.: The Story of Stax Records* (New York: Schirmer, 1997); Charles Hughes, *Country Soul: Making Music and Making Race in the American South* (Chapel Hill: University of North Carolina Press, 2015).

47 James McBride's *Kill 'Em and Leave: Searching for James Brown and the American Soul* (New York: Spiegel & Grau, 2016), R. J. Smith's *The One: The Life and Music of James Brown* (New York: Gotham, 2012) and Anne Danielsen's *Presence and Pleasure: The Funk Grooves of James Brown and Parliament* (Middletown, CT: Wesleyan University Press, 2006) are three recent works on Brown. Ramsey's *Race Music* and David Brackett's *Interpreting Popular Music* (New York: Cambridge University Press, 1995) also contain excellent considerations of Brown.

48 In 2008 the Pulitzer Prize committee awarded Dylan a special citation for "his profound impact on popular music and American culture, marked by lyrical compositions of extraordinary poetic power." "Bob Dylan Receives Honorary Pulitzer Prize," *MSNBC,* 10 Apr. 2008, available online at http://today.msnbc.msn.com/id/24000483/ns/today-entertainment/.

1. Darkness at the Break of Noon

Epigraphs: Cooke: "A Change Is Gonna Come." Words and Music by Sam Cooke. From the album *Ain't That Good News,* RCA–LPM–2899 [LP, Mono]/ RCA–LSP–2899 [LP, Stereo], Hollywood, California: RCA Victor Records,

1964. Copyright © 1964 (renewed) by ABKCO MUSIC, INC. Dylan: "It's Alright, Ma (I'm Only Bleeding)." Words and Music by Bob Dylan. From the album *Bringing It All Back Home,* Columbia—CS 9128 [LP, Stereo], New York City: Columbia Records, 1965. Copyright © 1965 by Warner Brothers Incorporated; Copyright © renewed 1993 by Special Rider Music, USA.

1 Sales numbers are from Robert Shelton's *No Direction Home: The Life and Music of Bob Dylan* (New York: William Morrow, 1985), 161.

2 Daniel Wolff, with S. R. Crain, Clifton White, and G. David Tenenbaum, *You Send Me: The Life and Times of Sam Cooke* (New York: William Morrow, 1995), 291.

3 Peter Guralnick, *Dream Boogie: The Triumph of Sam Cooke* (New York: Little, Brown, 2005), 541.

4 Ibid., 550. Sadly, no tape still exists of this performance.

5 Writes Dylan, in reference to a turning point in his Greenwich Village days, "Sometimes you know things have to change, are going to change, but you can only feel it—like in that song of Sam Cooke's 'Change Is Gonna Come'—but you don't know it in a purposeful way." Bob Dylan, *Chronicles, Volume One* (New York: Simon and Schuster, 2004), 61.

6 Sam Cooke, *The Man Who Invented Soul,* RCA 4500, 1968, 33rpm; Sam Cooke, *The Man Who Invented Soul,* RCA 67911, 2000, CD.

7 Elijah Wald, *Dylan Goes Electric! Newport, Seeger, Dylan, and the Night That Split the Sixties* (New York: HarperCollins, 2015).

8 Peter Doggett, *There's a Riot Going On* (New York: Canongate, 2008), 78.

9 Kevin J. H. Dettmar, "Introduction," in *The Cambridge Companion to Bob Dylan,* ed. Kevin J. H. Dettmar (New York: Cambridge University Press, 2009), 1.

10 Among just a few of the more well-known contemporary historians and cultural critics who have recently published booklength works on Dylan are Greil Marcus (*Like a Rolling Stone: Bob Dylan at the Crossroads* [New York: Public Affairs, 2005]), Sean Wilentz (*Bob Dylan in America* [New York: Doubleday, 2010]), and Christopher Ricks (*Dylan's Visions of Sin* [New York: Ecco, 2004]). *The Cambridge Companion to Bob Dylan* boasts contributions from Michael Denning, Eric Lott, and Jonathan Lethem, among many others.

11 "Bob Dylan Receives Honorary Pulitzer Prize," *MSNBC,* 10 Apr. 2008, available online at http://today.msnbc.msn.com/id/24000483/ns/today-entertainment/.

12 Bruce Eder, "Sam Cooke," *All Music Guide,* available online at http://www.allmusic.com/artist/sam-cooke-mn0000238115.

13 One significant exception to this is Mark Burford's "Sam Cooke as Pop Album Artist: A Reinvention in Three Songs," an excellent musicological exploration of Cooke's maturation as an album artist that addresses the critical dismissal of his "pop" material. Burford, "Sam Cooke as Pop Album Artist: A Reinvention in Three Songs," *Journal of the American Musicological Society* 65, no. 1 (Spring 2012): 113–178. A few others include Christopher Trigg's "A Change Ain't Gonna Come: Sam Cooke and the Protest Song," *University of Toronto Quarterly* 79, no. 3 (Summer 2010): 991–1003; Michelle Hartman's "'This Sweet / Sweet Music': Jazz, Sam Cooke, and Reading Arab American Literary Identities," *Arab American Literature* 31, no. 4 (Winter 2006): 145–165; and David Sanjek's "One Size Does Not Fit All: The Precarious Position of the African American Entrepreneur in Post–World War II American Popular Music," *American Music* 15, no. 4 (Winter 1997): 535–562.

14 "Motel Aide Exonerated in Slaying of Singer," *Los Angeles Times*, 17 Dec. 1964, 36.

15 Betty Washington, "L.A. Cops Deny 'Frame-Up' in Cooke's Death," *Chicago Defender*, 16 Dec. 1964, 1.

16 "Says Millions Reject Verdict On Sam Cooke," *Chicago Defender*, 9 Jan. 1965, 9.

17 Wolff et al., *You Send Me*, 346.

18 Craig Werner, *A Change Is Gonna Come: Music, Race, and the Soul of America* (New York: Plume, 1998), 31.

19 Nelson George, *The Death of Rhythm and Blues* (New York: E. P. Dutton, 1988), 81.

20 Brian Ward, *Just My Soul Responding: Rhythm and Blues, Black Consciousness and Race Relations* (Berkeley: University of California Press, 1998), 147; Dave Marsh, *The Heart of Rock and Soul* (New York: Da Capo, 1989), 252.

21 Amiri Baraka (as LeRoi Jones), *Blues People: Negro Music in White America* (1963; New York: Perennial, 2002).

22 Ibid., 137.

23 Burford, "Sam Cooke as Pop Album Artist," 115.

24 Radano has described this fantasy as "as a sonic beyondness in a world of disenchanted existence." Ronald Radano, *Lying Up A Nation: Race and Black Music* (Chicago: University of Chicago Press, 2003), 23.

25 Ralph Ellison, *Shadow and Act* (New York: Vintage, 1995), 116.

26 Unless otherwise noted, for basic biographical and historical information I relied on the two existent biographies of the singer, Guralnick's *Dream Boogie* and Wolff et al.'s *You Send Me*.

27 The gospel historian Anthony Heilbut has written that the Soul Stirrers "not only created but defined the terms of good quartet singing." Heilbut, *The Gospel Sound: Good News and Bad Times* (New York: Simon and Schuster, 1971), 113–114.

28 "Gospel Singers: They Move Millions with Their Ringing Voices," *Ebony,* Dec. 1950, 92.

29 For background on Rupe and his founding of Specialty, see Guralnick, *Dream Boogie,* 68–69.

30 Various Artists, *The Great Shrine Concert 1955,* Specialty SPCD-7045-2, 1993, CD.

31 Craig Werner has written that "the key to Cooke's success, even within the gospel world, lay in his provocative blending of sex and spirituality." Werner, *Change Is Gonna Come,* 36.

32 Guralnick, *Dream Boogie,* 87.

33 Ibid., 129.

34 The details of Cooke's falling-out with Specialty are extensively recounted in Guralnick, *Dream Boogie,* esp. 171–183.

35 Ernest Cofield, "Close Look at Sam Cooke," *Chicago Defender,* 18 Oct. 1958, 11.

36 David Yaffe has written of the ubiquity of the chord progression in "I Got Rhythm," noting that, "to this day, calling for 'Rhythm' changes is a universally understood directive on the bandstand." Yaffe, *Fascinating Rhythm: Reading Jazz in American Writing* (Princeton, NJ: Princeton University Press, 2006), 17.

37 All *Billboard* chart information is derived from Joel Whitburn's *Billboard Top Pop Singles: 1955–1999* (Menomonee Falls, WI: Record Research, 2000).

38 See Sandra Graham, "The Fisk Jubilee Singers and the Concert Spiritual" (Ph.D. diss., New York University, 2001). Anthony Heilbut's *The Gospel Sound* remains a classic study of African American gospel music. Jerma Jackson's *Singing in My Soul: Black Gospel Music in a Secular Age* (Chapel Hill: University of North Carolina Press, 2004) and Bernice Johnson Reagon's *If You Don't Go, Don't Hinder Me: The African American Sacred Song Tradition* (Lincoln: University of Nebraska Press, 2001) are more recent. On Thomas Dorsey, see Michael W. Harris, *The Rise of Gospel Blues: The Music of Thomas Andrew Dorsey in the Urban Church* (New York: Oxford University Press, 1992).

39 James Weldon Johnson and John Rosamond Johnson, *The Books of the Negro Spirituals* (Boston: Da Capo, 2002), 12; Alain Locke, *The New Negro*

(New York: Simon and Schuster, 1997), 199; W. E. B. Du Bois, *The Souls of Black Folk* (New York: Barnes and Noble Classics, 2003), 178.

40 Ronald Radano, "Denoting Difference: The Writing of the Slave Spirituals," *Critical Inquiry* 22, no. 3 (Spring 1996): 519.

41 See Karl Hagstrom Miller, *Segregating Sound: Inventing Folk and Pop Music in the Age of Jim Crow* (Durham, NC: Duke University Press, 2010), 73-74.

42 Werner's *A Change Is Gonna Come* and Guthrie P. Ramsey, Jr.'s *Race Music: Black Cultures from Bebop to Hip-Hop* (Berkeley: University of California Press, 2004) both employ the call-and-response framework to considerable success. Samuel A. Floyd, Jr.'s *The Power of Black Music: Interpreting Its History from Africa to the United States* (New York: Oxford University Press, 1996) offers the ring shout as meta-theory for African American music. Robert O'Meally's edited collection *The Jazz Cadence of American Culture* (New York: Columbia University Press, 1998), as its title suggests, presents jazz music as a metaphorical lens through which to understand large portions of American culture more generally.

43 Miller, *Segregating Sound,* 74.

44 Sam Cooke artist bio, 1961, Box 3, Folder 21, Michael Ochs Collection, Rock and Roll Hall of Fame Library and Archives.

45 Aretha Franklin and David Ritz, *Aretha: From These Roots* (New York: Villard, 1999), 77-78.

46 As Dylan told a *Playboy* magazine interviewer, Ron Rosenbaum, in 1978, "The first thing that turned me on to folk singing was Odetta"; he then goes on to list "Mule Skinner," "Jack of Diamonds," and other songs on *Odetta Sings Blues and Ballads.* In *Bob Dylan: The Essential Interviews,* ed. Jonathan Cott (New York: Wenner Books, 2006), 204. Odetta, *Odetta Sings Blues and Ballads,* Tradition TLP 1010, 1956, 33rpm.

47 Robert Alden, "Sam Cooke at the Copa," *New York Times,* 7 Jul. 1964, 27.

48 Sam Cooke, *Live at the Harlem Square Club, 1963,* RCA PCD1-5181, 1985, CD.

49 Alden, "Sam Cooke at the Copa," 27; Sam Cooke, *Sam Cooke at the Copa,* RCA LPM/LSP-2970, 1964, 33rpm.

50 Press release, "RCA Releases a Historic Live Concert LP by the Legendary Sam Cooke," 1985, Box 3, Folder 21, Michael Ochs Collection, Rock and Roll Hall of Fame Library and Archives.

51 Ward, *Just My Soul Responding,* 291.

52 Val Adams, "Satire on Birch Society Barred from Ed Sullivan's TV Show," *New York Times,* 14 May 1963, 61.

53 Wolff et al., *You Send Me,* 291.

54 Barry Shank, *The Political Force of Musical Beauty* (Durham, NC: Duke University Press, 2014), 69.

55 Ellison, *Shadow and Act,* 162–163.

56 Qtd. in Keith Negus, *Bob Dylan* (Bloomington: Indiana University Press, 2008), 95.

57 John Bauldie, liner notes to Bob Dylan, *Bootleg Series, Vol. 1–3,* Columbia C3K-47382, 1991, CD.

58 The song's lyrics first appeared in print under the title "Many Thousands Go" in *Atlantic Monthly* 19 (Jun. 1867): 692.

59 Lee Marshall, "Bob Dylan and the Academy," in *Cambridge Companion to Bob Dylan,* 105; Simon Frith, *The Sociology of Rock* (London: Constable, 1978), 186.

60 There are many biographies of Bob Dylan: three of the more thorough are Robert Shelton's *No Direction Home,* Bob Spitz's *Bob Dylan* (New York: McGraw-Hill, 1989), and Paul Williams's three-volume study *Bob Dylan: Performing Artist* (Vol. 1, Novato, CA: Underwood-Miller, 1990; Vols. 2 and 3, New York: Omnibus, 1994 and 2004, respectively).

61 Dylan, *Chronicles, Volume One,* 33.

62 Anthony Scaduto, *Bob Dylan* (New York: New American Library, 1973), 11.

63 Dylan, *Chronicles, Volume One,* 80.

64 Yearbook quote from Shelton, *No Direction Home,* 38; Wald, *Dylan Goes Electric!,* 41.

65 Williams, *Bob Dylan: Performing Artist,* Vol. 1, 38.

66 Robert Shelton, "Bob Dylan: A Distinctive Folk-Song Stylist," *New York Times,* 29 Sept. 1961, 31.

67 Bob Dylan, *Bob Dylan,* Columbia 62022, 1962, 33rpm.

68 See Dylan, *Chronicles, Volume One,* 32–33.

69 Neil Rosenberg, "Introduction," in *Transforming Tradition: Folk Music Revivals Examined,* ed. Neil Rosenberg (Urbana: University of Illinois Press, 1993), 8.

70 See David Allen Evans, "Folk Revival Music," record review, *Journal of American Folklore* 92 (1979): 110–111. Also Robert Cantwell, *When We Were Good: The Folk Revival* (Cambridge, MA: Harvard University Press, 1996), 34.

71 Robin D. G. Kelley, "Notes on Deconstructing the Folk," *American Historical Review* 97, no. 5 (Dec. 1992): 1403.

72 Miller, *Segregating Sound,* 6. Some of the foremost chroniclers and collectors of folk music brought such strong preconceptions and agendas to their ostensibly preservationist project that they were essentially inventing the musical spheres that they believed to be preserving. Miller reproduces a fascinating 1940 exchange between John Lomax and Blind Willie McTell in which Lomax asks McTell to play "complaining songs, complaining about the hard times and sometimes mistreatment of the whites." McTell responds that he does not know any such songs, but Lomax persists, asking him to play a song called "Ain't It Hard to Be a Nigger, Nigger." McTell again says he doesn't know the song; Lomax then observes that McTell seems "uncomfortable." Such an exchange demonstrates the ways that John Lomax, one of the most influential folklorists of the twentieth century, brought his own expectations to bear on McTell's music, and that what Lomax assumes to be "authentic" to McTell's musical journey is more fantasy of Lomax than lived reality of McTell. Ibid., 80.

73 See Ronald Cohen, *Rainbow Quest: The Folk Music Revival and American Society, 1940-1970* (Boston: University of Massachusetts Press, 2002), esp. 183-191.

74 Georgina Boyes, *The Imagined Village: Culture, Ideology and the English Folk Revival* (New York: Manchester University Press, 1993), 3.

75 Wald's *Dylan Goes Electric!* offers a terrific window into the realities and myths of this legendary encounter.

76 In an oft-quoted article penned for *Sing Out!* in 1964, Seeger wrote that the folksinger Ramblin' Jack Elliott (born Elliot Adnopoz in Brooklyn, New York) was a "fake":

> Jack Elliott is a self-made man. . . . When some people find that Jack Elliott was born in Brooklyn—he with his cowboy hat and boots, rough lingo and expert guitar playing—their first reaction is, "Oh, he's a fake." They're dead wrong. Jack reborned himself "in Oklahoma." He didn't just learn some new songs, but he changed his whole way of living.

This passage is notable for the way in which Seeger so forcefully articulates an alternative idea of musical and cultural authenticity. Jack Elliott's self-invention becomes evidence of his authenticity, and there's no bright line between playing a role and becoming a role. The phrase "Jack reborned himself 'in Oklahoma'" is particularly striking for its affected grammar: the intermingling of performance and identity here is so twisting it's almost indecipherable where one begins and the other ends. Pete Seeger, "Johnny Appleseed, Jr.," *Sing Out!,* February–March 1964, 71. Also qtd. in Cantwell, *When We Were Good,* 329.

77 John S. Wilson, "Program Given by Alan Lomax," *New York Times,* 4 April 1959, 13. The story of this event is the subject of some dispute. Lomax had originally booked a Harlem group called the Cadillacs to play the concert, and Ronald Cohen reports that they were widely booed (Cohen, *Rainbow Quest,* 140). However, Elijah Wald has since written that the Cadillacs in fact could not make the show and were hastily replaced with the Detroit group, who were the ones booed (Wald, *Dylan Goes Electric!,* 36).

78 *Little Sandy Review* 4 (1960): 21.

79 Wald, *Dylan Goes Electric!,* 50.

80 Jay Smith, "The Samplers in Person," *Little Sandy Review* 13 (1962): 8; "Odetta at Carnegie Hall," *Little Sandy Review* 9 (1961): 9; Bob Dahe, "Belafonte Returns to Carnegie Hall," *Little Sandy Review* 9 (1961): 11.

81 Tom Hayden and Students for a Democratic Society, *The Port Huron Statement: The Visionary Call of the 1960s Revolution* (New York: Public Affairs, 2005), 50–51.

82 See Doug Rossinow, *The Politics of Authenticity: Liberalism, Christianity and the New Left in America* (New York: Columbia University Press, 1998).

83 Hayden et al., *Port Huron Statement,* 45.

84 As Rossinow notes, the SDS leader, Tom Hayden, spoke openly of his hopes that his group would become a "counterpart to SNCC" but in the north (a significant qualification). Rossinow, *Politics of Authenticity,* 165. See also Grace Elizabeth Hale, *A Nation of Outsiders* (New York: Oxford University Press, 2011), 84–118.

85 Robert Shelton, "Songs a Weapon in Rights Battle," *New York Times,* 20 Aug. 1962, 1, 14.

86 Robert Shelton, "Freedom Songs Sweep North," *New York Times,* 6 Jul. 1963, 7.

87 "Blind Gary Davis—Harlem Street Singer," *Little Sandy Review* 11 (1962): 11.

88 Jim Rooney and Eric Von Schmidt, *Baby, Let Me Follow You Down: The Illustrated Story of the Cambridge Folk Years* (Boston: University of Massachusetts Press, 1994), 189.

89 Johannes Fabian, *Time and the Other: How Anthropology Makes Its Object* (New York: Columbia University Press, 2002).

90 Barry Hansen, "'"Spider" John Koerner, Dave "Snaker" Ray, and Tony "Little Sun" Glover'—*Blues, Rags, and Hollers," Little Sandy Review* 27

(1963): 3. Hansen frequently wrote on blues music and blues albums for *Little Sandy Review*. In an interesting and truly bizarre twist, he later went on to fame as the radio personality "Dr. Demento," a popular, nationally syndicated disc jockey perhaps best known for starting the career of the song parodist "Weird Al" Yankovic.

91 Barry Hansen, "Negro Folk Rhythms," *Little Sandy Review* 13 (1962): 11–12. Emphasis in original.

92 "John Lee Hooker—Folk Blues," *Little Sandy Review* 7 (1961).

93 "Robert Pete Williams—Angola Prisoner's Blues," *Little Sandy Review* 4 (1961): 29.

94 Neil Rosenberg observes that the fourth stage of the folk revival constantly dealt with inconsistencies reconciling "an intellectual music with an anti-intellectual ethos." "The *idea* that such a thing as folksong existed was an intellectual construct," writes Rosenberg, but "an essential aspect of the construct was that folk music was unselfconscious behavior." Rosenberg, "Introduction," 8.

95 Bob Dylan, *Bob Dylan*, Columbia 62022, 1963, 33rpm.

96 Negus, *Bob Dylan*, 82.

97 Barry Shank, " 'That Wild Mercury Sound': Bob Dylan and the Illusion of American Culture," *Boundary 2* 29, no. 1 (Spring 2002): 109.

98 This performance was originally released on Folkways' *Dave Van Ronk Sings, Vol. 2*, Folkways FA2383, 1961, 33rpm. It can also be heard on the Van Ronk compilation CD *Folkways Years, 1959–1961*, Smithsonian Folkways Recordings SF-40041, 1991, CD.

99 "I'd heard Van Ronk back in the Midwest on records and thought he was pretty great," writes Dylan in *Chronicles, Volume One*, "copied some of his recordings phrase for phrase . . . I loved his style" (15).

100 Bob Dylan, "Mixed-Up Confusion," Columbia 4-42656, 1962, 45rpm.

101 Bob Dylan, *Another Side of Bob Dylan*, Columbia 2193, 1964, 33rpm.

102 Nat Hentoff, "The Crackin, Shakin', Breakin' Sounds," *New Yorker*, 24 Oct. 1964, 66.

103 Ibid., 65.

104 Irwin Silber, "An Open Letter to Bob Dylan," *Sing Out!*, November 1964, 22–23.

105 Bob Dylan, "Subterranean Homesick Blues," Columbia 43242, 1965, 45rpm.

106 Bob Dylan, *Bringing It All Back Home*, Columbia 2328, 1965, 33rpm.

107 The Byrds, "Mr. Tambourine Man," Columbia 43271, 1965, 45rpm.

108 Bob Dylan, "Like a Rolling Stone," Columbia 43346, 1965, 45rpm. Information on recording dates are from Marcus, *Like a Rolling Stone,* 204–223.

109 Marcus, *Like a Rolling Stone,* 120.

110 Wald, *Dylan Goes Electric!,* 206.

111 Mary Campbell, "Rock 'n' Roll Music Gets Message, Man," *Los Angeles Times,* 20 Sept. 1965, C19; Thomas Meehan, "Public Writer No. 1?" *New York Times,* 12 Dec. 1965, 45.

112 "Nat Hentoff's American Airmail," *New Musical Express,* 15 Oct. 1965, 4.

113 Sylvie Reice, "Why Teens Switched to Folk Rock," *Los Angeles Times,* 6 Jan. 1966, E8.

114 Ellen Willis, "Dylan," in *Out of the Vinyl Deeps: Ellen Willis on Rock Music,* ed. Nona Willis Aronowitz (New York: New York University Press, 2011), 3–4.

115 In its December 9, 2004, issue, *Rolling Stone* magazine named the song number one on a list of "The 500 Greatest Songs of All Time." As the musicologist Wilfrid Mellers once wonderfully described it, "Although the words are dismissive, the music—with its jaunty repeated notes and eyebrow-charging rising thirds, its fragmented phrases that leave one agog for what's coming next—is positive in total effect. . . . He is putting down a girl who may have wanted to gobble him up like a lollypop, but music so affirmative cannot be finally destructive." Mellers, *A Darker Shade of Pale: A Backdrop to Bob Dylan* (New York: Oxford University Press, 1985), 104.

116 Transcript available online at http://rockhall.com/inductees/bob-dylan/transcript/bruce-springsteen-on-dylan/.

117 As Simon Frith argues, the cultural association of Dylan as a folksinger—an association that confirmed "his individual genius, his personal insights, his unique voice and style . . . dense poetic forms and rambling melodic structures that made audience participation impossible"—left important legacies for his emergence into rock stardom. Frith, *Sound Effects: Youth, Leisure, and the Politics of Rock 'n' Roll* (New York: Pantheon, 1981), 30.

118 Negus, *Bob Dylan,* 41.

119 See Theodore Gracyk, *Rhythm and Noise: An Aesthetics of Rock* (Durham, NC: Duke University Press, 1996), esp. 208–223.

120 Greil Marcus writes that Dylan allegedly suggested Spector as his next producer when he and Wilson parted ways shortly after "Like a Rolling Stone." Marcus, *Like a Rolling Stone,* 140.

121 Frith, *Sociology of Rock*, 181.

122 Dylan himself has occasionally played on the minstrelsy angle, most notably in the title of his acclaimed 2001 album *"Love and Theft"* (scare quotes in the original), widely believed to be a nod to Eric Lott's landmark 1993 study of antebellum blackface minstrelsy.

123 Hentoff, "Crackin, Shakin', Breakin' Sounds," 74.

124 Meehan, "Public Writer No. 1?," 132.

125 Williams, *Bob Dylan: Performing Artist*, Vol. 1, 35.

126 Jean Tamarin, "Bringing It All Back Home," in *Cambridge Companion to Bob Dylan*, 132.

127 For a recent consideration of the importance of black American blues on late 1960s British rock musicians, see Andrew Kellett, "Fathers and Sons: American Blues and British Rock Music, 1960–1970" (Ph.D. diss., University of Delaware, 2008). For a specific discussion of Eric Clapton and Cream's relationship to Robert Johnson, see Susan McClary, *Conventional Wisdom: The Content of Musical Form* (Berkeley: University of California Press, 2000), 32–62.

128 Muddy Waters, *Fathers and Sons*, Chess 127, 1969, 33rpm.

2. The White Atlantic

1 "Mailbag," *Melody Maker*, 27 Oct. 1962, 16.

2 Here are a few examples of such complaints: "Cliff Richard Slams British Stars," *Melody Maker*, 23 Jan. 1960, 20; "'Americanised' BBC & ITA Attacked," *Melody Maker*, 18 Feb. 1961, 1; "British Stars Don't Copy," *Melody Maker*, 5 Aug. 1961, 13; and "British Pop? The Yanks Don't Want to Know!" *Melody Maker*, 18 Aug. 1962.

3 "Top Fifty," *Melody Maker*, 27 Oct. 1962, 4.

4 Gary Edgerton, *The Columbia History of American Television* (New York: Columbia University Press, 2010), 261.

5 Barry Miles's *The British Invasion: The Music, The Times, The Era* (New York: Sterling, 2009) and Bill Harry's *The British Invasion: How the Beatles and Other UK Bands Conquered America* (New Malden, UK: Chrome Dreams, 2004) are two recent books on the subject, incidentally both by British authors; the number of compact discs, documentaries, television specials, and other tributes are too many to list.

6 "Rock 'n' Roll: Everybody's Turned On." *Time*, 21 May 1965, 66.

7 Charlie Gillett, *The Sound of the City: The Rise of Rock and Roll* (1970; Boston: Da Capo, 1996), 250.

8 Raymond Williams, *Marxism and Literature* (New York: Oxford University Press, 1977), 116.

9 Paul Gilroy, *The Black Atlantic: Modernity and Double Consciousness* (Cambridge, MA: Harvard University Press, 1993), 74–75.

10 Ibid., 3.

11 Lester Bangs, "The British Invasion," in *The Rolling Stone Illustrated History of Rock and Roll,* ed. Anthony DeCurtis, James Henke, Holly George-Warren, and Jim Miller (New York: Random House, 1992), 199.

12 Jack Maher and Tom Noonan, "Chart Crawling with Beatles," *Billboard,* 4 Apr. 1964, 1. The Beatles had twelve records on the Top 100 this week, including their new single "Can't Buy Me Love," which entered at number eleven.

13 Donald White, "Beatle Scourge Spreads," *Boston Globe,* 22 Nov. 1963, 24; "The Beatles Is Coming," *Newsweek,* 3 Feb. 1964, 77.

14 The Beatles, "Please Please Me," Vee-Jay 581, 1963; "From Me to You," Vee-Jay 522; *Introducing . . . The Beatles,* Vee-Jay 1062, 1963; "She Loves You," Swan 4152, 1963. All 45rpm.

15 The American rock and roll star Del Shannon actually released a cover of "From Me to You" in 1963 that outsold the original and beat the Beatles onto the American charts.

16 Chris Hutchins, "Roy Orbison Says 'The Beatles Could Be Tops in America,'" *New Musical Express,* 31 May 1963, 3.

17 All *Billboard* chart information is derived from Joel Whitburn's *Billboard Top Pop Singles: 1955–1999* (Menomonee Falls, WI: Record Research, 2000).

18 Dorothy Kilgallen, "New British Invaders Outdo Beatles," *Washington Post,* 26 May 1964, D5.

19 "Stones Roll Home Again," *New Musical Express,* 26 Jun. 1964, 4.

20 For an interesting history and analysis of this dichotomy, see John McMillian's *Beatles vs. Stones* (New York: Simon and Schuster, 2013).

21 Two prominent instances of this among many are the cover of *New Musical Express* from February 21, 1958, which announces "They're Coming Over!" with photos of Buddy Holly, Jerry Lee Lewis, and Paul Anka; and the cover story to the August 10, 1963, edition of *Melody Maker,* entitled "U.S. Stars Invade!" and featuring write-ups of Sam Cooke, Dinah Washington, and Josh White.

22 "The Pop Heroes," *Melody Maker,* 2 May 1964, 3.

23 Colin MacInnes, *Absolute Beginners* (1959; London: Allison and Busby, 2007), 12.

24 *Absolute Beginners* was particularly influential among British musicians: in 1986 David Bowie produced a musical film of the book starring himself and Ray Davies of the Kinks. The *Evening Standard* took a less charitable view of the book upon its release: "Here, you citizens, tax payers, oldsters, you conscripts, sordid and squares, dig this—This is what you and your city and the civilisation you have made there look like to an articulate teenager. It's not very pretty if you want to know." Qtd. in Arthur Marwick, *The Sixties: Cultural Revolution in Britain, France, Italy, and the United States* (Oxford: Oxford University Press, 1998), 62–63.

25 Some examples include Dick Hebdige, *Subculture: The Meaning of Style* (New York: Routledge, 1979); Stuart Hall and Tony Jefferson, eds., *Resistance through Rituals: Youth Subcultures in Post-War Britain* (1976; New York: Routledge, 1993); and Stanley Cohen, *Folk Devils and Moral Panics: The Creation of the Mods and the Rockers* (London: MacGibbon and Kee, 1972).

26 See Colin MacInnes, *England, Half English* (New York: Random House, 1961), 55.

27 Richard Hoggart, *The Uses of Literacy* (1957; New Brunswick, NJ: Transaction, 1998), 189. Hoggart's complaint about "echo-chamber recording" suggests this passage might describe an early encounter with Elvis Presley.

28 See E. P. Thompson, *The Making of the English Working Class* (New York: Vintage, 1963); Raymond Williams, *Culture and Society* (New York: Columbia University Press, 1958).

29 See Paul Gilroy, *"There Ain't No Black in the Union Jack": The Cultural Politics of Race and Nation* (Chicago: University of Chicago Press, 1991), esp. 11–42.

30 E. J. Hobsbawm, *Industry and Empire: 1750 to the Present Day* (New York: Penguin, 1999), 230–255.

31 George McKay, *Circular Breathing: The Cultural Politics of Jazz in Britain* (Durham, NC: Duke University Press, 2005), 10.

32 Ibid., 106–107. As Andrew Blake argues, American musics have long been "resisted from within and without the British musical establishment on the grounds that these were black or black-derived forms and that black music was dangerous.... There was a particular fear that eroticized and narcotized music would make white women open to the advances of black men, the common fear of 'miscegenation' around which many forms of racism have

been organized." Blake, *The Land without Music: Music, Culture, and Society in Twentieth-Century Britain* (New York: Manchester University Press, 1997), 85.

33 Tony Jefferson, "Cultural Responses of the Teds," in Hall and Jefferson, *Resistance through Rituals*, 86.

34 George Melly, *Revolt into Style: The Pop Arts* (1970; London: Faber and Faber, 2008), 32.

35 Stanley Cohen famously described the teddy boys as producers of a "moral panic." See Cohen, *Folk Devils and Moral Panics,* 1-3.

36 John Clarke, Stuart Hall, Tony Jefferson, and Brian Roberts, "Subcultures, Cultures and Class: A Theoretical Overview," in Hall and Jefferson, *Resistance through Rituals,* 15.

37 Hebdige, *Subculture,* 50.

38 The historian Edward Pilkington writes that "the phrase 'Rock 'n' Roll riot' was coined to describe their Saturday night escapades: instead of rocking in their seats the Teds took to ripping them up, which was much more fun." Pilkington, *Beyond the Mother Country: West Indians and the Notting Hill White Riots* (London: I. B. Tauris, 1988), 94. Following this, Dick Bradley writes that "if the cinema riots *fixed* the association of rock 'n' roll with teenagers, they also fixed another association, in the eyes of the parent culture—namely, that between rock 'n' roll and 'juvenile delinquency.'" Bradley, *Understanding Rock 'n' Roll: Popular Music in Britain 1955-1964* (Philadelphia: Open University Press, 1992), 56.

39 See Hebdige, *Subculture,* 50-51. The historian Bill Schwarz describes a "hardening" of British racial attitudes during this period, and by the late 1950s various polls revealed increasing hostility toward issues such as mixed marriages. Writes Schwarz: "To put this in abstract terms, one could conclude that in these years England was 're-racialised' . . . the rediscovery on the part of English people in this period of themselves as 'white' is as forceful a historical fact as any of the other more conventional ethnic discoveries of the 1950s and 1960s." Schwarz, "Black Metropolis, White England," in *Modern Times: Reflections on a Century of English Modernity,* ed. Mica Nava and Alan O'Shea (New York: Routledge, 1996), 199.

40 " 'Keep Britain White' Call in Notting Hill Area," *London Times,* 10 Sept. 1958, 5.

41 Pilkington, *Beyond the Mother Country,* 123.

42 "Four-Year Terms for Nine 'Nigger-Hunting' Youths," *London Times,* 16 Sept. 1958, 4.

43 Alan Travis, "After 44 Years Secret Papers Reveal Truth about Five Nights of Violence in Notting Hill," *Guardian,* 24 Aug. 2002, http://www.guardian.co.uk/uk/2002/aug/24/artsandhumanities.nottinghillcarnival 2002.

44 Hebdige, *Subculture,* 50.

45 Melly, *Revolt into Style,* 34.

46 See Linda Martin and Kerry Segrave, *Anti-Rock: The Opposition to Rock 'n' Roll* (New York: Da Capo, 1988), esp. 41–43.

47 An excellent treatment of trad as a political culture can be found in McKay, *Circular Breathing,* esp. 48–59.

48 There are numerous online trad communities at the time of this writing; see http://www.jazznorthwest.co.uk/ for just one example.

49 See, for instance, McKay, *Circular Breathing,* esp. 30–33, 47–86.

50 Chris Barber, "There's No U.S. Jazz Scene: It's Our Job to Teach the Americans about Jazz," *Melody Maker,* 30 May 1961, 2–3.

51 McKay, *Circular Breathing,* 98.

52 Chas McDevitt, *Skiffle: The Definitive Inside Story* (London: Robson, 1997), 5.

53 George Melly writes that Colyer and his acolytes "equated traditional jazz with left-wing protest and it was to the sound of a New Orleans marching band that the Ban-the-Bomb columns kept their spirits up on the road from Aldermaston." Melly, *Revolt into Style,* 60.

54 Qtd. in McKay, *Circular Breathing,* 93.

55 Harry Shapiro, *Alexis Korner* (London: Bloomsbury, 1996), 62.

56 Chas McDevitt, *Skiffle,* 17–18.

57 This prehistory of British skiffle in its American contexts can be found in McDevitt, *Skiffle,* 13–37.

58 Shapiro, *Alexis Korner,* 48.

59 All British chart information is derived from Neil Warwick, Jon Kutner, and Tony Brown, *The Big Book of British Charts: Singles and Albums,* 3rd ed. (London: Omnibus, 2004), 342.

60 McDevitt, *Skiffle,* 8.

61 Ibid., 6–7.

62 Donegan released "Pick a Bale of Cotton" as a single on Pye Records in 1962; it was his last to chart in England.

63 Paul Du Noyer, *Liverpool: Wondrous Place* (London: Virgin, 2002), vi.

64 The definitive biography of Korner is Harry Shapiro's, from which I draw biographical information here.

65 Alexis Korner, "'Skiffle' or 'Piffle'?" *Melody Maker,* 28 Jul. 1956, 5.

66 Keith Richards, *Life* (New York: Little, Brown, 2010), 83.

67 Shapiro, *Alexis Korner,* 102–103.

68 The first quote is from Chris Williams, "Rolling Stones R and B Champs," *New Musical Express,* 23 Aug. 1963, 8; the second quote is in Shapiro, *Alexis Korner,* 112.

69 Mick Jagger, "The Top Spot? I Don't Care a Damn . . . ," *Melody Maker,* 11 Jul. 1964, 3.

70 Blake, *Land without Music,* 125.

71 "Mystery Man of the Blues," *Melody Maker,* 11 Jan. 1963, 15.

72 The musicologist Susan McClary and the historian George Lipsitz have both written (quite critically) of the white blues obsession with Robert Johnson: McClary in *Conventional Wisdom* (Berkeley: University of California Press, 2000), 53–62; and Lipsitz in *The Possessive Investment in Whiteness* (Philadelphia: Temple University Press, 1998), 199–227.

73 The Rolling Stones, "Not Fade Away," Decca F11845, 1964, 45rpm.

74 Bo Diddley, "Bo Diddley," Checker 1098, 1955, 45rpm; Buddy Holly, "Not Fade Away," Brunswick 55035, 1957, 45rpm.

75 See Christopher Washburne, "The Clave of Jazz: A Caribbean Contribution to the Rhythmic Foundation of an African-American Music," *Black Music Research Journal* 17, no. 1 (Spring 1997): 59–80.

76 Richards, *Life,* 103.

77 The Rolling Stones, "Come On," Decca F11675, 1963, 45rpm.

78 Michael Coyle, "Hijacked Hits and Antic Authenticity: Cover Songs, Race, and Postwar Marketing," in *Rock Over the Edge,* ed. Roger Beebe, Denise Fulbrooke, and Ben Saunders (Durham, NC: Duke University Press, 2002), 146.

3. "Friends across the Sea"

Epigraph: Michael Goldberg, "Stevie Wonder," *Rolling Stone* 5 Nov. 1987, 153.

1 Chris Hutchins, "Beatles Soar to Success," *Billboard,* 2 Nov. 1963, 30.

2 "Beatles Score 2nd Million," *Billboard,* 14 Dec. 1963, 30; Chris Hutchins, "Dealer Unity Makes Strengths," *Billboard,* 14 Dec. 1963, 32.

3 "Hot 100," *Billboard*, 14 Dec. 1963, 24.

4 "Singles Reviews," *Billboard*, 4 Jan. 1964, 21.

5 See *Billboard*, 1 Feb. 1964, 1.

6 Jack Maher and Tom Noonan, "Chart Crawling with Beatles," *Billboard*, 4 Apr. 1964, 1.

7 In its 23 Nov. 1963 issue, *Billboard* featured an R&B Singles chart on page 22; the following week, it was gone.

8 See Chris Molanphy's terrific article, "I Know You Got Soul: The Trouble with *Billboard*'s R&B/Hip-Hop Chart," in *Pitchfork*, 14 Apr. 2014, http://pitchfork.com/features/articles/9378-i-know-you-got-soul-the-trouble-with-billboards-rbhip-hop-chart/. David Brackett has also considered this moment extensively in his article "The Politics and Practice of 'Crossover' in American Popular Music, 1963 to 1965," *Musical Quarterly* 78, no. 4 (1994): 774–797. *Billboard* has never given a definitive answer for why the chart was discontinued and then reinstated.

9 All *Billboard* chart information is derived from Joel Whitburn's *Billboard Top Pop Singles: 1955–1999* (Menomonee Falls, WI: Record Research, 2000).

10 "Tamla-Motown Goes Outside to Get Talent," *Billboard*, 4 Sept. 1965, 10.

11 Brian Ward, *Just My Soul Responding: Rhythm and Blues, Black Consciousness, and Race Relations* (Berkeley: University of California Press, 1998), 268.

12 "Rock 'n' Roll: Everybody's Turned On," *Time*, 21 May 1965, 86.

13 Robert Shelton, "The Beatles Will Make the Scene Here Again . . . ," *New York Times*, 11 Aug. 1965.

14 Ray Coleman, "George Harrison—Exclusive!" *Melody Maker*, 21 Mar. 1964, 10–11.

15 Peter Guralnick, *Sweet Soul Music* (Boston: Back Bay, 1999), 1–2.

16 Nelson George, *The Death of Rhythm and Blues* (New York: E. P. Dutton, 1988), 88–89.

17 Andrew Flory, "I Hear a Symphony: Making Music at Motown, 1959–1979," Ph.D. diss., University of North Carolina at Chapel Hill, 2006, 131.

18 Perhaps the most extreme example of this is found in George's *Death of Rhythm and Blues*, in a chapter entitled "R&B Yin and Yang" in which he (unfavorably) judges Motown against Stax (86). Stax artists actually covered Motown songs with some frequency, with notable examples including Otis Redding's versions of Smokey Robinson's "My Girl" and "It's Growing."

19 "Motown's Musical Education Makes Four Tops Classy Act," *Billboard,* 24 Dec. 1966, 8.

20 "The Supremes Ask: 'What's Happened to Show Business?,'" Box 11, Folder 11, Michael Ochs Collection, Rock and Roll Hall of Fame Library and Archives.

21 William Buchanan, "The Supremes—A 'Pop' Sound for Young, Old," *Boston Globe,* 10 Nov. 1966, 38.

22 Nancy Moss, "The Supremes: 11 Frantic Hours, 50 Screaming Minutes," *Chicago Tribune,* 20 Mar. 1966, 131.

23 Richard Goldstein, "Super Supremes: 'Stop in the Name of Love,'" *New York Times,* 23 Jul. 1967, 75.

24 Fred Moten, *In the Break* (Minneapolis: University of Minnesota Press, 2003), 149.

25 See Bob Spitz, *The Beatles* (New York: Little, Brown, 2005), 111.

26 There are numerous histories of Motown: the most foundational is Nelson George's *Where Did Our Love Go? The Rise and Fall of the Motown Sound* (1985; Urbana-Champaign: University of Illinois Press, 2007), while Gerald Posner's more recent *Motown: Music, Money, Sex, and Power* (New York: Random House, 2002) is also excellent. Gerald Early's *One Nation under a Groove: Motown and American Culture* (Ann Arbor: University of Michigan Press, 2004) is a short but highly insightful work on the label's cultural significance, and Suzanne Smith's *Dancing In the Street: Motown and the Cultural Politics of Detroit* (Cambridge, MA: Harvard University Press, 2001) is an outstanding study of Motown's relationship with the city that spawned it. The number of biographies, histories, and critical studies of the Beatles is too vast to begin to list them. The earliest major effort was Hunter Davies's *The Beatles,* written with the band's cooperation and originally published in 1968 (New York: W. W. Norton, 2010). Perhaps the most widely read is Philip Norman's *Shout!* (New York: Simon and Schuster, 1981). Recent books include Jonathan Gould's *Can't Buy Me Love* (New York: Harmony, 2007), Steven Stark's *Meet the Beatles* (New York: HarperEntertainment, 2005), and Spitz's *The Beatles.*

27 On the *New Musical Express* charts "Love Me Do" hit number twenty-one, whereas "Please Please Me" stalled out at number two. "From Me to You" and "She Loves You" hit the top spot on both.

28 The Beatles, *Please Please Me,* Parlophone PMC 1202, 1963, 33rpm. All recording dates are from Mark Lewisohn, *The Complete Beatles Chronicle* (London: Pyramid, 1992).

29 The Beatles, *With the Beatles,* Parlophone PMC 1206, 1963, 33rpm; *Meet the Beatles!,* Capitol 2047, 1964, 33rpm.

30 The Marvelettes, "Please Mr. Postman," Tamla 54046, 1961, 45rpm; The Miracles, "You've Really Got a Hold on Me," Tamla 54073, 1962, 45rpm; Barrett Strong, "Money," Anna 1111, 1960, 45rpm.

31 As Jonathan Gould has argued, "Each of the three Motown-derived songs on *With the Beatles* represented a landmark in the rise of [Gordy's] label." Gould, *Can't Buy Me Love: The Beatles, Britain, and America* (New York: Harmony, 2007), 192.

32 In 2011 BBC Four ran a documentary on the Motown Revue's 1965 tour entitled *Motown Invasion,* in an interesting reversal of the British Invasion concept. While the tour itself was largely seen as a flop at the time, the exposure generated from the *Ready, Steady, Go!* "Sounds of Motown" special, filmed during the visit, soon led to considerable U.K. chart success for numerous Motown artists.

33 Maurice Williams and the Zodiacs, "Stay," Herald 552, 1960, 45rpm.

34 Jacqueline Warwick, *Girl Groups, Girl Culture: Popular Music and Identity in the 1960s* (New York: Routledge, 2007), 46.

35 In 1964, a New York publisher even released a small novelty book entitled *Love Letters to the Beatles* that anthologized the band's more memorable correspondence. Bill Adler, *Love Letters to the Beatles* (New York: G. P. Putnam's Sons, 1964).

36 Tim Riley notes that "where the Miracles sound elegant, Lennon sounds ruthless. . . . The politesse it took for a black man to make this hunger for love acceptable gets drowned in Lennonesque revenge." Riley, *Tell Me Why: A Beatles Commentary* (Boston: Da Capo, 2002), 80.

37 Dave Marsh, *The Heart of Rock and Soul* (Boston: Da Capo, 1999), 163.

38 Writes Berry Gordy in his memoir: "Janie didn't realize I was serious about using the line. . . . She was more convinced when she saw the songwriter's contract. Thinking her verse was the best of all, I gave her fifty percent." Gordy, *To Be Loved: The Music, the Magic, the Memories of Motown* (New York: Warner, 1994), 122.

39 Ian MacDonald, *Revolution in the Head: The Beatles' Records and the Sixties* (London: Fourth Estate, 1997), 77–81.

40 Alex Weheliye, *Phonographies: Grooves in Sonic Afro-Modernity* (Durham, NC: Duke University Press, 2005), 3.

41 See, for instance, Karl Hagstrom Miller, *Segregating Sound: Inventing Folk and Pop Music in the Age of Jim Crow* (Durham, NC: Duke University

Press, 2010), and Scott DeVeaux, *The Birth of Bebop: A Social and Musical History* (Berkeley: University of California Press, 1997).

42 According to Dave Laing's thorough catalogue of the band's early repertoire, for the most part the Beatles didn't even start performing Motown songs until early 1963, by which point they'd already made the British charts with "Love Me Do" and "Please Please Me." Laing, appendix to "Six Boys, Six Beatles: The Formative Years, 1950-1962," in *The Cambridge Companion to the Beatles,* ed. Kenneth Womack (New York: Cambridge University Press, 2009), 27-32.

43 Reebee Garofalo describes Boone as "the singer who represents the epitome of cultural theft," noting that "the 'white buck' shoes that became his signature only reinforced the racist implications of his 'white bread' delivery," while Craig Werner explicitly links Boone to minstrelsy and argues that "the long-standing segregation of the record charts encouraged white artists to release sanitized 'cover' versions of black hits." Garofalo, *Rockin' Out: Popular Music in the U.S.A.,* 4th ed. (Upper Saddle River, NJ: Pearson Prentice Hall, 2008), 139; Werner, *A Change Is Gonna Come: Music, Race, and the Soul of America* (New York: Plume, 1998), 86.

44 Gordy, *To Be Loved,* 95-96.

45 This story is recounted in Posner, *Motown,* 137.

46 "Ravings," *Melody Maker,* 22 Jun. 1963, 5.

47 The Beatles, *A Hard Day's Night,* Parlophone PMC 1230, 1964, 33rpm (UK); United Artists 6366, 1964, 33rpm (US).

48 Allan "Dr. Licks" Slutsky, *Standing in the Shadows of Motown: The Life and Music of Legendary Bassist James Jamerson* (Wynnewood, PA: Dr. Licks Publishing, 1989), 183.

49 George, *Where Did Our Love Go?,* 110.

50 Slutsky, *Standing in the Shadows of Motown,* xii.

51 "James Jamerson Dies at 45: Bassist Backed Detroit Stars," *New York Times,* 6 Aug. 1983, 26.

52 Marshall Crenshaw, "James Jamerson: 1938-1983," *Rolling Stone,* 29 Sept. 1983, 60.

53 Slutsky, *Standing in the Shadows of Motown,* 190.

54 All biographical information on Jamerson is from Slutsky's *Standing in the Shadows of Motown,* unless otherwise noted. Berry Gordy was born November 28, 1929; Paul McCartney was born June 18, 1942.

55 Ibid., 10.

56 Posner, *Motown,* 141.

57 As Motown arranger Dave Van Depitte described it, "What James contributed to the music was a sense of jazz as opposed to basic R&B. When he came on the scene in the early '60s, bass parts hung on the roots and fifths and then called it a day . . . even his simple lines were far more complex than what anybody had been doing up to that time." Slutsky, *Standing in the Shadows of Motown,* 188.

58 Ibid., 12.

59 Mary Wells, "My Guy," Motown 1056, 1964, 45rpm.

60 Martha and the Vandellas, "Nowhere to Run," Gordy 7039, 1965, 45rpm; The Four Tops, "It's the Same Old Song," Motown 1081, 1965, 45rpm; The Temptations, "Get Ready," Gordy 7049, 1966, 45rpm. As Nelson George writes, "On some Motown recordings it's hard to hear the piano, the organ, and vibes blend together, the sax solo is bland, and even Benny's drums, buried beneath tambourines and guitars, are sometimes lost in a [Holland-Dozier-Holland] mix. But never, never does anyone forget the bass lines." George, *Where Did Our Love Go?,* 110.

61 Fontella Bass, "Rescue Me," Checker 1120, 1965, 45rpm. "Rescue Me" went to number one on the R&B charts and number four on the Pop charts.

62 Slutsky, *Standing in the Shadows of Motown,* 38.

63 "Record Reviews," *Variety,* 8 Dec. 1965, 54; Allen Evans, "Rubber Soul," *New Musical Express,* 3 Dec. 1965, 8.

64 Tim Riley has written that "with *Rubber Soul* the Beatles come of age musically as their subject matter matures emotionally." Riley, *Tell Me Why,* 155. The Beatles, *Rubber Soul,* Parlophone PMC 1267, 1965, 33rpm (UK, Mono); Capitol 2442, 33rpm (US).

65 Gould, *Can't Buy Me Love,* 294. As Jonathan Gould writes, "The title *Rubber Soul* was suggested by Paul McCartney and meant as a self-deprecating pun on the relationship between white musicians and black music."

66 MacDonald, *Revolution in the Head,* 180. McCartney quoted in Barry Miles, *Paul McCartney: Many Years from Now* (London: Secker and Warburg, 1997), 277-228.

67 McCartney told an interviewer, Barry Miles, of "You Won't See Me," "To me it was very Motown-flavoured. It's got a James Jameson [*sic*] feel. He was the Motown bass player, he was fabulous, the guy who did all those great melodic bass lines." Miles, *Paul McCartney,* 271.

68 Transcriptions of select Jamerson bass lines can be found in the appendix to Slutsky's *Standing in the Shadows of Motown.* Full transcriptions of

all McCartney bass lines can be found in *The Beatles: Complete Scores* (New York: Hal Leonard, 1993).

69 James M. Decker, *"Rubber Soul* and the Transformation of Pop," in Womack, *Cambridge Companion to the Beatles,* 80–81.

70 For a detailed summation of these circumstances, see Dave Marsh, *The Beatles' Second Album* (New York: Rodale, 2007).

71 "Nowhere Man" was released as a single in the United States on March 5, 1966. The Beatles, "Nowhere Man," Capitol 5587, 1966, 45rpm.

72 Perhaps the most energetic and thorough excoriation of Dexter can be found in Dave Marsh's *The Beatles' Second Album,* esp. 120–151.

73 The emergence and implications of folk rock are discussed in depth in Chapter 1.

74 Marsh, *Beatles' Second Album,* 122.

75 Sylvie Reice, "Why Teens Switched to Folk Rock," *Los Angeles Times,* 6 Jan. 1966, E8.

76 The Beatles, "Paperback Writer" b/w "Rain," Parlophone R5452 (UK), Capitol 5651 (US), 1966, 45rpm.

77 The Four Tops, "Standing in the Shadows of Love," Motown 1102, 1966, 45rpm; Marvin Gaye, "What's Going On," Tamla 54201, 1971, 45rpm.

78 The Beatles, *Revolver,* Parlophone PMC 7009 (UK), Capitol 2576 (US), 1966, 33rpm.

79 Russell Reising, ed., *Every Sound There Is: The Beatles' "Revolver" and the Transformation of Rock and Roll* (Burlington, VT: Ashgate, 2002), 1.

80 "Revolver," *Rolling Stone,* 11 Dec. 2003, 86.

81 An exception to this tendency is Walter Everett's short essay entitled "Detroit and Memphis: The Soul of *Revolver,*" in which Everett explores the influence of black music on the songwriting and production of *Revolver,* arguing that the album "shows a strong continuing dependence on American R&B." Everett, "Detroit and Memphis: The Soul of *Revolver,*" in Reising, *Every Sound There Is,* 27.

82 "Memphis Gears for Beatles Disk Session," *Variety,* 6 Apr. 1966, 51. See also "Beatles Will Record in U.S. during Tour," *Billboard,* 23 Apr. 1966, 34.

83 Robert M. J. Bowman, *Soulsville, U.S.A.: The Story of Stax Records* (New York: Schirmer, 1997), 94.

84 It has been frequently speculated that "Here, There, and Everywhere" was strongly influenced by the Beach Boys' *Pet Sounds,* but Ian MacDonald has debunked this by pointing out that the album had not been released in the

United Kingdom at the time of the track's recording. MacDonald, *Revolution in the Head,* 210.

85 Everett, "Detroit and Memphis," 33.

86 The Miracles, "(Come Round Here) I'm the One You Need," Tamla 54140, 1966, 45rpm; The Four Tops, "Bernadette," Motown 1104, 1967, 45rpm.

87 The Beatles, *Sgt. Pepper's Lonely Hearts Club Band,* Parlophone PMC 7027 (UK), Capitol 2653 (US), 1967, 33rpm. For a thorough discussion of *Sgt. Pepper's* reception, see Michael Frontani, *The Beatles: Image and the Media* (Jackson: University of Mississippi Press, 2007), 148. Also see Bernard Gendron's *Between Montmartre and the Mudd Club: Popular Music and the Avant-Garde* (Chicago: University of Chicago Press, 2002), esp. 189–226, for a discussion on the Beatles' impact on music criticism and ideas about popular music as art.

88 Richard Poirier, "Learning from the Beatles," *Partisan Review* 34 (Fall 1967): 526.

89 Carl Bernstein, "Beatles' 'Band,'" *Washington Post,* 18 Jun. 1967, L1.

90 Jim Hoagland, "Pop Goes on a Trip," 18 Jun. 1967, L1.

91 Elijah Wald, *How the Beatles Destroyed Rock 'n' Roll* (New York: Oxford University Press, 2009), 238–239.

92 Russell Reising and Jim LeBlanc note that "critics have since gradually begun to acknowledge the importance of *Revolver* as the most significant advance in the Beatles' work." Reising and LeBlanc, "Magical Mystery Tours, and Other Trips: Yellow Submarines, Newspaper Taxis, and the Beatles' Psychedelic Years," in Womack, *Cambridge Companion to the Beatles,* 97.

93 "Presenting: Marvin Gaye, Tamla Recording Star," Box 5, Folder 15, Michael Ochs Collection, Rock and Roll Hall of Fame Library and Archives; David Ritz, *Divided Soul: The Life of Marvin Gaye* (Boston: Da Capo, 2009), 29.

94 Ritz's *Divided Soul,* originally intended as Gaye's memoir until Gaye's untimely death in 1984, is the definitive biographical account of Marvin Gaye; biographical information here comes from Ritz's book.

95 Ibid., 106–107.

96 See Flory, "I Hear a Symphony," 139–143; Marvin Gaye, *That's the Way Love Is,* Tamla 299, 33rpm, 1969.

97 See Miles, *Paul McCartney,* 203.

98 MacDonald, *Revolution in the Head,* 157.

99 Flory, "I Hear a Symphony," 188.

100 Frank Sinatra, *My Way,* Reprise 1020, 1969, 33rpm.

101 Marvin Gaye, *What's Going On,* Tamla 310, 1971, 33rpm.

102 For biographical information on Wonder I relied on Craig Werner's *Higher Ground: Stevie Wonder, Aretha Franklin, Curtis Mayfield and the Rise and Fall of American Soul* (New York: Crown, 2004).

103 Posner, *Motown,* 156.

104 "I just dug the effects they got, like echoes and the voice things, the writing, like 'For the Benefit of Mr. Kite.' I just said, 'Why Can't I?' I wanted to do something else, go other places." Qtd. in Werner, *Higher Ground,* 148.

105 Stevie Wonder, *Signed Sealed & Delivered,* Tamla 304, 1970, 33rpm.

106 Stevie Wonder, "We Can Work It Out," Tamla 54202, 1971, 45rpm.

107 The Beatles, "We Can Work It Out," Parlophone 5389, 1965, 45rpm.

108 By the late 1960s Jamerson's alcoholism was increasingly affecting his performances, and Babbitt was frequently employed as a substitute. By Babbitt's own account on his website, "We Can Work It Out" was the first Motown session he ever played on. See http://www.bobbabbitt.com/about.htm.

109 Jann Wenner, "John Lennon: The Rolling Stone Interview," *Rolling Stone,* 21 Jan. 1971, 35.

4. "Being Good Isn't Always Easy"

Epigraph: "Comment No. 1." Poem by Gil Scott-Heron. From the album *Small Talk at 125th and Lenox* FD–10131 [LP, Stereo], New York: Flying Dutchman Records, 1970. Copyright © 1970 Gil Scott-Heron. Courtesy of the estate of Gil Scott-Heron/Rumal Rackley administrator.

1 Keith Richards, *Life* (New York: Little, Brown, 2010), 177.

2 Stephen Davis, *Old Gods Almost Dead: The 40-Year Odyssey of the Rolling Stones* (New York: Random House, 2001), 129.

3 "Hot 100," *Billboard,* 10 Jul. 1965, 26.

4 All *Billboard* chart information, unless otherwise noted, is from Joel Whitburn's *Billboard Top 10 Singles Charts, 1955–2000* (Menonomee Falls, WI: Record Research, 2001) and Whitburn's *Billboard Top R&B Singles 1942–1995* (Menonomee Falls, WI: Record Research, 2001).

5 The Rolling Stones, *Out of Our Heads,* Decca/London 429, 1965, 33rpm.

6 Aretha Franklin, *Aretha Arrives,* Atlantic Records 8150, 1967, 33rpm.

7 David Llorens, "Miracle in Milwaukee," *Ebony,* Nov. 1967, 29.

8 Dusty Springfield, *Dusty in Memphis,* Atlantic 8214, 1969, 33rpm.

9 Emily Lordi has written extensively of Franklin's role as a musical muse to the Black Arts Movement during this period. See Emily J. Lordi, *Black Resonance: Iconic Women Singers and African American Literature* (New Brunswick, NJ: Rutgers University Press, 2013), 173–208.

10 Amiri Baraka (as LeRoi Jones), *Blues People: Negro Music in White America* (1963; New York: Perennial, 2002).

11 For an example of the first, see Nelson George, *The Death of Rhythm and Blues* (New York: E. P. Dutton, 1988); for the second, see Brian Ward, *Just My Soul Responding: Rhythm and Blues, Black Consciousness, and Race Relations* (Berkeley: University of California Press, 1998); for the third, see Peter Guralnick, *Sweet Soul Music: Rhythm and Blues and the Southern Dream of Freedom* (Boston: Back Bay, 1999). It's also not uncommon that these threads overlap in a sort of self-corroboration: for instance, one critic writes that "soul music represented the conflation of polytonal vocal expression, over a layered musical landscape of rhythm and blues and gospel," then argues that "the soul singer emerges as the popular representation of an emerging postcolonial sensibility among the black community, despite the perpetual constraints placed on black public expression that could be deemed as expressions of resistance." While this description isn't necessarily inaccurate, its first part ignores the significant influences of country music and mainstream pop on Southern soul music, while the second reduces the soul musician to a primarily symbolic position and obscures the specific, lived practice of music itself. Mark Anthony Neal, *What the Music Said: Black Popular Music and Black Public Culture* (New York: Routledge, 1998), 40.

12 Charles Hughes, *Country Soul: Making Music and Making Race in the American South* (Chapel Hill: University of North Carolina Press, 2015), 6.

13 Karl Hagstrom Miller, *Segregating Sound: Inventing Folk and Pop Music in the Age of Jim Crow* (Durham, NC: Duke University Press, 2010), 15.

14 As Richard Middleton has argued, rock ideology often searches for a literal ideal of the artistic self, in which the narrative voice of the song and the actual embodied voice of the singer are somehow related. See Middleton, *Voicing the Popular: On the Subjects of Popular Music* (New York: Routledge, 2006), esp. 200–201. Simon Frith suggests that this "originalism" is tied to anxieties over popular music's proximity to market capitalism, and the critical tendency that "equates bad music with imitative music" carries a "critical assumption . . . that this reflects a cynical or pathetic production decision." Frith, *Performing Rites: On the Value of Popular Music* (Cambridge, MA: Harvard University Press, 1996), 69.

15 Ellen Willis, "Janis Joplin," in *The Rolling Stone Illustrated History of Rock and Roll*, ed. Anthony DeCurtis, James Henke, Holly George-Warren, and Jim Miller (New York: Random House, 1992), 383.

16 Simon Frith and Angela McRobbie, "Music and Sexuality," in *On Record: Rock, Pop, and the Written Word*, ed. Simon Frith and Andrew Goodwin (New York: Routledge, 1990), 373.

17 "Wilson Pickett Blasts Afro Records Boycott," *Los Angeles Sentinel*, 14 May 1970, B. Emphasis added.

18 Fillmore West Press Release, March 1969, Box AF6, Folder 31, *Rolling Stone* Records, Rock and Roll Hall of Fame Library and Archives.

19 Chris Porterfield, "Lady Soul, Singing It Like It Is," *Time*, 28 Jun. 1968, 62–66.

20 For an excellent genealogy of the word "soul" in its relationship to African American music and culture, see Joel Dinerstein, "The Soul Roots of Bruce Springsteen's American Dream," *American Music* 25, no. 4 (Winter 2007): 441–476; "Democrats: Soul Brother Humphrey," *Time*, 10 May 1968.

21 "Who's Got Soul?," *Esquire*, Apr. 1968, 89.

22 Porterfield, "Lady Soul," 62.

23 Ibid.

24 "An Introduction to Soul," *Esquire*, Apr. 1968, 79.

25 Thaddeus T. Stokes, "This Is 'Soul,'" *Atlanta Daily World*, 29 Mar 1968, 6.

26 Al Rutledge, "The Root of All Soul," *Baltimore Afro-American*, 20 Jul. 1968, A1.

27 Albert Murray, "'Soul': 32 Meanings Not in Your Dictionary," *Chicago Tribune*, 23 Jun. 1968, J6.

28 Wrote Garland, "Its essence is indisputably black; for in the long and dismal decades that must have seemed like eons to those forced to endure them, chants and hollers not markedly unlike those to be heard in the popular music of today were sent up from rural Dixie's cotton fields by sackcloth-clad black men and women who labored under a relentless sun from predawn to postdusk knowing that no matter *how* hard they worked or how many bales they picked, tomorrow would be no better than today and might well be far worse." Phyl Garland, *The Sound of Soul* (Chicago: Henry Regnery, 1969), 2.

29 Clayton Riley, "If Aretha's Around, Who Needs Janis?," *New York Times*, 8 Mar. 1970, M1.

30 Amiri Baraka (as LeRoi Jones), *Black Music* (New York: Akashic, 2010), 230.

31 Ibid., 235.

32 Albert Goldman, "Why Do Whites Sing Black?," *New York Times,* 14 Dec. 1969, D25.

33 "Music Mailbag: 'No Matter How Whites Sing, It's Not Black,'" *New York Times,* 18 Jan. 1970, 113.

34 "Music Mailbag," *New York Times,* 15 Feb 1970, 108.

35 Bill Millar's article "Blue-Eyed Soul: Colour Me Soul" for *The History of Rock* (1983, archived online at http://www.rocksbackpages.com/article.html ?ArticleID=783) credits Woods with the term, as do a number of other sources, including Woods's online biography at the Broadcast Pioneers of Philadelphia Hall of Fame (http://www.broadcastpioneers.com/georgiewoods.html). A 1965 article from *Billboard* on "blue-eyed soul" also quotes Woods extensively. Claude Hall, "R&B Stations Open Airplay Gates to 'Blue-Eyed Soulists,'" *Billboard,* 9 Oct. 1965, 1, 49.

36 Porterfield, "Lady Soul," 63–64.

37 Michael Awkward, *Soul Covers: Rhythm and Blues Remakes and the Struggle for Artistic Identity* (Durham, NC: Duke University Press, 2007), 46.

38 Writes Franklin, "The article also painted me as a woman trapped by the blues, like Bessie Smith or Billie Holiday. Nothing could be further from the truth. I am Aretha, upbeat, straight-ahead, and not to be worn out by men and left singing the blues. . . . Due to the stature of *Time,* the mistakes were picked up by countless writers in the years ahead." Aretha Franklin and David Ritz, *Aretha: From These Roots* (New York: Crown, 1999), 123.

39 For basic biographical information on Aretha Franklin I relied on Mark Bego's *Aretha Franklin: The Queen of Soul* (New York: St. Martin's, 1989), Matt Dobkin's *I Never Loved a Man the Way I Love You: Aretha Franklin, Respect, and the Making of a Soul Music Masterpiece* (New York: St. Martin's, 2004), and Franklin's own autobiography, *Aretha: From These Roots.*

40 An article in the March 30, 1957, Norfolk, Virginia, *New Journal and Guide,* "Capacity Audience Hears Rev. Franklin at Newport," mentions the reverend's daughter Aretha being "accorded a great ovation" for her performance on page B11. Robert Shelton mentions the singer in a July 25, 1961, *New York Times* article ("Wandering Minstrel Is in Town," 19): "A recent gospel graduate, 18-year-old Aretha Franklin, is winning ovations at the Village Gate with the sort of entertainment genius that makes her something of a female Ray Charles."

41 "Aretha Wins New Honors," *Pittsburgh Courier,* 25 Nov 1961, 15.

42 For details on this incident, see chapter 7 of Dobkin, *I Never Loved a Man the Way I Love You,* esp. 136–154.

43 Unless otherwise noted, for basic biographical information on Janis Joplin I relied primarily on Alice Echols's excellent biography, *Scars of Sweet Paradise: The Life and Times of Janis Joplin* (New York: Henry Holt, 1999), as well as Laura Joplin's *Love, Janis* (New York: Villard, 1992) and Ellen Willis's essay "Janis Joplin" in *The Rolling Stone Illustrated History of Rock and Roll.*

44 Michael Lydon, "The Janis Joplin Philosophy: Every Moment Is What She Feels," *New York Times Magazine,* 23 Feb. 1969, SM41.

45 "I heard Leadbelly," Joplin told *Newsweek* in 1969, "and it was like a flash. It *mattered* to me." "Rebirth of the Blues," *Newsweek,* 26 May 1969.

46 Threadgill's, the famed Austin restaurant and music venue where Joplin first drew audiences while a student at the University of Texas, was not integrated until 1966, after Joplin had departed for San Francisco. Echols, *Scars of Sweet Paradise,* 57.

47 Michael Rogin, *Blackface, White Noise: Jewish Immigrants in the Hollywood Melting Pot* (Berkeley: University of California Press, 1996), 37.

48 Pete Johnson, "Hippies at Their Happiest at Monterey Pop Festival," *Los Angeles Times,* 20 Jun. 1967, D1.

49 Nat Hentoff, "We Look at Our Parents and . . . ," *New York Times,* 21 Apr. 1968, D19.

50 Robb Baker, "The Sound," *Chicago Tribune,* 31 Mar. 1968, G16.

51 Ralph Gleason, "Pop's Explosive Little Flower Girl," *San Francisco Chronicle,* 16 Mar. 1969.

52 Rasa Gustaitis, "Janis Joplin," *Los Angeles Times,* 24 Nov. 1968, O42; Nick Logan, "Explosive Legend of Janis Joplin," *New Musical Express,* 12 Apr. 1969, 14.

53 William Kloman, "Rock: The 50s Come Back," *New York Times,* 1 Sept. 1968, D18.

54 Hollie I. West, "Blacks and Whites and the Blues," *Washington Post,* 22 Jun. 1969, 131.

55 A search of the *Atlanta Daily World, Baltimore Afro-American, Los Angeles Sentinel, New York Amsterdam News, Norfolk Journal and Guide, Philadelphia Tribune, Pittsburgh Courier, Cleveland Call and Post,* and *Chicago Defender* from 1967 through 1970 yields a mere fifty-five results combined, and most of these articles mention the singer only in passing.

56 Stanley G. Robertson, "L.A. Confidential," *Los Angeles Sentinel*, 28 Sept. 1967, A7.

57 Hollie I. West, "Black Tune," *Washington Post*, 13 Mar. 1969, L1.

58 Robb Baker, "Groovin' with Janis," *Chicago Tribune*, 11 May 1969, K27.

59 Robert Shelton, "Janis Joplin Is Climbing Fast in the Heady Rock Firmament," *New York Times*, 19 Feb. 1968.

60 Paul Nelson, "Janis: The Judy Garland of Rock and Roll?," *Rolling Stone*, 15 Mar. 1969, 6.

61 "Biography from Columbia Records: Big Brother and the Holding Company," ca. 1967, Box RG1, Folder 10, Jeff Gold Collection, Rock and Roll Hall of Fame Library and Archives.

62 Julie Smith, "What Makes Janis Sing—Ol' Kozmic Blues?," *San Francisco Chronicle*, 26 May 1970.

63 Robb Baker, "The Sound," *Chicago Tribune*, 31 Mar. 1968, G16.

64 Goldman, "Why Do Whites Sing Black?," D25.

65 Julie Smith, "Janis Joplin and the Saturday Night Swindle," *Chicago Tribune*, 12 Jul. 1970, J2.

66 Nelson, "Janis," 6.

67 Sue C. Clark, "Wexler: A Man of Dedication," *Rolling Stone*, 9 Sept. 1968, 8–10. In Wexler's papers at the Rock and Roll Hall of Fame Library and Archives there is a fascinating correspondence where the critic Ralph Gleason wrote to Wexler to defend "hippies" using the word. Writes Gleason: "This leads into, I think, the question of the use of the word 'spade' by hippies et al. That problem is complicated by the fact that these people meet many black cats who themselves use the word 'spade' in mixed company in the same way. It astonished me at first and it still does sometimes when, under certain conditions I sense it being wrong. But I am forced to admit the possibility that perhaps there is a time and place when they CAN use it." Box 22, Folder 19, Jerry Wexler Papers, Rock and Roll Hall of Fame Library and Archives.

68 Unless otherwise noted, for basic biographical information on Dusty Springfield I relied on Penny Valentine and Vicki Whickham's *Dancing with Demons: The Authorised Biography of Dusty Springfield* (London: Hodder and Stoughton, 2000), Annie Randall's *Dusty! Queen of the Postmods* (New York: Oxford University Press, 2009), and Laurence Cole's *Dusty Springfield: In the Middle of Nowhere* (Middlesex, UK: Middlesex University Press, 2008).

69 Randall, *Dusty!*, 71.

70 Ibid, 19. Dusty Springfield, *A Girl Called Dusty*, Philips Records BF 7594, 1964, 33rpm.

71 "Dusty Ordered 'Hit the Road,'" *Chicago Defender*, 17 Dec. 1964, 2.

72 *Ready Steady Go!* "The Sound of Motown," Rediffusion, 28 Apr. 1965.

73 Ray Coleman, "Pop Probe: Dusty," *Melody Maker*, 21 Nov. 1964, 3.

74 Cole, *Dusty Springfield*, 4.

75 Erma Franklin, "Piece of My Heart," Shout Records 221, 1967, 45rpm.

76 Both of these songs were written under the pseudonym "Bert Russell."

77 Ragovoy wrote "Time Is on My Side" under the pseudonym "Norman Meade."

78 It is worth mentioning that this is the same chord progression to "Twist and Shout" and nearly identical to the progression of "Hang on Sloopy." Bert Berns knew his formulas.

79 The final line of the chorus occurs over a IV-I cadence, the song's only real deviation from the I-IV-V progression noted above.

80 Dusty Springfield, *Dusty . . . Definitely*, Philips Records SBL 7864, 1968, 33rpm.

81 Big Brother and the Holding Company, *Cheap Thrills*, Columbia Records 9700, 1968, 33rpm.

82 Echols, *Scars of Sweet Paradise*, 197.

83 John Hardin, "Cheap Thrills," *Rolling Stone*, 14 Sept. 1968, 21.

84 By his own account, while producing the album Simon relied heavily on studio edits to cover up the band's mistakes, which is ironic since the record was also deliberately recorded with a murky, low-fi mix intended to simulate the experience of a live concert, widely agreed to be the optimal setting in which to enjoy Big Brother's music. For more information on the recording of *Cheap Thrills*, see Echols, *Scars of Sweet Paradise*, 202–210.

85 Nelson, "Janis," 6.

86 Robert Hilburn, "Janis Joplin: Rock 'n' Roll's Biggest Female Star," *Los Angeles Times*, 12 Oct. 1969, V16.

87 Kloman, "Rock," D18.

88 John Hardin, "Cheap Thrills," *Rolling Stone*, 14 Sept. 1968, 21.

89 Recalled Jerry Wexler, "I brought it to her, and she said, 'I'm not gonna do this song.' And I think, 'Well, it's got something to do with the church,' and I will always respect that." Bego, *Aretha Franklin*, 129.

90 Dusty Springfield, "Son of a Preacher Man," Atlantic 2580, 1968, 45rpm.

91 Aretha Franklin, *This Girl's in Love with You*, Atlantic 8248, 1970, 33rpm.

92 Dobkin, *I Never Loved a Man the Way I Love You*, 174.

93 These would be "Share Your Love with Me" (originally performed by Bobby Bland); "Eleanor Rigby" and "Let It Be" (both by the Beatles, the latter version of which Franklin actually released first but had heard a demo sent by Paul McCartney); "The Weight" (the Band), and "The Dark End of the Street" (James Carr).

94 "I was trying to make a bridge over to the 'flower children,' and it was a mistake," recalled Wexler. Bego, *Aretha Franklin,* 130.

95 Led Zeppelin is a massively important band whom, largely due to periodization, I've mostly left out of this book. I have written about them extensively elsewhere, though: see Jack Hamilton, "Good Times Bad Times," *Slate,* 18 June 2014, available at http://www.slate.com/articles/arts/culturebox/2014/06/led_zeppelin_how_jimmy_page_robert_plant_et_al_invented_modern_rock.html, and Jack Hamilton, "Robert Plant's Second Act," *The Atlantic,* 1 Nov. 2010, available at http://www.theatlantic.com/entertainment/archive/2010/11/robert-plants-second-act/65278/.

96 Valentine and Whickham, *Dancing with Demons,* 87.

97 The Beatles, *Revolver,* Capitol 2576, 1966, 33rpm.

98 As the critic Ian MacDonald has argued, "Death is a subject normally avoided in pop music. . . . Consequently the downbeat demise of a lonely spinster in 'Eleanor Rigby'—not to mention the brutal image of the priest 'wiping the dirt from his hands as he walks from the grave'—came as quite a shock to pop listeners in 1966." MacDonald, *Revolution in the Head: The Beatles' Records and the Sixties* (London: Pimlico, 2005), 203.

99 Gayle Wald, "One of the Boys? Whiteness, Gender, and Popular Music Studies," in *Whiteness: A Critical Reader,* ed. Mike Hill (New York: New York University Press, 1997), 158.

100 Garland, *Sound of Soul,* 162.

5. House Burning Down

Epigraph: Qtd. in Henry Mitchell, "The Death of Jimi Hendrix," *Washington Post* 19 Sept. 1970, C1.

1 Ritchie York, " 'I'm into Different Things,' Says Jimi Hendrix," *Los Angeles Times,* 7 Sept. 1969, Q20.

2 Ernie Santosuosso, "Epitaph for Jimi Hendrix," *Boston Globe,* 19 Sept. 1970, 10.

3 See, for instance, *Forrest Gump* ("All along the Watchtower," 1994), *In the Name of the Father* ("Voodoo Child [Slight Return]," 1993), *Mean Streets* ("Jumpin' Jack Flash," 1972), and *The Departed* ("Gimme Shelter," 2006).

4 "Jimi Hendrix Has a Brand New Bass," *Rolling Stone,* 12 Jul. 1969, 10; "Jimi Hendrix 1945–1970," *Rolling Stone,* 15 Oct. 1970, 6.

5 B. P. Fallon, "Jimi Hendrix—the Pop Sound of the Year," *Melody Maker,* 23 Dec. 1967, 14.

6 Paul Gilroy, *Darker Than Blue: On the Moral Economies of Black Atlantic Culture* (Cambridge, MA: Harvard University Press, 2010), 132.

7 Simon Frith, *Performing Rites: On the Value of Popular Music* (Cambridge, MA: Harvard University Press, 1996), 67.

8 Richard Goldstein, "Pop Eye," *Village Voice,* 16 Jun. 1966, 16.

9 Richard Goldstein, "Pop Eye: Evaluating Media," *Village Voice,* 14 Jul. 1966, 6.

10 Richard Goldstein, "We Still Need the Beatles, But . . . ," *New York Times,* 18 Jun. 1967, 104.

11 Jon Landau, "Rock 1970: It's Too Late to Stop Now," *Rolling Stone,* 10 Dec. 1970, 41.

12 Richard Goldstein, "Pop Eye: The Soul Sound from Sheepshead Bay," *Village Voice,* 23 Jun. 1966, 7; Goldstein, "Pop Eye: Phillers," *Village Voice,* 23 Feb. 1967, 14.

13 Richard Goldstein, "Why Do the Kids Dig Rock . . . ," *New York Times,* 24 Nov. 1968, H1, H14. Two months earlier the *Chicago Tribune* had run an extensive article on the same theme: Robb Baker, "Revolutionary, Satanic Imagery Sweeping the Rock World," *Chicago Tribune,* 8 Sept. 1968, SC1.

14 "This equation," writes Bryan Wagner, "does not put the outlaw in the singer's place; it conjoins outlaw and singer without dissolving one into the other, yielding a common sense." Wagner, *Disturbing the Peace: Black Culture and the Police Power after Slavery* (Cambridge, MA: Harvard University Press, 2009), 57.

15 Mike Gershman, "The Blues, Once Black, Now a Shade Whiter," *Los Angeles Times,* 19 Jan. 1969, Q37.

16 Ralph J. Gleason, "Like a Rolling Stone," *American Scholar* (Autumn 1967): 557.

17 Ibid., 559.

18 Ibid.

19 Ibid.

20 Greil Marcus writes about Cohn's book extensively in Marcus's magnificent *Lipstick Traces: A Secret History of the Twentieth Century* (Cambridge, MA: Harvard University Press, 1989).

21 From the preface to the 2001 edition of Nik Cohn, *Awopbopalaloobop Alopbamboom: The Golden Age of Rock* (1969; New York: Grove, 2001), 5.

22 Ibid., 58, 33, 146.

23 Ibid., 115.

24 Ibid., 117.

25 For basic biographical information on Hendrix, I relied primarily on Charles Cross's *Room Full of Mirrors* (New York: Hyperion, 2005), David Henderson's *'Scuse Me While I Kiss the Sky* (1978; New York: Atria, 2008), and Charles Shaar Murray's *Crosstown Traffic: Jimi Hendrix and the Rock 'n' Roll Revolution* (New York: St. Martin's, 1989).

26 Keith Altham, "New to the Charts: Wild Jimi Hendrix," *New Musical Express,* 14 Jan. 1967, 26; "It's Jumping Jimi!" *Melody Maker,* 4 Feb. 1967, 1.

27 Nick Jones, "Hendrix—On the Crest of a Fave Rave," *Melody Maker,* 21 Jan. 1967, 8.

28 "Rolling Stone Interview: Eric Clapton," *Rolling Stone,* 11 May 1968, 12.

29 Murray, *Crosstown Traffic,* 91.

30 In 1986 Reprise Records released Hendrix's entire performance from Monterey on the album *Jimi Plays Monterey,* Reprise 25358, 1986, CD.

31 Steve Waksman, *Instruments of Desire: The Electric Guitar and the Shaping of Musical Experience* (Cambridge, MA: Harvard University Press, 1998), 188.

32 Germaine Greer, *The Madwoman's Underclothes: Essays and Occasional Writings* (New York: Atlantic Monthly Press, 1994), 41.

33 Robert Christgau, "Anatomy of a Love Festival," *Esquire,* Jan. 1970, 153, 154.

34 Ibid., 147.

35 Jim Hoagland, "Jimi Hendrix Socks It to 'Em," *Washington Post,* 11 Mar. 1968, C12.

36 Richard Goldstein, "Pop Eye: The Hip Homunculus," *Village Voice,* 29 Jun. 1967, 17.

37 Tony Glover, "Electric Ladyland," *Rolling Stone,* 9 Nov. 1968, 20.

38 Albert Goldman, "The Blues Today: SuperSpade Raises Atlantis," *New York,* 2 Sept. 1968, 53.

39 Lee Ivory, "Among the Stars," *Chicago Defender,* 21 Dec. 1967, 17.

40 Hollie I. West, "Blacks and Whites and the Blues," *Washington Post,* 22 Jun. 1969, 131.

41 The Jimi Hendrix Experience, *Electric Ladyland,* Reprise 6307, 1968, 33rpm.

42 Richard Goldstein, "Pop Eye: The Hip Homunculus," *Village Voice,* 29 Jun. 1967, 17.

43 Joan Deppa, "British Pop Grows to Stupefying Bang," *Los Angeles Times,* 11 Nov. 1967, 17.

44 Hoagland, "Jimi Hendrix Socks It to 'Em," C12; Robb Baker, "The Shattering Hendrix Experience," *Chicago Tribune,* 26 Feb. 1968, B12.

45 John Morthland, "Jimi Hendrix," in *The Rolling Stone Illustrated History of Rock and Roll,* ed. Anthony DeCurtis, James Henke, Holly George-Warren, and Jim Miller (New York: Random House, 1992), 415. Harmonically, "Voodoo Child" departs from the conventional twelve-bar blues form in its verses by hanging on the tonic chord for the first eight bars, before moving to a standard V-IV turnaround in the ninth and tenth bars followed by two more bars of I. The song's chorus is only four bars long, an ascending bVI–bVII progression that comes on the heels of each twelve-bar verse.

46 Nolen's "chicken scratch" innovation has been widely acknowledged and is referenced in Michael Veal's *Fela: The Life and Times of an African Musical Icon* (Philadelphia: Temple University Press, 2000), 269.

47 "All along the Watchtower" was released as a 45rpm single in 1968 (Reprise 0767).

48 The chord structure is Im–bVII | bVI–bVII.

49 Dylan's influence on Hendrix's singing style was enormous, and plainly audible—Hendrix claimed that hearing Dylan was what convinced him to try singing in public. See Steven Roby and Brad Schreiber, *Becoming Jimi Hendrix* (Cambridge, MA: Da Capo, 2010), 152.

50 Dylan's version of "All along the Watchtower" can be heard on Bob Dylan, *John Wesley Harding,* Columbia 2804, 1968, 33rpm.

51 Albin Zak, "Bob Dylan and Jimi Hendrix: Juxtaposition and Transformation in 'All along the Watchtower,'" *Journal of the American Musicological Society* 57, no. 3 (Fall 2004): 600–601.

52 Steve Waksman, "Black Sound, Black Body: Jimi Hendrix, the Electric Guitar, and Musical Blackness," *Popular Music and Society* 23, no. 1 (Spring 1999): 76.

53 "Third Dimension: Hendrix the Man," *Melody Maker,* 8 Mar. 1969, 12–13.

54 Greg Tate has a less sanguine view of the situation, writing that a "profound irony of Hendrix's career is that even after shredding racial shibboleths

by the dozens he discovered a gate at the country's color-obsessed edge he was not able to bust wide . . . the gate that has kept Black people from embracing him as one of their own to this day." Tate, *Midnight Lightning: Jimi Hendrix and the Black Experience* (Chicago: Lawrence Hill, 2003), 11.

55 As Charles Shaar Murray notes, the fact that Hendrix's music first appeared on the Pop charts made it unlikely that *Billboard* would consider tracking his music in terms of R&B numbers. Murray, *Crosstown Traffic*, 82.

56 This introduction can be heard on Jimi Hendrix, *Live at the Fillmore East,* MCA 11931, 1999, CD.

57 William K. De Fossett, Jr., "Jimi Hendrix at UBA Block Party," *New York Amsterdam News,* 13 Sept. 1969, 1.

58 "Third Dimension: Hendrix the Man," 12–13.

59 "Jimi Hendrix Sings at Harlem Benefit," *New York Times,* 6 Sept. 1969, 18.

60 John Burks, "Hendrix: The End of a Beginning Maybe," *Rolling Stone,* 19 Mar. 1970, 40.

61 Jay Ruby, "Jimi Hendrix," *Jazz & Pop,* Jul. 1968, 17.

62 Jimi Hendrix, *Band of Gypsys,* Capitol 472, 1970, 33rpm.

63 An account of this incident can be found in Henderson, *'Scuse Me While I Kiss the Sky,* 346–347.

64 Hendrix's "Star Spangled Banner" can be heard on Jimi Hendrix, *Live at Woodstock,* Experience Hendrix 11987, 1999, CD. Al Aronowitz gushed in the *New York Post* that Hendrix's anthem was "the single greatest moment of the sixties," and Greil Marcus has called it "the greatest protest song of all time." Aronowitz qtd. in Cross, *Room Full of Mirrors,* 271; Greil Marcus, *Bob Dylan by Greil Marcus: Writings 1968–2010* (New York: Public Affairs, 2010), 419.

65 Cross, *Room Full of Mirrors,* 271.

66 Ibid., 289.

67 "Black Rock Singer Died Happy Man, Blond Moans," *Philadelphia Tribune,* 29 Sept. 1970, 1.

68 Robert Hilburn, "Jimi Hendrix: Quality Made Him 'Something Else,'" *Los Angeles Times,* 4 Oct. 1970, Q1; "Jimi Hendrix's Ascent to 'Sex God' Began in Phila.," *Philadelphia Tribune,* 22 Sept. 1970, 1.

69 For a discussion of Hendrix's position as the lone black hero in rock iconography, see Maureen Mahon, *Right to Rock: The Black Rock Coalition and the Cultural Politics of Race* (Durham, NC: Duke University Press, 2004), 231–256.

70 Simon Frith and Angela McRobbie, "Rock and Sexuality," in *On Record: Rock, Pop, and the Written Word,* ed. Simon Frith and Andrew Goodwin (New York: Routledge, 2000), 319.

71 Tate, *Midnight Lightning,* 66.

72 Robert Walser, *Running with the Devil: Power, Gender, and Madness in Heavy Metal Music* (Middletown, CT: Wesleyan University Press, 1993), 110.

73 Steve Waksman, *This Ain't the Summer of Love: Conflict and Crossover in Heavy Metal and Punk* (Berkeley: University of California Press, 2009), 150.

74 Charles Shaar Murray has argued that Hendrix's music is rather unique in the sensitivity with which it portrays women, particularly in comparison to other music of the period. Murray, *Crosstown Traffic,* 74.

75 Mahon, *Right to Rock,* 235.

76 Ben Fong-Torres, "The Resurrection of Carlos Santana," *Rolling Stone,* 7 Dec. 1972, 40–41.

77 John Mendelsohn, "The Cream Returns Via Film at the Rose Palace," *Los Angeles Times,* 13 May 1969, C17; "Santana Group and Staple Singers Are Here Friday at Allen Theatre," *Cleveland Call and Post,* 16 May 1970, 11A; James D. Dilts, "Santana Comes On Strong in Peaceful Civic Center Concert," *Baltimore Sun,* 17 Aug. 1970, B6; Mike Jahn, "Santana's Rhythms Heard in 2 Concerts," *New York Times,* 11 Nov. 1969, 40; John Mendelsohn, "Santana Plays Two Rock 'n' Roll Shows," *Los Angeles Times,* 3 Mar. 1970, F11; Steve Starger, "Columbia Presents Robert Johnson Blues Release," *Hartford Courant,* 10 Apr. 1971, 8; Lynn Van Matre, "Santana Just Keeps Hanging On," *Chicago Tribune,* 14 Jun. 1971, B14.

78 *Rolling Stone* was one of the few venues to pan Santana's first album, calling the band "terrible." Langdon Winner and John Morthland, "Santana," *Rolling Stone,* 18 Oct. 1969, 38.

79 Dilts, "Santana Comes On Strong," B6; Don Owen, "Aretha Socks It to Fans," *Baltimore Afro-American,* 6 Nov. 1971, 20.

80 "Mandrill Rocks in Latin Tempo," *New York Times,* 16 May 1971, 73; Starger, "Columbia Presents Robert Johnson Blues Release," 8.

81 Jim Nash, "Abraxas," *Rolling Stone,* 24 Dec. 1970, 52.

82 Ned Sublette, *Cuba and Its Music: From the First Drums to the Mambo* (Chicago: Chicago Review Press, 2007).

83 For instance, in a 1971 slam of *Led Zeppelin III,* the *New York Times* wrote that "what is so annoying about their music is the fact that its starting point— black American blues—has such a beautifully rich spectrum of artistic

expression." Don Heckman, "Sally's Psyche on a Journey," *New York Times,* 28 Feb. 1971, D30.

84 Ralph J. Gleason, "Miles and Carlos: Music of Philosophy and the Street," *Rolling Stone,* 7 Dec. 1972, 62.

6. Just around Midnight

Epigraphs: Stanley Booth, *The True Adventures of the Rolling Stones* (Chicago: A Cappella, 1984), 394. Woman in the crowd (Madison Square Garden, November 28, 1969): From the album *Get Yer Ya-Ya's Out! The Rolling Stones in Concert,* Decca–SKL 5065 [LP, Stereo], London: The Decca Record Co., Ltd. Copyright © 1970, The Decca Record Company Limited.

1 The Rolling Stones, "Jumpin' Jack Flash," London 908, 1968, 45rpm.

2 The Rolling Stones, *Their Satanic Majesties Request,* London 2, 1967, 33rpm.

3 "3-D Stones Try for Big League," *Melody Maker,* 2 Dec. 1967, 21.

4 Jon Landau, "Stones," *Rolling Stone,* 10 Feb. 1968, 18; Pete Johnson, "Can't Tell an Album by Its Cover," *Los Angeles Times,* 3 Dec. 1967, D24.

5 All chart position information is from Joel Whitburn's *The Billboard Albums, Sixth Edition* (Menomonee Falls, WI: Record Research, 2006), Joel Whitburn's *Top Pop Singles, 1955–2006* (Menomonee Falls, WI: Record Research, 2007), and Neil Wawick, Jon Kutner, and Tony Brown, *The Complete Book of the British Charts* (London: Omnibus, 2004).

6 Robb Baker, "The Sound," *Chicago Tribune,* 28 May 1968, B17.

7 As Steve Waksman writes, "The Rolling Stones were as integral to the early history of arena rock as were any of the bands that fell under the metal category." Steve Waksman, *This Ain't the Summer of Love: Conflict and Crossover in Heavy Metal and Punk* (Berkeley: University of California Press, 2009), 21.

8 "Biography: Decca Group Records," Jul. 1964. Box 11, Folder 2, Michael Ochs Collection, Rock and Roll Hall of Fame Library and Archive.

9 Pete Hamill, "The Enemy Camp," *New York Post,* 31 Oct. 1965.

10 LeRoi Jones, Martin Williams, and John Szwed are three prominent writers who have accused the Rolling Stones (and particularly Jagger) of minstrelsy. See Amiri Baraka (as LeRoi Jones), *Black Music* (1967; Westport, CT: Akashic, 2010), 234; Williams, *Jazz Heritage* (New York: Oxford University Press, 1985), 94–95; and Szwed, "Race and the Embodiment of Culture," *Ethnicity* 2, no. 1 (1975): 27.

11 Chris Williams, "Rolling Stones R and B Champs," *New Musical Express,* 23 Aug. 1963, 8.

12 Adam Gussow, *Seems Like Murder Here: Southern Violence and the Blues Tradition* (Chicago: University of Chicago Press, 2002).

13 "The Pursuers: The Big Beat Boys Chart-Chasing the Beatles," *Melody Maker,* 11 Jan. 1964, 8-9.

14 Upon the release of the band's first album, Jagger remarked that "to those who listen to groups like ours, and think we are originators, we say—don't listen to us. Listen to the men who inspire us. Buy their records." Ray Coleman, "The Pop Heroes," *Melody Maker,* 2 May 1964, 3.

15 "We're Not on the Wagon," *Melody Maker,* 21 Mar. 1964, 3.

16 Maydiea Cole, "Star-Studded TAMI Rock 'n' Roll Show Thrills Teens," *Los Angeles Sentinel,* 5 Nov. 1964, C10.

17 Terry, Penny, Pip, Brandy, and Tee, "The Low Down," *Chicago Defender,* 12 Jun. 1965, 30.

18 Pip, Brandi, Penni, Terry, and Joe, "The Low Down," *Chicago Defender,* 16 Oct. 1965, 28.

19 "Not Fade Away" also reached number forty-eight on the U.S. charts. The Rolling Stones, "Not Fade Away," London 9657, 1964, 45rpm.

20 Ray Coleman, "Rebels with a Beat!," *Melody Maker,* 6 Feb. 1964, 10–11.

21 Ray Coleman, "Mick Jagger of the Rolling Stones Asks . . . Why Do Parents Hate Us?" *Melody Maker,* 7 Mar. 1964, 9.

22 Ray Coleman, "Would You Let Your Sister Go with a Rolling Stone?," *Melody Maker,* 14 Mar. 1964, 8-9.

23 The aforementioned Pete Hamill column also contains a reference, although there it's been changed to "would you let your daughter marry a Rolling Stone?" Hamill, "Enemy Camp." A column in the *Evening Standard* entitled "But Would You Let Your Daughter Marry One?" (a clear reference to the *Melody Maker* headline) declared that "never have middle-class virtues . . . been so lacking as they are in the Rolling Stones." Qtd. in Mark Paytress, *The Rolling Stones: Off the Record* (New York: Omnibus, 2003), 48.

24 Martha Olson, "Beatles Surpassed," *Chicago Tribune,* 29 Jun. 1964, 14.

25 Louise Hutchinson, "Barber Gives Scare to Five Fuzzy Singers," *Chicago Tribune,* 12 Jun. 1964, 20.

26 Gloria Emerson, "British 'His and Her' Haircuts Blur 'Him-Her' Line," *New York Times,* 23 Jul. 1964, 29; Andrew Carthew, "Shaggy Englishmen

Story," *New York Times,* 6 Sept. 1964, SM18, "Cleveland to Bar Beatles and the Like in Public Hall," *New York Times,* 4 Nov. 1964, 46.

27 Bill Whitworth, "After the Beatles Came the Deluge," *Los Angeles Times,* 6 Dec. 1964, 26.

28 Paul Richard, "Rolling Stones Lacking in Beatle-Like Finesse," *Washington Post,* 14 Nov. 1965, B3.

29 Robert Musel, "Singer Puts Blame on Parents," *Chicago Tribune,* 29 Jan. 1967, A4.

30 "Who Breaks a Butterfly on a Wheel?," *London Times,* 1 Jul. 1967, 11.

31 Richards writes extensively of his discovery of open tunings in his autobiography, declaring "it transformed my life." Richards, *Life* (New York: Little, Brown, 2010), esp. 241–244.

32 The chord progression for the chorus of "Jumpin' Jack Flash" is bIII–bVII–IV–I. Note the preponderance of fourths. As Rob Walser has argued, Aeolian later became the dominant mode of hard rock and heavy metal in the 1970s and 1980s, a legacy that can to some degree be traced to Richards's open tunings and the innovations they brought to his guitar technique and songwriting. Robert Walser, *Running with the Devil: Power, Gender, and Madness in Heavy Metal Music* (Middletown, CT: Wesleyan University Press, 1993), 40–53.

33 The Rolling Stones, *Beggars Banquet,* London 33, 1968, 33rpm.

34 Jann Wenner, "Rolling Stones Comeback: Beggars' Banquet," *Rolling Stone,* 10 Aug. 1968, 1. *Rolling Stone* (magazine) and the Rolling Stones (band) share no connection other than a name.

35 Carl Bernstein, "Rolling Stones: Contempt for Just about Everything," *Washington Post,* 12 Jan. 1969, 182.

36 Robb Baker, "Revolutionary, Satanic Imagery Sweeping the Rock World," *Chicago Tribune,* 8 Sept. 1968, SC1.

37 Patrick Lydon, "Mick Jagger: A Churning Writhing Paradox." *New York Times,* 20 Jul. 1969, D26.

38 For just a few famous instances of this, see Robert Johnson's "Hellhound on My Trail," Skip James's "Devil Got My Woman," and Lonnie Johnson's "Devil's Got the Blues."

39 The Rolling Stones, "Street Fighting Man," London 909, 1968.

40 Stephen Davis, *Old Gods Almost Dead: The 40-Year Odyssey of the Rolling Stones* (New York: Random House, 2001), 257,

41 In 2011 an original sleeve sold for more than $17,000 at a Los Angeles auction. http://www.bonhams.com/auctions/19045/lot/2264/.

42 LeRoi Jones wrote that "Dancing in the Street" "provided a legitimate core of social feeling, though mainly metaphorical and allegorical for Black people." Amiri Baraka (as LeRoi Jones), *Black Music* (1967; New York: Akashic, 2010), 238.

43 Richard Goldstein, "Why Do the Kids Dig Rock . . . ," *New York Times,* 24 Nov. 1968, H1, H14.

44 "The Rolling Stone Interview: Mick Jagger," *Rolling Stone,* 12 Oct. 1968, 17.

45 Lydon, "Mick Jagger," D26.

46 The Rolling Stones, *Let It Bleed,* London 4, 1969, 33rpm.

47 Don Heckman, "Pop: No, the Rolling Stones Are Not Fascists," *New York Times,* 28 Dec. 1969, D24. "What we're left with is still basically the Stones' own hard, gritty, matter-of-fact, blues-based musicianship. Oozing all over. Let it bleed," wrote Robb Baker in "Rolling Stones Ooze in Latest: 'Let It Bleed,'" *Chicago Tribune,* 14 Dec. 1969, SC2.

48 Greil Marcus, "You Get What You Need," *Rolling Stone,* 27 Dec. 1969, 52.

49 Chuck Berry's "Roll over Beethoven" and "Johnny B. Goode" were released in 1956 and 1958, respectively.

50 W. B. Yeats, "The Second Coming," in *The Poems,* ed. Richard J. Finneran (New York: Macmillan, 1983), 187. Charley Patton's "High Water Everywhere" can be found on *Charley Patton: Complete Recorded Works, Vol. 2,* Document Records 5010, 1990, CD.

51 Farah Jasmine Griffin, "When Malindy Sings: A Meditation on Black Women's Vocality," in *Uptown Conversation: The New Jazz Studies,* ed. Robert G. O'Meally, Brent Hayes Edwards, and Farah Jasmine Griffin (New York: Columbia University Press, 2004), 104.

52 According to research conducted on the Internet Movie Database (www .imdb.com) and All Music Guide (www.allmusic.com), "Gimme Shelter" has appeared in more films and television programs, from Vietnam War documentaries to police thrillers to gangster epics, than any other Rolling Stones song.

53 Charles T. Powers, "Bizarre Tale of 'Black Magic': Manson 'Black Magic' Told by Ex-Followers," *Los Angeles Times,* 5 Dec. 1969, 1.

54 *Gimme Shelter,* DVD, directed by Albert Maysles, David Maysles, and Charlotte K. Swerin (1970; Los Angeles: Criterion Collection, 2000).

55 Lester Bangs et al., "Let It Bleed," *Rolling Stone,* 21 Jan. 1970, 1–36.

56 John Burks, "Rock and Roll's Worst Day," *Rolling Stone,* 7 Feb. 1970.

57 Sol Stern, "Altamont: Pearl Harbor to the Woodstock Nation," reprinted in *Conversations with the New Reality,* ed. Martin Singer (San Francisco: Canfield, 1971), 45–68.

58 Pauline Kael, "Beyond Pirandello." *New Yorker,* 19 Dec. 1970, 112.

59 Vincent Canby, "Making Murder Pay?," *New York Times,* 13 Dec. 1970, 118.

60 Albert Goldman, "Or a 'Whitewash of Jagger'?," *New York Times,* 3 Jan. 1971, D9.

61 Bangs et al., "Let It Bleed," 32.

62 William F. Buckley, "Rock Fest Murder Makes Subject for Youth Movie," *Los Angeles Times,* 11 Dec. 1970, D11; Joel Haycock, "Gimme Shelter," *Film Quarterly* 24, no. 4 (1971): 60.

63 Simon Frith, "Letter from Britain: Join Together with the Band," *Creem,* Sept. 1972, 32.

64 Brian Ward, *Just My Soul Responding* (Berkeley: University of California Press, 1998), 360.

65 The Rolling Stones, *Sticky Fingers,* Rolling Stones 59100, 1971, 33rpm.

66 The Rolling Stones, "Brown Sugar," Rolling Stones 19100, 1971, 45rpm.

67 Martin Elliott, *The Rolling Stones: Complete Recording Sessions* (London: Cassell, 1990), 102.

Acknowledgments

Before counting this off properly I want to express my undying appreciation and admiration to every musician responsible for every note of every performance discussed in these pages. It is such an immense privilege to work with this music, and to live in the world with it. I hope I've honored that, and I hope that one day James Jamerson is mentioned in the same breath as Louis Armstrong, Charlie Parker, and other giants of American instrumental music.

And now, from the top. This book was shaped and nurtured by the most generous and brilliant advising committee I could have dreamed of. Werner Sollors and Carol Oja have both been with this project since before any of us even knew it existed; the countless hours I've spent in their classrooms, offices, living rooms, Venetian balconies, and everywhere else make me so grateful that they took me under their wings. You are both such wonderful role models, as scholars and as human beings. Ingrid Monson provided some of my fondest memories of graduate school, inside the classroom and out, and her writing, teaching, and open-heartedness are an inspiration.

Eric Lott has always been unreasonably generous to me in every way. His lightning-in-a-bottle friendship remains one of the best things about this strange and wonderful profession.

My friends and colleagues in American Studies and Media Studies at the University of Virginia are nothing short of amazing. My deep and profound thanks to Hector Amaya, Grace Hale, Siva Vaidhyanathan, and Bruce Williams, all of whom provided valuable feedback on this book as it was rounding into the homestretch. I have tremendous respect and affection, professional and personal, for Christopher Ali, Wyatt Andrews, Lawrie Balfour, Coy Barefoot, Emily Blout, Aniko Bodroghkozy, Anna Brickhouse, Andre Cavalcante, Sylvia Chong, Shilpa Davé, Kevin Driscoll, Lisa Goff, Jennifer Greeson, Matt Hedstrom, Carmenita Higginbotham, Aynne Kokas, William Little, Elliot Majerczyk, Maurie McInnis, Jennifer Petersen, Andrea Press, Nick Rubin, Sandhya Shukla, Lana Swartz, Chad Wellmon, and Ashley Williams. Thanks also to other friends and colleagues across the university: Sophie Abramowitz, Bonnie Gordon, Njelle Hamilton, Andrew Kahrl, Kyrill Kunakhovich, Lisa Messeri, Karl Hagstrom Miller, Sarah Milov, and Joey Thompson. Barbara Gibbons makes everything happen and has helped me in more ways than I can begin to count, so extra thanks to her.

I am tremendously grateful to everyone at Harvard University Press for the excellent job they did with this book, starting with my editor, the great Lindsay Waters, and his right hand, the magnificent Amanda Peery. Stephanie Vyce provided helpful counsel on many occasions, and Timothy Jones designed a phenomenal cover. Thanks to Mary Ribesky, who shepherded this through the later stages, and to my cousin, Anne Peckham, who proofread this out of the goodness of her heart. I feel grateful to all my students over the years but particularly to the wonderful and talented Jasmine Lee, who worked tirelessly as a research assistant in helping bring this book to completion.

Adam Bradley gave me an invaluable opportunity as a postdoctoral fellow for the Laboratory for Race and Popular Culture at the University of Colorado, and I'm profoundly indebted to his generosity and friendship. Thanks as well to Lisa Bailey and Amber and Lola Lloyd. My tremendous gratitude also goes to the Charles Warren Center for American History, Harvard University's American Studies program, and the University of Virginia for providing funding for this project at various stages in its development. I am enormously appreciative of the wonderful librarians and staff members at Harvard University, the British Library at St. Pancras and Colindale, the Rock and Roll Hall of Fame Library and Archive, the University of Virginia, the University of Colorado, New York University, the University of Southern California, and Berklee College of Music. Special thanks to Kirsta Anderson, Carol and Ken Hochman, and Nora and Stephen McGregor, who opened their homes to me on various research trips over the years.

Many scholars and friends were extraordinarily generous in providing feedback and insight into this project over the years that it progressed, and their intellectual influence is all over these pages. Daphne Brooks, Glenda Carpio, Glenda Goodman, Maggie Gram, Brian Hochman, Hua Hsu, Josh Kun, and Karl Hagstrom Miller all read significant portions of this at various stages and provided invaluable suggestions, commentary, and advice. Carlo Rotella has offered me so much valuable professional advice over the years, and Greil Marcus's support and encouragement early on were the most humbling endorsement I could imagine.

The number of friends, mentors, and partners-in-crime I've met over the years through the Experience Music Project's annual Pop Conference is a staggering thing, starting with the brilliant and intrepid Eric Weisbard and Ann Powers—what an extraordinary community of people and music you have built. Regina Bradley, Robert Christgau, Meghan Drury, Charles Hughes, Emily Lordi, Michelangelo Matos, Charlie McGovern, Chris Molanphy (special thanks to Chris, for indulging and answering every esoteric chart question I've ever thrown his way), Jody Rosen, Barry Shank, Elijah Wald, Gayle Wald, Oliver Wang, Carl Wilson: you are all amazing, and it is an honor to know and learn from you. Thanks also to Yago Colas, Alex Corey, Erica Fretwell, Phil Nel, Erich Nunn, and Matt Treon for their great friendship and insights in various academic and nonacademic settings over the years.

Outside of my committee I enjoyed a wonderful community of teachers and colleagues in graduate school. Nancy Cott, Andy Jewett, and Tommie Shelby all played sizable roles in the beginnings of this project. To Ryan Bañagale, William Bares, Andrea Bohlman, Brian Goodman, Mike Heller, Sheryl Kaskowitz, Eitan Kensky, Drew Massey, Liz Maynes-Aminzade, Danny Mekonnen, Eva Payne, Kathryn Roberts, Meredith Schweig—thanks for your insights and friendship over the years. Thanks also to Arthur

Patton-Hock and Christine McFadden, without whom none of this would have happened.

I've spent a perhaps inadvisable portion of my life as a working musician, and those experiences have shaped this work as much as any archive. No two people have had more impact on how I think about music as a living act than Mike Welch and Alec Derian. I owe so much to them, and to Jan Welch for a chance she took on me long ago that changed my life. Abbie Barrett, Warren Grant, Brad Hallen, Josh Kiggans, Steve Levy, and Mike Oram are just a few others I've had the privilege to perform with regularly over the years.

I'd also like to thank my friends and colleagues at *Slate* magazine, where I've been lucky enough to write regularly for several years now. My particular gratitude to John Swansburg and Josh Levin, who've read more of my writing over the years than any sane person should and who are such great people and friends. The editing talents of Laura Bennett, Tommy Craggs, David Haglund, Dan Kois, Jeremy Stahl, and Forrest Wickman have all made me a better writer, and my conversations with Aisha Harris, Derreck Johnson, Ben Mathis-Lilley, and Leon Neyfakh have made me a better thinker. Thanks as well to Julia Turner, for bringing it all together. Amanda Hess has been a great friend since before *Slate* and has remained one since taking a job at a local newspaper. Megan Greenwell doesn't work at *Slate* but she is one of the best editors and people on earth and I am grateful for her friendship, intellectual generosity, and frequent hospitality.

I feel so fortunate for the community of friends I have here in Charlottesville, nonwork-related variety. Adam, Kate Lynn, and Jack Nemett welcomed me before I even got to town, as did Emma Rathbone and Adam Brock. I can't imagine these past few years without you guys. Thanks to Nell Boeschenstein, Tom Breihan, Moby Brown, Sarah Burke, Garnette Cadogan, Aaron Fein, Coby and Sopher Fein, Kristen Finn, Seth Green, Melissa Henriksen, Kelley Libby, Dahlia Lithwick, Amy Hagstrom Miller, Molly Minturn, Sarah Mullen, Liz Russell, Paige Ryan, Rebecca Taylor, Scott Wilcox, Allison Wright, Bill Wylie, and Sherman for making this such a great place to live. Being back in the same neck of the woods as my old and dear friends Alex Stephenson and Dave Zielke is a tremendous pleasure.

And to others, far and wide: Jon Abraham and Shannon Abraham-Cook, Andy Almeter, Jed Berger and Nicki Pombier-Berger, Ben Bradlow and Fenna Krienen, Zach Church, Andy and

Prudence Diamond, Catharine Dill, Andrew and Melissa DuBeau, Tania Friedel, Nathaniel Friedman, Peter Gelling and Retno Prawati, Tim Grimes, Jesse Herman, Nate Jaffee and Marisa Tom, Leila Jamal and Chad Hochberg, Jake Kissell and Mariam Levy, David Moore and Chrissy O'Brien, Alissa Roeder, Erik Rune and Bonnie Reese, Oliver Sellers-Garcia and Tom McHale, Adriana Schick, Delfo and Karen Trombetta, Paul Venuti, Gina Welch, Matt and Leah Wiacek, Taylor and Dana Wolfe, and all the people I'm immediately going to hate myself for forgetting: I couldn't have done any of this without you.

I can't say enough about the friends I made in Harvard's American Studies program while working on this project. Tenley Archer, Eli Cook, Hillary Hochman, David Kim, and Katherine Stevens are among the finest people to have never seen a documentary about Phil Spector. Scott Poulson-Bryant makes me smarter every time I talk to him, even when we're having the same conversation about Michael Jackson albums for the millionth time. Brian and Laura McCammack opened their home and refrigerator to me on many an occasion; Buddy and Tippy McCammack are missed dearly. Pete L'Official is the kind of friend who watches World Cup games in Italy with me and flies to Seattle to be on EMP panels about Future with me. Nick Donofrio is one of my all-time favorite conversationalists: come back to Thanksgiving, Nicky. There are numerous ways in which I could thank the magnificent George Blaustein. Tim McGrath's friendship and erstwhile housemateship were one of the best parts of grad school, and remain one of the best parts of everything since. During graduate school Maggie Gram and Brian Hochman probably read more of this than anyone besides myself and my advisors, so special thanks and gratitude to them—I've now thanked you both twice, and it still isn't enough. Becca Bailey, Bianca Etkin, Derek Etkin, and Juniper Etkin are like a second family to me, and even though none of them were actually in graduate school with me I can't imagine those years without them. And thanks of course to the ACBL, always in overtime and never ending.

And my family. My lifelong love and affection to David, Ruth, Nick, and Katherine Rose, who aren't blood relatives but that's always felt like a technicality. Rob Hamilton is one of the smartest and funniest people I know, and I'd feel lucky just having him as a friend, but having him as a brother is such a privilege. And to my parents, who have been with all of this since the beginning, literally: I know there were times when you weren't totally sure what to make of me, of my strange preoccupations and obsessions that you didn't really share, nor should you have. But you loved and supported me and never once tried to make me into anyone but myself, which is all that any weird and dreamy kid could ever ask for. I dedicate this to you.

Finally, in the early stages of this project I lost a dear friend, tragically and senselessly, the kind of person you can't imagine your world without until one day when you suddenly have no choice. No one has had a bigger impact on the way I read, write, think, and laugh than Neil Chamberlain, and I miss him every day. Neil, I dedicate this to you as well, even if doing so seems redundant, since no small part of everything here has always felt like it's already yours.

Credits

Music Example 4.1. "Nowhere to Run," bass guitar as played by session musician James Jamerson. Music by Holland-Dozier-Holland. Performed by Martha and the Vandellas. Recorded: Hitsville, U.S.A. (Studio A), Detroit, Michigan, October 21, 1964. EMI Music Publishing. © 1965, 1973, 1977 (Renewed 1993, 2001, 2005) JOBETE MUSIC CO., INC. Score transcription by the author.

Music Example 4.2. "Nowhere Man," bass guitar as played by Paul McCartney. Music by Lennon/McCartney. Performed by the Beatles. Recorded: EMI Studios, London, October 21–22, 1965. Sony/ATV Music Publishing. Copyright © 1965 Sony/ATV Songs LLC. Score transcription by the author.

Music Example 4.3. "Rain," bass guitar as played by Paul McCartney. Music by Lennon/McCartney. Performed by the Beatles. Recorded: EMI Studios, London, April 14 and 16, 1966. Sony/ATV Music Publishing. Copyright © 1966 Sony/ATV Songs LLC. Score transcription by the author.

Music example 4.4. "Bernadette" bass guitar as played by session musician James Jamerson. Music by Holland-Dozier-Holland. Performed by The Four Tops. Recorded: Hitsville, U.S.A. (Studio A), Detroit, Michigan, 1966. EMI

Music Publishing. © 1967 (Renewed 1995) JOBETE MUSIC CO., INC. Score transcription by the author.

Music Example 4.5. "And Your Bird Can Sing," bass guitar as played by Paul McCartney. Music by Lennon/McCartney. Performed by the Beatles. Recorded: EMI Studios, London, April 14 and 16, 1966. Sony/ATV Music Publishing. Copyright © 1966 Sony/ATV Songs LLC. Score transcription by the author.

Index